LEARN CHINESE:

A Beginner's Guide to Mandarin Chinese

简体字

Chinese for Beginners

Copyright © 2016 Daniel Schoeman
All rights reserved.
ISBN-13: 978-0-620-71353-5

DEDICATION

This book is dedicated to all students of Mandarin, who strive and work at bringing humans together. Through language we learn to understand, to cooperate and to advance. It is this beautiful endeavor, that allows continents and oceans to be bridged and for humans to walk this earth as one.

Remember To Access All Bonus Audio Information On Page 423

HOW TO USE THIS BOOK

This book functions as a self-study guide for the beginner student and content is laid out in a simple format that's easy to follow.

The units are in order of difficulty, and we recommend that you work through the book from beginning to end.

- Start on the first page of every unit by reading the *dialog* and *dialog description* at the bottom of the page. We provide you with the (1) *Chinese sentences* (characters), (2) the *Pinyin* and (3) *English translation*.

- The second page of the unit consists of the *New Vocabulary* as used in the dialog and also *Useful Vocabulary* to compliment the theme of the lesson.

- The third page of the unit has a section with *Revision Vocabulary* which consists of *old* vocabulary used in the dialog. It allows for constant revision and progressive learning. At the bottom of the page, the lesson explanation starts with a sentence from the dialog. Keywords are highlighted and explained.

- The lesson explanation continues on the fourth and fifth pages of every unit. A breakdown of the lesson is given and the different parts of speech are identified and discussed.

- The sixth page of every unit consists of simple *practice activities*. Follow the instructions and work through them at your own pace.

- The seventh page of the unit is for writing practice. In units 1-19 we provide both *radicals* and *new characters* to be practiced. From units 20-49 we provide both *useful* and *new characters*. Knowledge of radicals is essential and must be mastered before we attempt actual characters. Unit 50 is dedicated to the practice of radicals.

- The last page of the unit is for self-practice. Write and practice the characters on your own.

You can, of course, also use this book as a reference guide, to consult when necessary.

CONTENTS

1. Introduction: The Basics you need to know ix
2. Unit 1 1
3. Unit 2 9
4. Unit 3 17
5. Unit 4 25
6. Unit 5 33
7. Unit 6 41
8. Unit 7 49
9. Unit 8 57
10. Unit 9 65
11. Unit 10 73
12. Unit 11 81
13. Unit 12 89
14. Unit 13 97
15. Unit 14 105
16. Unit 15 113
17. Unit 16 121
18. Unit 17 129
19. Unit 18 137
20. Unit 19 145
21. Unit 20 153
22. Unit 21 161
23. Unit 22 169
24. Unit 23 177
25. Unit 24 185
26. Unit 25 193
27. Unit 26 201
28. Unit 27 209

29. Unit 28 217
30. Unit 29 225
31. Unit 30 233
32. Unit 31 241
33. Unit 32 249
34. Unit 33 257
35. Unit 34 265
36. Unit 35 273
37. Unit 36 281
38. Unit 37 289
39. Unit 38 297
40. Unit 39 305
41. Unit 40 313
42. Unit 41 321
43. Unit 42 329
44. Unit 43 337
45. Unit 44 345
46. Unit 45 353
47. Unit 46 361
48. Unit 47 369
49. Unit 48 377
50. Unit 49 385
51. Unit 50 393
52. Practice Radicals 396
53. Word Index 418
54. Answers 419
54. Bonus Material 423
55. About The Author 423

INTRODUCTION

The 21st century is often described as the Chinese Century or even more dramatically, the Century of the Dragon. For this very reason, an increasing amount of people around the world are studying Mandarin as a foreign language. What sets Mandarin apart from other languages is that not only does it consist of characters and tones, but it also follows a very peculiar word order and sentence structure. To make head or tail of all of this, it's essential that new students be guided in the right direction from the start.

To The Student

In picking up this guide, you've shown that you are serious about becoming a student of Mandarin. This book was designed for students like you, who want to learn.

You can use this guide without a teacher. We provide you with the Chinese characters, their Pinyin and the English translations. The content is intended for students who are completely new to the basics of Mandarin.

Throughout we will make reference to Verbs, Nouns, Adjectives and all other sentence parts. Make sure that you are familiar with all parts. We will provide you with a condensed version of Sentence Parts at the end of this introduction. Knowing these elements is of vital importance in order for you to start *thinking* like a native speaker. Be aware of the fact, that every word has a function in the sentence and that you should be familiar with these functions.

Pinyin is used throughout and the words and sounds will be unfamiliar at first. Have a look at our Pinyin explanation to educate yourself with the tones and how to read them. (Audio download information can be found on page 420.)

This guide, for beginner students, was designed to make the process of Chinese learning as clear and as simple as possible. It is very easy to use and it should provide you with all the knowledge that you need. You can work through it at your own pace and initially, if the characters seem to complicated, you can stick to the Pinyin provided.

Let's take a quick look at the basics of Mandarin.

Pinyin

Pinyin allows non-Mandarin speakers to read and to pronounce the unfamiliar characters. It is this Romanization of Mandarin that allows new students to read Chinese characters, as English words.
To put it plainly: You can read Mandarin, through the use of Pinyin.

English	I don't know.
Mandarin	我不知道.
Pinyin	Wǒ bú zhī dào.

Look closely at the little marks placed on top of the vowels of the last Pinyin phrase.

The Pinyin system makes use of a diacritical mark (a small mark added on top of a letter) that refers to the tone of a character.

These are placed on top of vowels (a, e, i, o, u) and indicate the tone of the specific character. If a syllable has no tone mark, it indicates a neutral tone. It is pronounced in a normal tone.

Tones

There are four basic tones in Chinese. The tone refers to variations in highs and lows, in the sound of each syllable. Different tones have different meanings.

You can distinguish the different tones as a 1st (high), 2nd (high rising), 3rd (low dipping) and a 4th (high falling) tone.

ā	1st tone
á	2nd tone
ǎ	3rd tone
à	4th tone

If there is no tone mark above a syllable, it means that the tone is neutral. Just pronounce it normally, depending on the syllable preceding it. (Download audio files for samples of 4 tones of "ma".)

New students need not feel overwhelmed. Pay attention and listen to the sounds and try to get a general feel for the four basic tones. Through practice, it gets easier and you will become more aware of when and how to apply certain tones. Some students approach it intuitively and compare it to music. Learning the lyrics of a song you become quickly aware of tempo and pitch. Most serious students simply memorize the character with its tone. Practice is the key and in this case, practice certainly makes perfect!

Sentence Parts

A summary of the Sentence parts, used in this Grammar guide:

Sentence Part	Function	Example Words	Sentences
Noun	person or a thing	school, food, places, objects	This my house. I live in Japan.
Adjective* (Stative Verb)	describes a Noun	new, salty, nice, red	My house is small. It is white.
Verb	action or state	to be, have, like, sing	I like my house. I built it.
Adverb	describe a Verb, Adjective, Adverb	quickly, well, badly, really	I work really hard, but I drive slowly.
Pronoun	replaces a Noun	I, you, he, she	She is good. They are my friends.
Conjunctions	to join two or more words	and, or	The apples and oranges are mine.

*(In Chinese, Adjectives are called Stative Verbs.)

Make sure that you are familiar with all sentence parts.
Also take note that throughout this book we will mention Subjects and Objects. In grammar, the sentence is the simplest manner that we use to express a thought. A typical sentence will have a Subject, a Verb and an Object.

xi

A Subject is the **doer** of the action that takes place. It can be a person, a place, a thing or an idea.

A Verb is of course the **action** that takes place.

An Object is that upon which the Verbs acts. It is the **receiver** of the action. It can also be a person, a place, a thing or an idea.

Writing

Writing Chinese characters might seem a daunting task, but it is something that can be mastered by any student willing to apply a little bit of patience and effort.

We decided to dedicate a whole unit (50) to the writing of characters and it starts on p.393.

Please work through the Writing Unit 50 and the practice sheets for the radicals before you start with Unit 1.

第一课　　　Unit 1

Dialog

你好!
Nǐ hǎo !
Hello!

你好!
Nǐ hǎo !
Hello!

再见!
Zài jiàn !
Good-bye!

再见!
Zài jiàn !
Good-bye!

This is a dialog between two friends who bump into each other. Both are in a hurry and there is no time for pleasantries.

Dialog Vocabulary

你好	nǐ hǎo	hello
你	nǐ	you
好	hǎo	to be good
再见	zài jiàn	good-bye

Useful Vocabulary

我	wǒ	I/ me
不	bù	not/ no
不好	bù hǎo	not good
再	zài	again
见	jiàn	to meet

Revision Vocabulary

From Unit 2 onwards, you can view the vocabulary used in the previous lesson.

This provides you with an opportunity to review what you have learned and to incorporate it into the current lesson.

This "progressive learning" allows for constant revision.

Lesson Breakdown

你好!

Nǐ hǎo!

Hello!

This sentence functions as a **greeting**.

Not only is it a very important greeting, but it is also considered one of the most commonly used phrases found in Mandarin.

Pay special attention to the tones of the two words and note that the mood is *friendly and polite*.

This greeting literally means: "You good?", and translates to *Hello*.

Let's look at the breakdown of every component.

你　　nǐ　　you

This Pronoun acts as the Subject (S) of the sentence.
As the Subject, it is also the main *topic* of the sentence.

好　　hǎo　　good

This is the Adjective (Adj) of the sentence. (Also called a Stative Verb.)

The role of the Adjective "good", is to help us to describe the Subject, "you". It indicates the *degree* of the Subject, because in this case, it tells us more about how he or she is doing.

> 再见!
> Zài jiàn !
> Good-bye!

Traditionally this **expression** is used at the end of a conversation when we *take leave of someone*. The tones of the two words are important and the mood is friendly and polite; very typical of Chinese conversations.

It literally means: "To see again", and translates to "Good-bye" or "See you next time."

再　　zài　　again

This is the Adverb (Adv) of the sentence.

An Adverb is a word that modifies or qualifies an Adjective, Verb or another Adverb. In the example provided, it is used to describe the Verb [jiàn], meaning *to meet*.

In describing the Verb, it tells us "when" or "how" they will *meet*.

见   jiàn   to meet

This is the Verb (V) of the sentence.
It indicates the *action* to take place.
Pay attention to the sentence structure and word order used.
It is one of the more challenging aspects of mastering Mandarin.

Supplementary

Tones:

nǐ hǎo

Look at the 3rd tone present in both words.
They are pronounced *slowly* and with a "dip" in the middle.
Greeting someone is obviously a commonly used phrase and you should put extra effort into this one.
Note that Pinyin uses its own pronunciation system and that you simply have to practice the tones as often as possible.

zài jiàn

These words are both in the 4th tone.
Note the *speed* of the 4th tone.
It is a tone filled with purpose.
We will continue to point out the tones of the words introduced.
Practice, repeat, practice, repeat; it just gets easier with time.

Download The Bonus Audio Files To Practice Your Pronunciation

My Progress

Words	QW's	MW's	TW's	Total
Count	0	0	0	4

Hint

Remember to practice tones and expressions as often as possible. Role-play is a great method.

Practice

Connect and match:

你	•	• zài •	• good-bye
再	•	• jiàn •	• you
好	•	• nǐ hǎo •	• to be good
见	•	• nǐ •	• no/ not
你好	•	• hǎo •	• again
再见	•	• zài jiàn •	• hello
不	•	• bù hǎo •	• bad
不好	•	• bù •	• to meet

Rewrite the following words into Pinyin:

1. 再见 _____
2. 好 _____
3. 见 _____
4. 你好 _____
5. 再 _____
6. 你 _____
7. 不好 _____
8. 不 _____

Circle the correct character in every line:

1. 你 , 妳 , 祢 , 侭 , 尔
2. 妤 , 奸 , 妡 , 好 , 奴
3. 贝 , 见 , 兄 , 冗 , 几
4. 冉 , 甫 , 禹 , 再 , 用

● Radical Stroke Order　　Character Stroke Order ●

丿	亻	儿	土	冂
子	你	好	再	见

Trace the following characters

丿									
亻									
儿									
土									
冂									
子									
你									
好									
再									
见									

Self-Practice

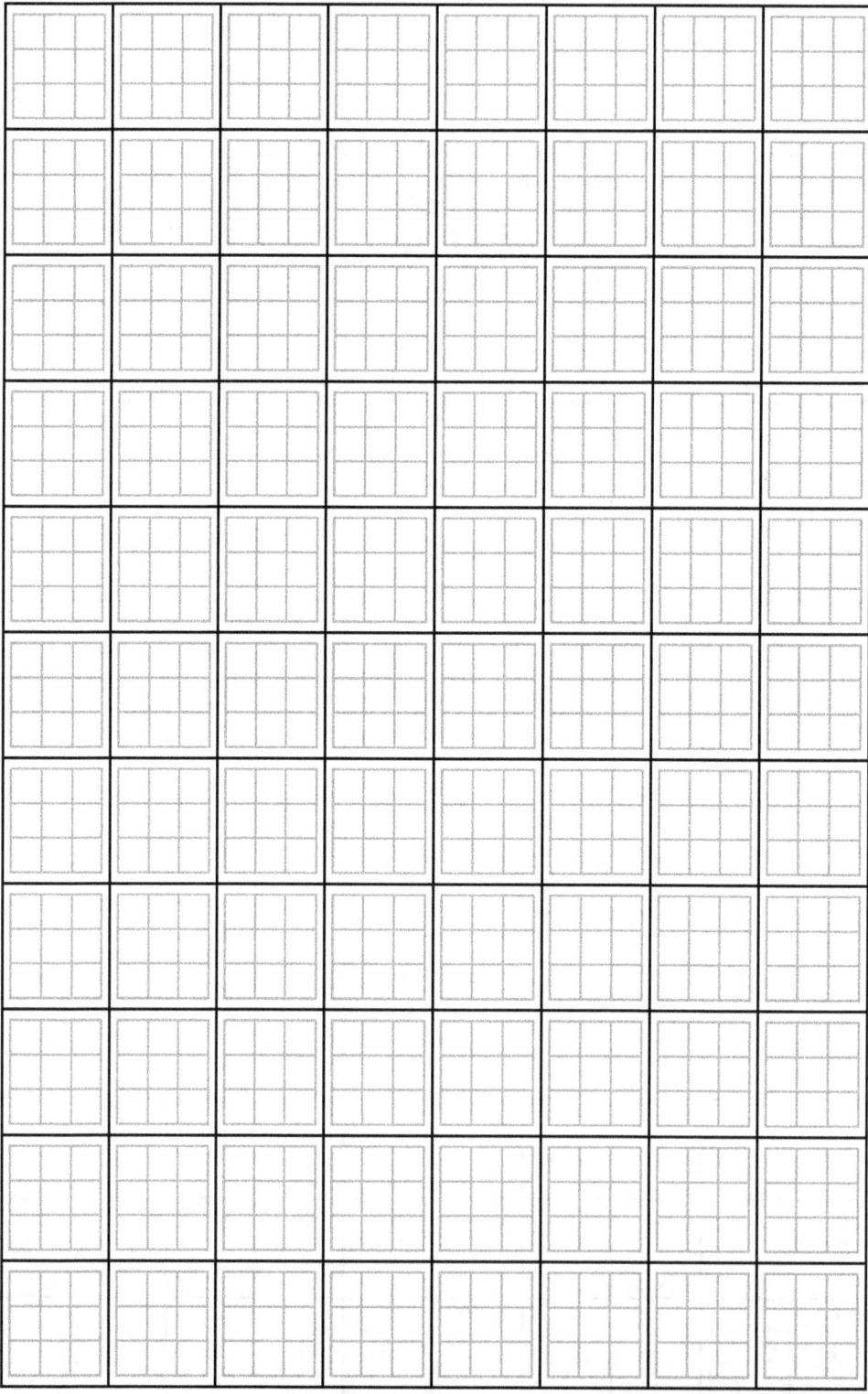

第二课　　　Unit 2

你好！我叫 Ben。
Nǐ hǎo！Wǒ jiào Ben.
Hello! I am Ben.

什么？
Shén me？
What?

我叫 Ben。
Wǒ jiào Ben.
I am Ben.

你好, Ben！我叫 Roy。
Nǐ hǎo, Ben！Wǒ jiào Roy.
Hello Ben! I am Roy.

This is a dialog between two kids who meet on the playground. Both are very young and eager to make new friends.

Dialog Vocabulary

我	wǒ	I/ me
叫	jiào	to be called
什么	shén me	what

Useful Vocabulary

是	shì	to be
名字	míng zi	name
为什么	wèi shén me	why
人	rén	people

Revision Vocabulary

你好	nǐ hǎo	hello
你	nǐ	you
好	hǎo	to be good

Lesson Breakdown

> 我 叫 Ben 。
> Wǒ jiào Ben.
> I am Ben.

This is an **informal and casual way to introduce** oneself.
Introductions are very important in Chinese culture and as such, some introductions are considered more polite than others.
This sentence literally means: "I am, to be called, Ben".
Correctly translated it means: "I am Ben."
Let's take a look at the main Verb and its position in this sentence.

> 叫   jiào   to be called

This is a Verb (V) used to introduce a **first name** or a **full name**. We do not use this Verb for surnames!

When using this Verb, we have to follow a very specific structure:

Subject + 叫 + Name

A name can be a simple English name, as in our example, or it can be a proper Chinese first name. Chinese names follow a very specific order:

Surname + First names

Example:

王 ＋ 文美 ＝ 王文美

> 什么?
> Shén me ?
> What?

Note that this is what's known as a Chinese Question Word (QW) and that it **asks a simple question**.

Chinese QWs are very similar to their English counterparts:

> Why/ When/ Where/ Who/ What/ How?

These words play an important role in understanding Chinese grammar.

Question Words assist us in asking specific questions where we do not expect a Yes/No answer.

More about QWs in later lessons.

Supplementary

Tones:

shén me

Let's 'look at the 2nd tone in [shén]. The 2nd tone tends to be the tricky one and you really have to concentrate to distinguish it from the 1st and 3rd tones.

It is a rising tone. It begins in the mid-tone zone, then rises to a high tone, as if asking a question. (Similar to, "Are you *coming*?", note the rise in the last word.)

The last part of the word, [me], has no tone and thus no tone mark. We call this the neutral tone or 5th tone. The neutral tone's exact pitch depends on the tone that came before it. There is no need to complicate this tone. Words without tone marks are pronounced in a normal, flat tone with no emphasis.

Remember that words do not start with the neutral tone. They are always found at the back-end of the word and also as sentence-final particles like 吗 , 吧 , 呢.

什 + 么 = 什么

Take note of this word's character make-up. We notice that there are *two characters* present and that combined they form *one word*:

Sometimes we are able to separate the individual characters of a word and to look at individual meanings.

In this case the individual characters cannot be separated and have no meaning on their own. One word in Mandarin, can consist of one, two or even three characters.

Download The Bonus Audio Files To Practice Your Pronunciation

My Progress

Words	QW's	MW's	TW's	Total
Count	1	0	0	7

Hint

Remember that QWs help us ask questions. Look online and get yourself a relevant Chinese name.

Practice

Connect and match:

我	•	• jiào •	• name
再	•	• shì •	• I / me
叫	•	• míng zi •	• to be
人	•	• wǒ •	• people
什么	•	• rén •	• again
名字	•	• wèi shén me •	• what
是	•	• shén me •	• why
为什么	•	• zài •	• to be called

Rewrite the following words into Pinyin:

1. 为什么 _____
2. 人 _____
3. 是 _____
4. 名字 _____
5. 我 _____
6. 叫 _____
7. 什么 _____
8. 再 _____

Circle the correct character in every line:

1. 找 , 我 , 掛 , 扰 , 犹
2. 叫 , 叭 , 叮 , 吟 , 吧
3. 仟 , 件 , 什 , 仔 , 仕
4. 仫 , 幺 , 厶 , 么 , 公

● Radical Stroke Order   Character Stroke Order ●

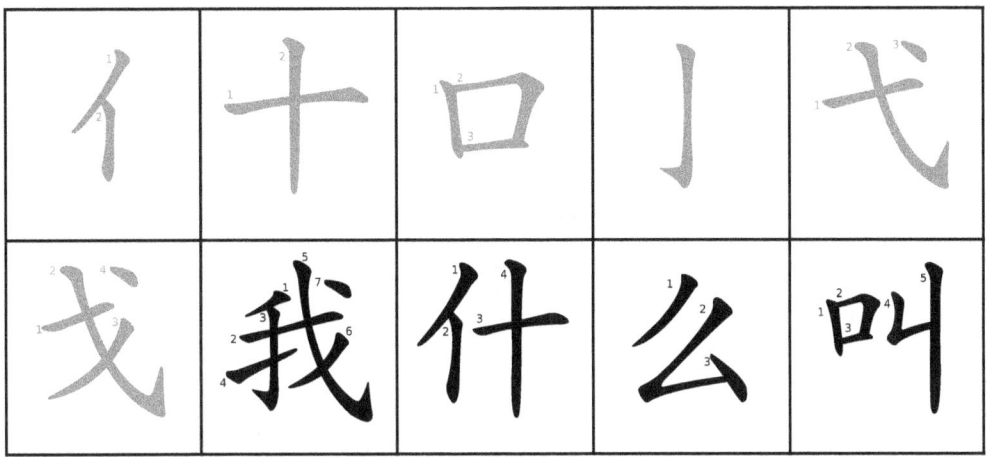

Trace the following characters

Unit 2   15

Self-Practice

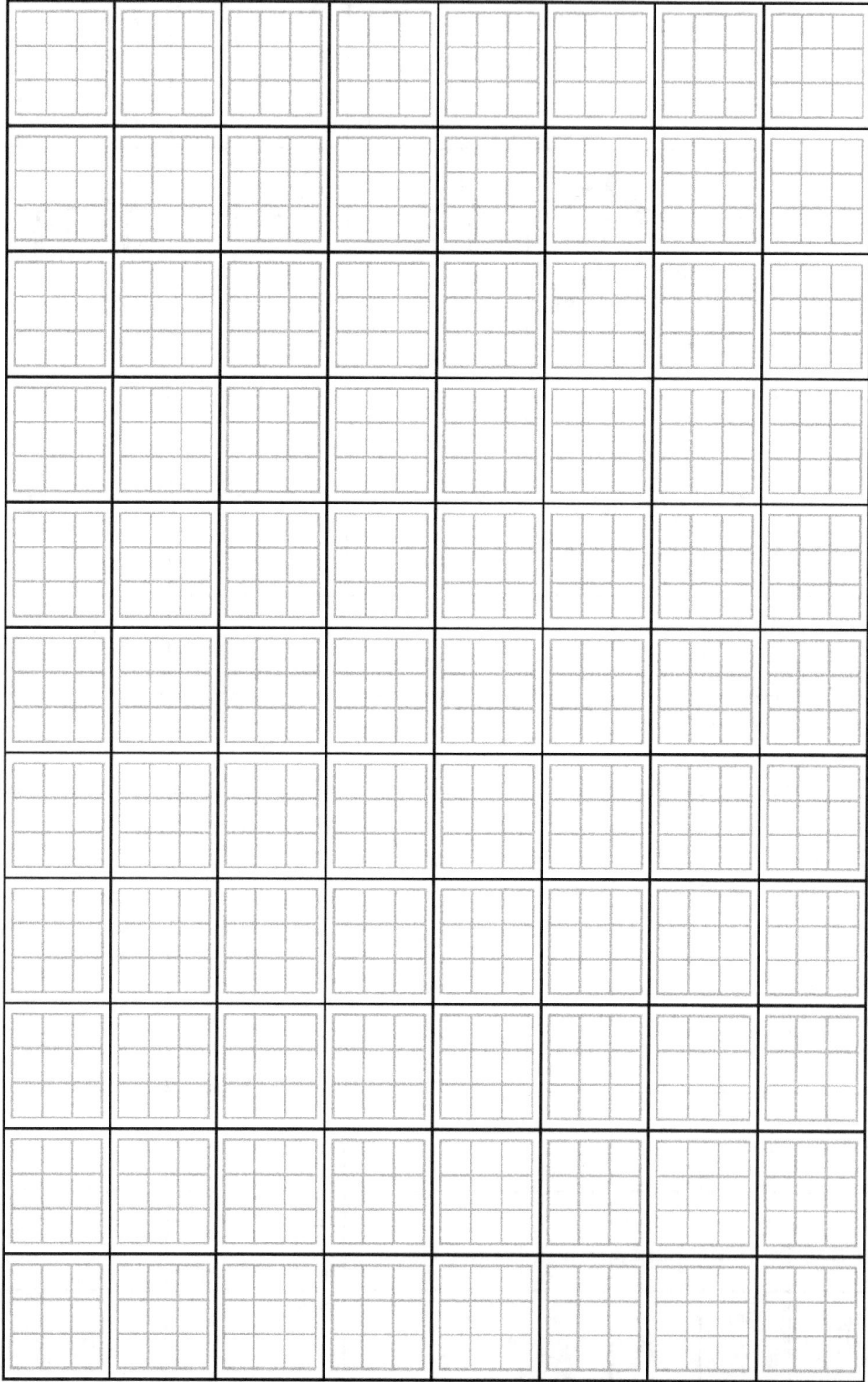

第三课　　　　Unit 3

你好！你叫什么名字？
Nǐ hǎo! Nǐ jiào shén me míng zi?
Hello! What is your name?

我叫 James。
Wǒ jiào James.
My name is James.

你好, James! 我是 Alice。
Nǐ hǎo, James! Wǒ shì Alice.
Hello, James! I am Alice.

你好, Alice。
Nǐ hǎo, Alice.
Hello, Alice!

This is a dialog between two people (of similar status and age) who meet on a business trip. Both are relaxed and eager to make friends.

Dialog Vocabulary

我	wǒ	I/ me*
叫	jiào	to be called*
什么	shén me	what*
名字	míng zi	name
是	shì	to be (am/ is/ are)

* Repeated to assist with introductions (Important!)

Useful Vocabulary

不是	bù shì	not
姓	xìng	family name
名片	míng piàn	name card
名车	míng chē	luxury car
有名	yǒu míng	famous

Revision Vocabulary

你好	nǐ hǎo	hello
你	nǐ	you
好	hǎo	good

Lesson Breakdown

你叫什么名字?
Nǐ jiào shén me míng zi ?
What is your name?

This is a phrase that we can expect to hear around any casual meeting or introduction. It is an informal inquiry about someone's name, where the speakers are of similar age or status.

Literal meaning: "You, are called, by what name?"

When looking at this sentence, we become aware of the specific word order used to express something.

This brings us to a very common sentence pattern in Mandarin namely, the **SVO sentence structure**.

Subject + Verb + Object

你 (Subject)　叫 (Verb)　什么名子 (Object)?

This structure is common to most languages:
I eat food. (S+V+O)

This structure allows us to form grammatically correct sentences. It clearly indicates who the Subject is and what action (Verb) he/ she is performing.

Make sure that your basic sentences follow the SVO order.

> 我 是 Alice。
> Wǒ shì Alice.
> I am Alice.

Literally: "I am Alice."

This is another informal way to introduce oneself.

We already know how to use 叫 for casual introductions. For **introductions with a slightly more polite tone**, we will use the Verb, 是 .

| 是 | shì | am, is, are |

This Verb is used in different contexts, but always means "to be".
Depending on the sentence and which Noun is used, it can indicate: *am, is or are*.

For introductions, the Verb is normally followed by a **Title** or a person's **full name**.

A full name can be an English name or a Chinese name consisting of the family name followed by the first names.

Supplementary

名字　　　míng zi　　name

This word is a Noun.

Get used to seeing two characters that represent one word.

As seen in the vocabulary list, the root 名 is also present in numerous other words.

The suffix 子 indicates that the word is used as a Noun (person).

In this case it makes 名 a person, literally meaning: name of person.

Titles:

Using the correct title is very important in China.

Certain introductions require the formal use of titles and this will encourage further conversation.

Basic list of common titles used during introductions:

小姐 [xiǎo jiě] Miss/ Ms
先生 [xiān shēng] Mister/ Sir
太太 [tài tai] Mrs.

(Take note that in certain cities the use of 小姐 [xiǎo jiě] is frowned upon. Nowadays it can also mean a female of ill-repute.)

Download The Bonus Audio Files To Practice Your Pronunciation

My Progress

Words	QW's	MW's	TW's	Total
Count	1	0	0	9

Hint

Remember that 是 is used for informal introductions and followed by a title or full name.

Self-Practice

Circle the Pinyin for the character:

1. 叫 : nǐ   jiào   shì   me

2. 是 : wǒ   shì   hǎo   zài

3. 名字 : shén me   míng zi   nǐ hǎo   zài jiàn

4. 再见 : shén me   míng zi   nǐ hǎo   zài jiàn

Rewrite the following sentences into Pinyin:

1. Hello. _____
2. I am Jack. _____
3. What's your name? _____
4. Good bye. _____
5. I am Mary. _____
6. What? _____

Arrange the words into sentences:

1. jiào   nǐ   shén me   míng zi ?
   _____

2. Jack   jiào   wǒ.
   _____

3. wǒ   Amy   shì.
   _____

4. John   nǐ   hǎo.
   _____

● Radical Stroke Order　　Character Stroke Order ●

口	了	足	宀	厶
名	字	是	什	么

Trace the following characters

口									
了									
足									
宀									
厶									
名									
字									
是									
什									
么									

Self-Practice

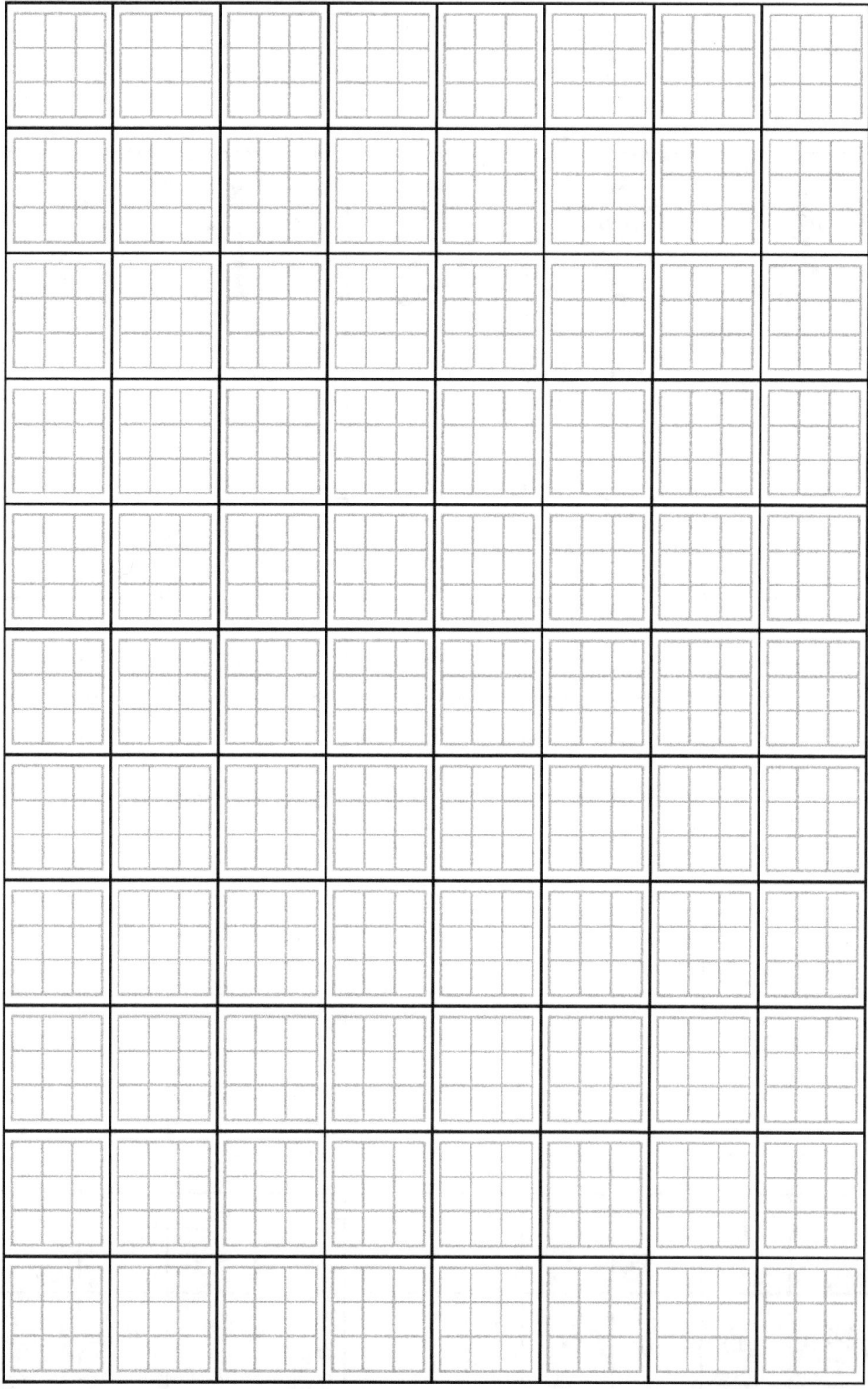

第四课 Unit 4

您好!您贵姓?
Nín hǎo! Nín guì xìng?
Hello. What is your last name?

我姓马。
Wǒ xìng Mǎ.
My last name is Ma.

您好,马先生!我姓王。
Nín hǎo, Mǎ xiān shēng! Wǒ xìng Wáng.
Hello Mr. Ma! My last name is Wang.

您好,王先生。
Nín hǎo, Wáng xiān shéng.
Hello, Mr. Wang.

This is a dialog between two people who meet at a function. Both are on best behavior and the mood is formal.

Dialog Vocabulary

您	nín	you (polite)
姓	xìng	surname
先生	xiān shéng	Mr.
马	Mǎ	Ma
王	Wáng	Wang
贵姓	guì xìng	What's your surname?

Useful Vocabulary

小姐	xiǎo jiě	Miss
小	xiǎo	small
王	wáng	king
马	mǎ	horse
姐姐	jiě jie	older sister
姐	jiě	for young women

Revision Vocabulary

我	wǒ	I/ me
好	hǎo	good

Lesson Breakdown

> 您好!您贵姓?
> Nín hǎo ! Nín guì xìng ?
> Hello. What is your last name?

您	nín	you

This is a Pronoun (PN) and it is the **polite form** of 你 [nǐ].

Mandarin is considered a language with a distinct polite tone and we use this Pronoun when addressing superiors, older people or when being **formal**.

We can therefore conclude that, 您好 [**nín hǎo**] is a formal way of saying *hello* to someone.

Note that 贵 [guì] has, on its own, no specific meaning in the sentence. During introductions, it is always used in conjunction with 姓 [xìng] to introduce (or inquire after) a Surname.

New students should memorize this phrase, since it's frequently used by Chinese speakers.

> 我 姓 马。
> Wǒ xìng Mǎ.
> My last name is Ma.

This sentence literally means: "I, am Surnamed, Ma".

You will use this expression when meeting new people. In order to do this, you must have a *Chinese name* with a *surname*.
1

> 姓   xìng   Surname

This Verb literally means: "to be Surnamed" and it is commonly used at first-time introductions.

It has a polite tone and it is **used only with Surnames**.

You cannot say : 我 姓 Ben。

Ben is a name and not a surname.

For a name you have to say : 我 叫 Ben。

> 您 好, 王 先 生。
> Nín hǎo, Wáng xiān shéng.
> Hello, Mr. Wang.

This is a proper and polite greeting and therefore the person's **Title** is mentioned. The tone is formal and you sense a mood of respect. Titles and respect go hand in hand in Chinese culture.

Let's look at the individual components involved.

王 先生　　　Wáng xiān shéng　　　Mr. Wang

These three characters can be broken down into the following:

Chinese Surname + Title

王　[Wáng] is a common Chinese surname.

先生　[xiān shéng] means Mister and it is a Title.

Surnames are always placed in front of titles.

No matter what the title, it must always follow the surname.

(Note that 先生 can also mean husband.)

Supplementary

Writing: Radicals

您 and 你

您 (polite) is a different character from 你 (casual).

Both mean you, but they are written differently:

There is a 亻 [rén] radical at the front of both 你 and 您 meaning "person".

There is a 心 [xīn] radical at the bottom of 您 meaning "heart".

Tones:

xiān shéng

Look at the tone in [xiān].

This is the **1st tone** and it is a *high* and long tone.

This tone has no pitches, rises or dips.

It just holds a steady high note.

Download The Bonus Audio Files To Practice Your Pronunciation

My Progress					Hint
Words	QW's	MW's	TW's	Total	Remember that characters are compiled of radicals and different radicals have different meanings.
Count	1	0	0	15	

Self-Practice

Connect and match:

你 •   • mǎ •   • king
您 •   • wáng •   • you
姓 •   • xiān shéng •   • horse
马 •   • nǐ •   • ...your surname?
先生 •   • xìng •   • surname
小姐 •   • guì xìng •   • you (polite)
王 •   • xiǎo jiě •   • Miss
贵姓 •   • nín •   • Mr.

Rewrite the following sentences into Pinyin:

1. Hello (polite). _____
2. My surname is Wang. _____
3. What's your surname? _____
4. Hello Mr. Wang. _____
5. Good bye. _____
6. I am John. _____

Circle the correct character in every line:

1. 玛 ，码 ，妈 ，吗 ，马
2. 性 ，姓 ，鮏 ，娃 ，姃
3. 王 ，玉 ，壬 ，仟 ，仕
4. 老 ，光 ，先 ，告 ，尭

● Radical Stroke Order　　Character Stroke Order ●

心	女	中	土	王
您	姓	贵	先	生

Trace the following characters

心	心	心	心	心	心	心	心	心
女	女	女	女	女	女	女	女	女
中	中	中	中	中	中	中	中	中
土	土	土	土	土	土	土	土	土
王	王	王	王	王	王	王	王	王
您	您	您	您	您	您	您	您	您
姓	姓	姓	姓	姓	姓	姓	姓	姓
贵	贵	贵	贵	贵	贵	贵	贵	贵
先	先	先	先	先	先	先	先	先
生	生	生	生	生	生	生	生	生

Self-Practice

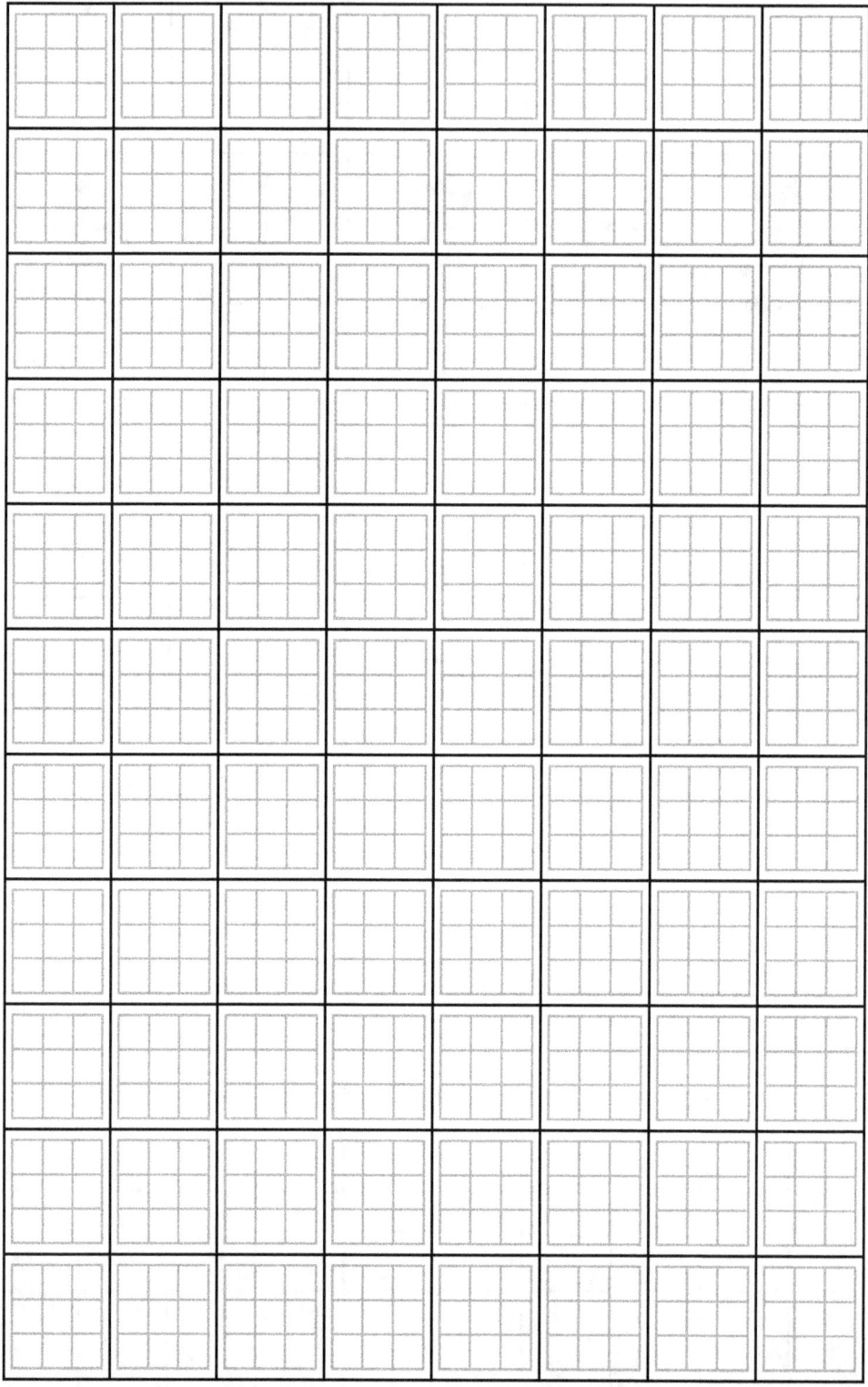

第五课　　　　Unit 5

马 先生, 早!
Mǎ xiān shēng, zǎo!
Morning, Mr. Ma!

赵 小姐, 早!
Zhào xiǎo jiě, zǎo!
Morning, Miss Zhao!

我 叫 Alice。你 好 吗?
Wǒ jiào, Alice. Nǐ hǎo ma?
I am Alice. How are you?

我 叫 John。我 很 好!
Wǒ jiào, John. Wǒ hěn hǎo!
I am John. I am very well!

This is a dialog between two people who are acquaintances. They decide that the time is right to become more familiar with each other.

Dialog Vocabulary

小姐	xiǎo jiě	Miss
早	zǎo	Morning
很	hěn	very/ quite
吗	ma	question suffix
赵	Zhào	Zhao (surname)

Useful Vocabulary

午安	wǔ ān	Good afternoon!
晚安	wǎn ān	Good evening!
早安	zǎo ān	Good morning!
她	tā	she/ her
早上好	zǎo shang hǎo	Good morning!

Revision Vocabulary

叫	jiào	to be called
先生	xiān shēng	Mr.
马	Mǎ	Ma (surname)

Lesson Breakdown

马 先生, 早!

Mǎ xiān shēng, zǎo !

Morning, Mr. Ma!

This sentence is another common greeting, that's used daily in China. It is a casual way of saying *Good morning*.

Typical of greeting used in Mandarin, the tone is polite and friendly.

Take note of the fact that the name and title are both placed at the beginning of the sentence and the greeting at the end of the sentence.

Let's look at the actual vocabulary used.

> 早   zǎo   Morning!

This is a **casual** way to greet someone in the morning. This expression is used daily, by millions of Chinese and therefore both the tone and pronunciation are very important. Interesting to note that this word can also mean *to be early* (Adj).

Let's look at another, less casual, morning greeting:

> 早安   zǎo ān   Morning!

This is a proper morning greeting and it is used in a **polite** tone. It is important to note that the character 安 means *peace* (Adj.).
It literally means: "morning peace".

> 早上好   zǎo shàng hǎo   Morning!

This is a slightly more formal way to say *good morning*. It is a longer greeting and it is used in a **formal** tone.

> 赵 小姐, 早!
> Zhào xiǎo jiě, zǎo !
> Morning, Miss Zhao!

Titles are very important and are always used during meetings.

> 小姐   xiǎo jiě   Miss

This is a title for a *young, unmarried lady* and in this case it is preceded by a surname.

Surnames are always placed in front of titles.

> 你 好 吗?
>
> Nǐ hǎo ma ?
>
> How are you?

This sentence literally means: "Are you good?".

Let's look at the particle used at the end of this sentence.

| 吗 | ma | Question particle |

This question particle is placed at the end of a sentence, similar to the use of a question mark (?). It indicates that a question is being asked. **It is used for simple questions where a Yes/No answer is expected.**

Keep in mind that you still have to place the actual question mark behind the 吗 .

> 我 很 好!
>
> Wǒ hěn hǎo !
>
> I am very well!

| 很 | hěn | very/quite |

This Adverb means *very or quite* and is used to express *degree* or feeling. It indicates just "how" good the Subject is.
Pay attention to this Adverb because you will see in later lessons that it is a multipurpose word.

(Download The Bonus Audio Files To Practice Your Pronunciation)

My Progress

Words	QW's	MW's	TW's	Total
Count	1	0	0	20

Hint

Remember, Surnames are placed in front of Titles. The question particle is for Yes/ No answers.

Self-Practice

Connect and match:

马 •	• zǎo ǎn •	• question particle
早 •	• ma •	• good
好 •	• hǎo •	• Good morning!
很 •	• zǎo •	• Miss
先生 •	• hěn •	• Morning!
小姐 •	• mǎ •	• Mr.
吗 •	• xiān shéng •	• horse
早安 •	• xiǎo jiě •	• very, quite

Circle the Pinyin for the character:

1. 很: hǎo   hěn   shì   zǎo

2. 早: zǎo   mǎ   hǎo   ma

3. 吗: mǎ   ma   má   ǎn

4. 早安: xiān shéng   míng zi   zǎo ǎn   xiǎo jiě

Arrange the words into sentences:

1. 我   叫   Alice。

   _____

2. 先生   马   早。

   _____

3. 很   我   好。

   _____

4. 吗   你   好。

   _____

● Radical Stroke Order　　Character Stroke Order ●

艮	曰	丨	且	马
很	早	小	姐	吗

Trace the following characters

艮									
曰									
丨									
且									
马									
很									
早									
小									
姐									
吗									

Unit 5

Self-Practice

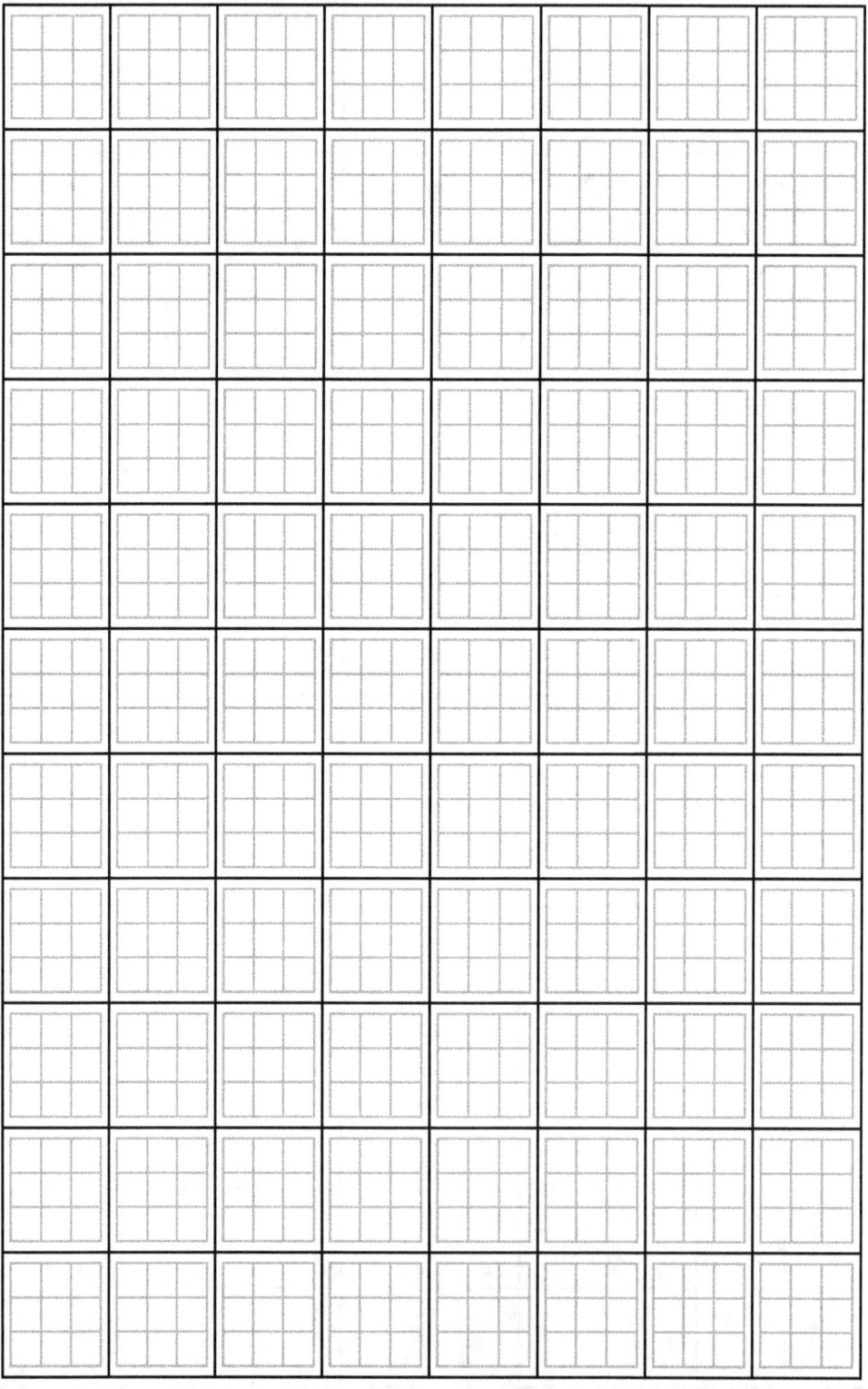

第六课　　　　Unit 6

您好,我姓王。您贵姓?
Nín hǎo, wǒ xìng Wáng. Nín guì xìng?
Hello! My last name is Wang. What's your last name?

您好,王先生,我姓陈。
Nín hǎo, Wáng xiān shéng, wǒ xìng Chén.
Hello Mr. Wang. My last name is Chen.

她是我太太 (1)。
Tā shì wǒ tài tai.
She is my wife.
(Pointing to his companion)

早上好,王太太 (2)!
Zǎo shàng hǎo, Wáng tài tai!
Good morning, Mrs. Wang!

This is a dialog between two couples who meet at a formal venue. The mood is formal and polite.

Dialog Vocabulary

太太(1)	tài tai	wife
太太(2)	tài tai	Mrs.
她	tā	she/ her
早上好	zǎo shàng hǎo	Good morning!
陈	Chén	Chen (surname)

Useful Vocabulary

他	tā	he/ him
太	tài	too
男	nán	male
女	nǚ	female
人	rén	person/ people
早上	zǎo shàng	(early) morning

Revision Vocabulary

早	zǎo	Morning!
姓	xìng	surname
您	Nín	you (polite)
王	Wáng	Wang
先生	xiān shéng	Mr./ husband
是	shì	to be (am,is,are)
贵姓	guì xìng	your last name?

Lesson Breakdown

> 您 贵 姓?
> Nín guì xìng ?
> What's your last name?

This is a very important expression that's often used during new introductions.

It is a **polite and formal** way to ask: "What is your **surname**?".

Note the 您 is indicating a polite tone, as discussed in a previous lesson.

您 (polite) is a different character from 你 (casual).

Both mean *you*, but they are written differently.

As mentioned earlier, 贵 [guì] has, on its own, no specific meaning in this sentence.

During an introduction, **it** is used in conjunction with 姓 [xìng] to introduce (or inquire after) a Surname.

> 早上好, 王太太(2)！
> Zǎo shàng hǎo, Wáng tài tai !
> Good morning, Mrs. Wang!

This is a more formal morning greeting and is used when greeting people at formal events, ceremonies or in the work environment.

It is also used when greeting older people or someone in a position of authority.

| 太太 | tài tai | Mrs. (Title) |

This is a *title* and it indicates that somebody is married.

Titles are preceded by surnames.

As seen in the provided dialog, the word 太太 , can also mean *wife*.

> 她 是 我太太(1)。
> Tā shì wǒ tài tai.
> She is my wife. (Pointing to his companion)

| 是 | shì | am, is, are |

We already know that this Verb is used to express **to exist and to be** through the use of *am, is, are*.

We can expand on that and use this Verb to explain the **relationship between two Nouns**.

In using this Verb, we can explain the relationship between a husband and his wife and we can thus put **emphasis on this relationship.**

We use the following structure:

N1 + 是 + N2

Example:

他 是 老师。

[tā shì lǎo shī]

He is a teacher.

The use of this structure implies a definite meaning and truth.

Supplementary

Writing: Radicals

她 and 他

The character for "she" is written as 她 and consists of a *female* radical 女 placed in front of 也.

女 + 也 = 她

The character for "he" is written as 他 and has the *person* radical 亻 in front of 也.

亻 + 也 = 他

Keep an eye open for radicals that define certain characters. It can be very beneficial in the long run.

Download The Bonus Audio Files To Practice Your Pronunciation

My Progress					Hint
Words	QW's	MW's	TW's	Total	是 is the Verb "to be", or *am, is, are*. It connects two Nouns and emphasizes their relationship.
Count	1	0	0	25	

Self-Practice

Connect and match:

太太 •	• nǔ •	• Good morning!
她 •	• chén •	• she
男 •	• nán •	• he
他 •	• tài tai •	• female
好 •	• tā •	• male
陈 •	• tā •	• to be good
女 •	• zǎo shàng •	• wife
早上 •	• hǎo •	• Chen

Rewrite the following sentences into Pinyin:

1. How are you? _____
2. Morning! _____
3. What's your surname? _____
4. Good morning Mr. Wang. _____
5. She is my wife. _____
6. My last name is Wang. _____

Circle the correct character in every line:

1. 大 , 太 , 哭 , 尢 , 犬
2. 早 , 車 , 串 , 旱 , 年
3. 始 , 也 , 她 , 祂 , 如
4. 是 , 走 , 足 , 起 , 先

● Radical Stroke Order　　Character Stroke Order ●

阝	上	大	也	三
陈	上	太	她	王

Trace the following characters

阝	阝	阝	阝	阝	阝	阝	阝	阝
上	上	上	上	上	上	上	上	上
大	大	大	大	大	大	大	大	大
也	也	也	也	也	也	也	也	也
三	三	三	三	三	三	三	三	三
陈	陈	陈	陈	陈	陈	陈	陈	陈
上	上	上	上	上	上	上	上	上
太	太	太	太	太	太	太	太	太
她	她	她	她	她	她	她	她	她
王	王	王	王	王	王	王	王	王

Self-Practice

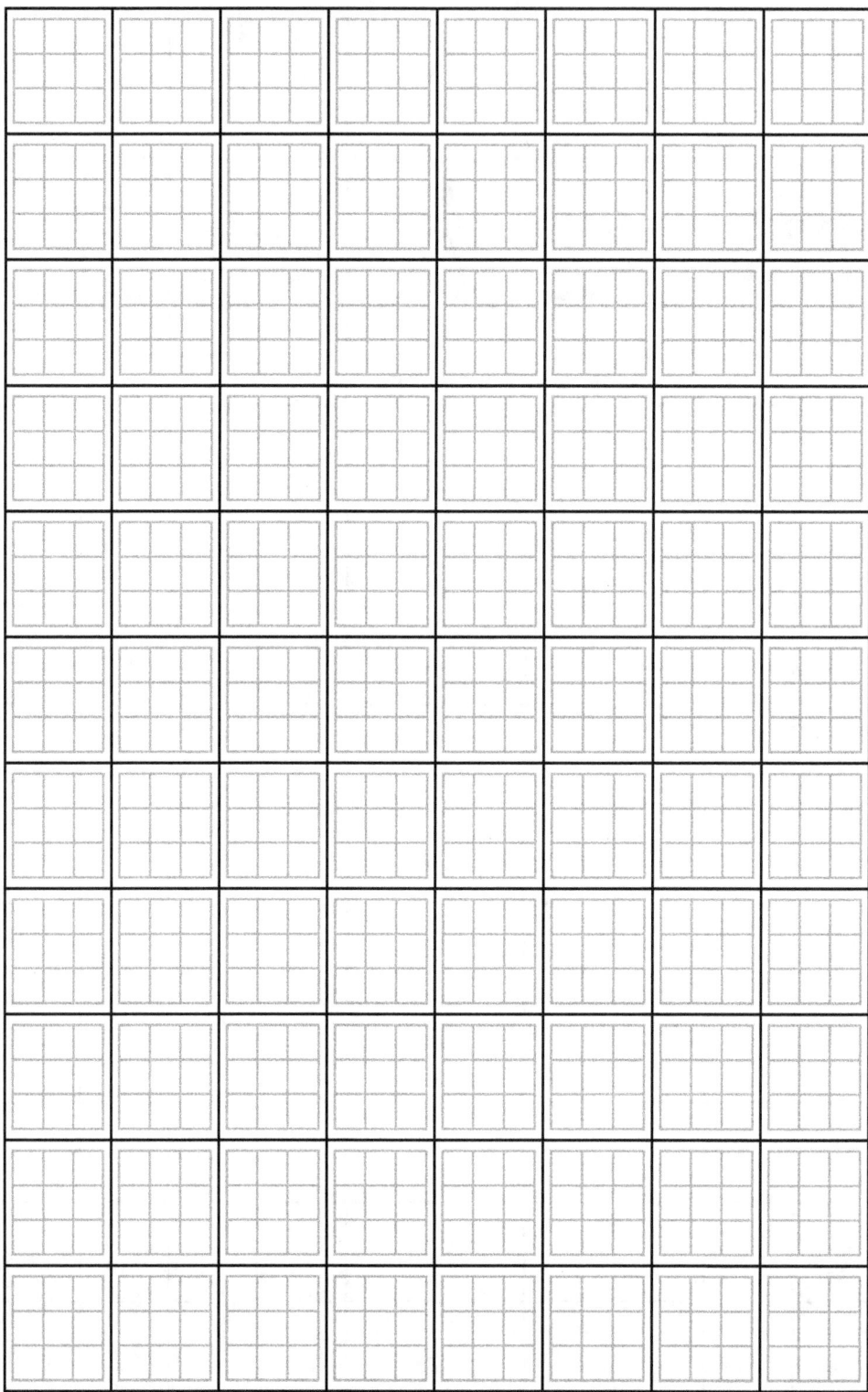

弟七课   Unit 7

田 小姐, 你 今天 忙 不 忙?
Tián xiǎo jiě, nǐ jīn tiān máng bù máng?
Miss Tien, are you busy today?

我 不 太 忙, 你 呢?
Wǒ bú tài máng, nǐ ne?
I am not too busy and you?

我 今天 不 忙。
Wǒ jīn tiān bù māng.
I am not busy today.

很好!
Hěn hǎo!
That is nice.

This is a dialog between two coworkers. Both work in the same department and the mood is friendly and casual.

Dialog Vocabulary

今天	jīn tiān	today
忙	máng	busy
不	bù	not/ no
太	tài	too
呢	ne	-and you?
田	Tián	Tian (surname)

Useful Vocabulary

天	tiān	day
天天	tiān tiān	every day
明天	míng tiān	tomorrow
昨天	zuó tiān	yesterday

Revision Vocabulary

小姐	xiǎo jiě	Miss
很	hěn	very
你	nǐ	you

Lesson Breakdown

我不太忙,你呢?
Wǒ bú tài máng, nǐ ne ?
I am not too busy and you?

This is an interesting sentence not only because it introduces a question particle, but also because it shows us *how to redirect a question back at the other speaker.*

It basically involves making a statement and ending it with ... *what about...?*

Let's have a look at the question particle used.

呢   ne   what about...?

呢 is a question particle with many uses. In this case it means: - and you? It is connected to a Pronoun and asks a related question:

I am hungry, **and you?**

We use this structure:

Statement + 呢

When using this structure, you first make a statement about your own situation, then redirect by asking what the other speaker thinks about it.

Take note, that we still place a question mark behind 呢.

> 我 今天 不忙。
> Wǒ jīn tiān bù māng.
> I am not busy today.

今天   jīn tiān   today

The use of 今天 is important because it is a Time Word (TW).

Time-words indicate when an action takes place and are placed at the beginning of a sentence.

Note!

Try not to say: 我 不忙 今天。 [Wǒ bù māng jīn tiān] Incorrect!

不   bù   no/ not

This Adverb means "no/ not" and it usually **precedes a Verb or an Adjective**.

I am not hungry, tired, thirsty, busy, etc.

> 你 今天 忙不忙?
> Nǐ jīn tiān máng bù máng ?
> Are you busy today?

| 忙不忙 | máng bù máng | busy or not |

This literally means: busy or not busy? One way to ask a question in Chinese, is to **place emphasis on the Adjective** through the use of the negative 不 meaning *not*. We do this by asking a **question with alternatives**. The structure used is:

Adjective + 不 + Adjective

Example:
你 累 不 累?
[nǐ lèi bú lèi]
You tired or not tired?

This is a casual way to ask if someone is tired.

Note that besides Adjectives, we can also formulate questions with alternatives through the use of Verbs.

Supplementary

Writing: Radicals

呢 has the 口 radical at the front which means: *mouth*.
This means that we use it for a *spoken* expression.

忙 has the 忄 radical at the front which means: *heart*.
This means that there is an *emotion* involved.

Download The Bonus Audio Files To Practice Your Pronunciation

My Progress

Words	QW's	MW's	TW's	Total
Count	1	0	1	31

Hint

TWs belong at the front of sentences. Remember, question particles are not QWs.

Self-Practice

Connect and match:

忙 •	• ne •	• particle -and you?
呢 •	• tài •	• day
天 •	• bù •	• yesterday
不 •	• tiān •	• busy
今天 •	• zuó tiān •	• no/ not
明天 •	• míng tiān •	• too
太 •	• jīn tiān •	• today
昨天 •	• máng •	• tomorrow

Write questions for the following answers:

1. _____?
我很好。
2. _____?
我姓王。
3. _____?
我叫 James。
4. _____?
今天我不忙。

Arrange the words into sentences:

1. 不　你　忙　今天　忙。

2. 忙　太　我　不。

3. 很　我　忙。

4. 不　你　忙。

● Radical Stroke Order　　Character Stroke Order ●

Trace the following characters

忄									
七									
丁									
今									
大									
忙									
呢									
不									
今									
天									

Self-Practice

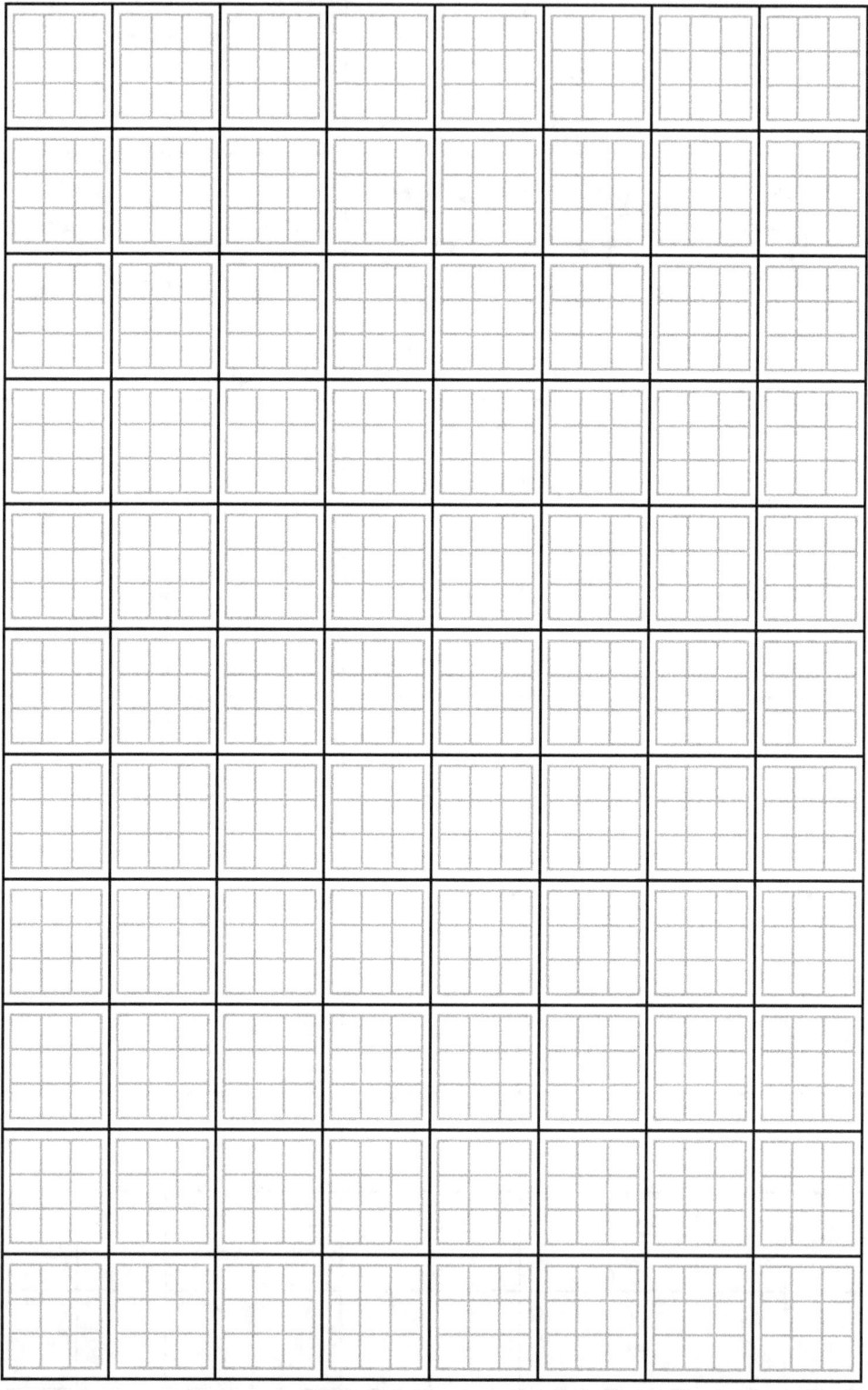

第八课　　　　Unit 8

你好！你是 美国人 吗？
Nǐ hǎo ! Nǐ shì Měi guó rén ma ?
Hello! Are you American?

是的, 我是 美国人。你 呢？
Shì de, wǒ shì Měi guó rén. Nǐ ne ?
Yes, I am an American. How about you?

我是 法国人。我的 名字 是 David。
Wǒ shì Fǎ guó rén. Wǒ de míng zi shì David.
I am French. My name is David.

你好, David！我的 名字 是 Jeff。
Nǐ hǎo, David! Wǒ de míng zi shì Jeff.
Hello David! My name is Jeff.

This is a dialog between two students who meet at the International Language Institute. Both are eager to reach out to make new friends.

Dialog Vocabulary

人	rén	person
国	guó	country/ nation
法国人	Fǎ guó rén	Frenchman
美国人	Měi guó rén	American
我的	wǒ de	my/ mine
是的	shì de	yes/ right
的	de	possessive

Useful Vocabulary

美	měi	beautiful
美国	Měi guó	U.S.A.
中国	Zhōng guó	China
男人	nán rén	men
女人	nǚ rén	women

Revision Vocabulary

你呢	nǐ ne	-and you?
名字	míng zi	name
是	shì	to be (am,is,are)
吗	ma	question particle?

Lesson Breakdown

你是 美国人 吗?

Nǐ shì Měiguó rén ma ?

Are you American?

是　　　shì　　　am/is/are

We can use this Verb to explain the relationship between *two Nouns*. In this case it is used to explain the relationship between a person and his nationality.

This Verb is used to point out "to be". It implies a definite meaning and truth and it puts emphasis on the phrase following 是 .

> 是的, 我是 美国人。你 呢?
> Shì de, wǒ shì Měi guó rén. Nǐ ne ?
> Yes, I am an American. How about you?

| 是的 | shì de | yes/ correct |

This word literally means: " yes, it is".

You will notice in many instances, that the Verb 是 is used on its own, to imply "yes". This begs the question, what is the difference in adding or omitting the particle 的 ?

The 的 particle is added just for **emphasis** and as such, it implies that the **speaker concurs**.

For general statements we omit this particle.

| 美国人 | Měi guó rén | American |

In the sentence the actual country, 美国 , is followed by the character for person, 人 [rén].

This literally means: "American person".

Thus, placing the character for person (人) behind the name of the country, presents us with the *person who inhabits that country*.

Interesting to note, that 美 [Měi] means *beautiful* and 国 [guó] means *country*.

The reason for this, is not because the Chinese admire America as a beautiful country. It is because the 2nd syllable sounds like "mei", as in A-**me**-ri-ca.

It allows the Chinese word to sound similar to the English word in pronunciation.

In Mandarin neutral words, or words positive in meaning, are used as country names.

> 我的 名字 是 Jeff。
> Wǒ de míng zi shì Jeff.
> My name is Jeff.

的   de   possessive particle

We use this particle to indicate **possession**. The sentence structure for possession is:

Subject + 的 + Noun

Example:

我 的 房子。

[**wǒ de** fáng zi]

My house.

It is similar to the use of the apostrophe (') in English.

The Subject can be a person, Pronoun, name, animal, place or object and the Noun, to be possessed, can be any object, physical or abstract in nature.

Examples of Pronouns:

我 的   [wǒ de] means: mine

他 的   [tā de] means: his

她 的   [tā de] means: her

It can be used with Pronouns like *mine* and *his*, but it can also be used with Nouns, Adjectives and Verbs. This is a **very important particle** that is used very, very often!

Download The Bonus Audio Files To Practice Your Pronunciation

My Progress

Words	QW's	MW's	TW's	Total
Count	1	0	1	38

Hint

Particle 的 is used for **emphasis** or for **possession**. For possession, it's followed by a Noun.

Unit 8

Self-Practice

Connect and match:

人 •   • měi guó •   • person
国 •   • de •   • my/ mine
法国人 •   • fǎ guó rén •   • possessive
是 的 •   • guó •   • Frenchman
法国 •   • shì de •   • America
美国 •   • fǎ guó •   • country
的 •   • wǒ de •   • France
我的 •   • rén •   • yes

Rewrite the following sentences into Pinyin:

1. Are you French? _____
2. Yes, I am French. _____
3. How about you? _____
4. My wife is French. _____
5. My name is Dave. _____
6. Mr Wang is an American. _____

Circle the correct character in every line:

1. 口 , 玉 , 国 , 凶 , 团
2. 亻 , 人 , 认 , 入 , 八
3. 的 , 昀 , 铂 , 肐 , 朐
4. 去 , 法 , 丢 , 圭 , 王

● Radical Stroke Order Character Stroke Order ●

亻 玉 氵 羊 勺

人 国 法 美 的

Trace the following characters

亻									
玉									
氵									
羊									
勺									
人									
国									
法									
美									
的									

Unit 8

Self-Practice

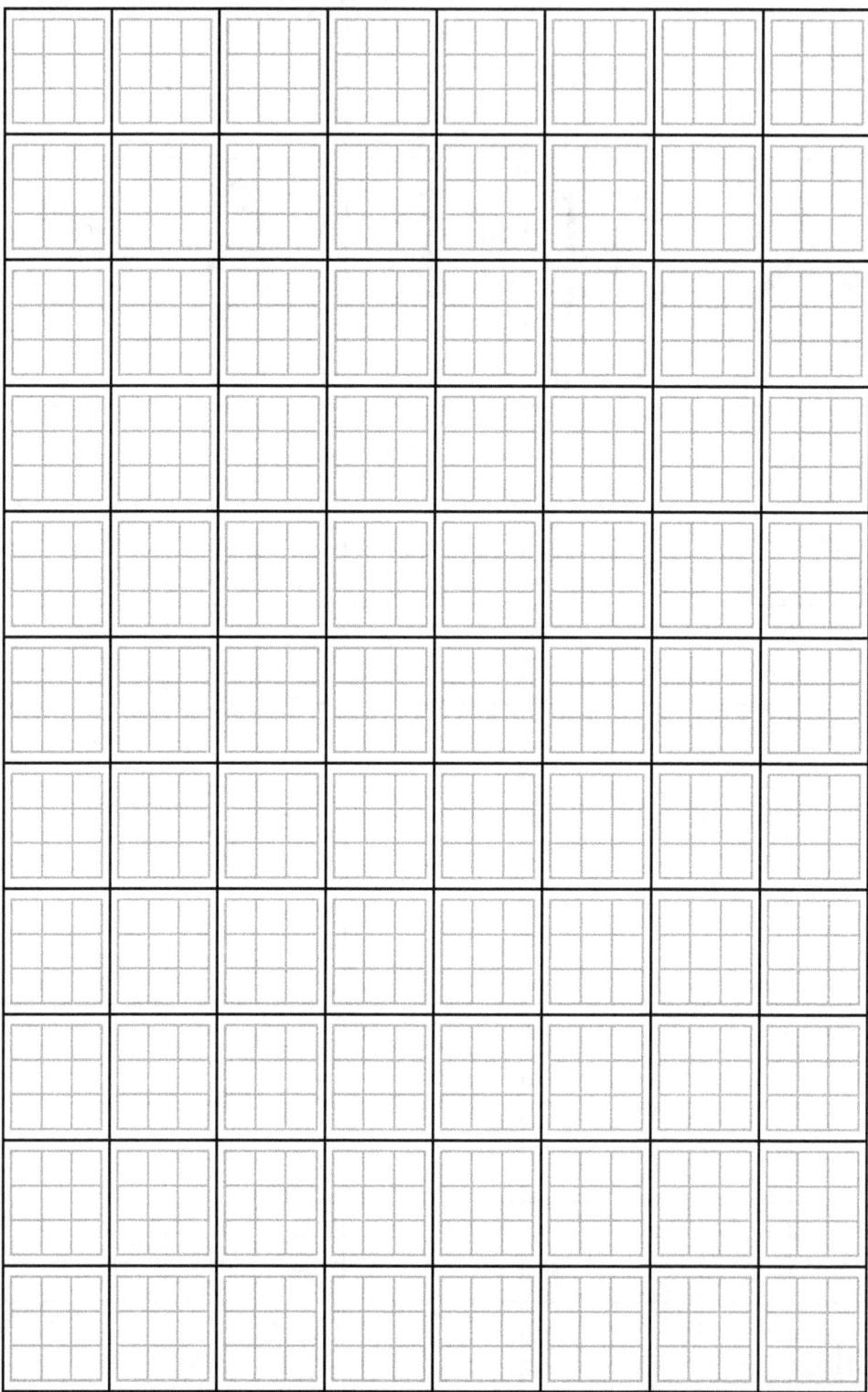

第九课　　　Unit 9

李小姐,他是谁?他很帅!
Lǐ xiǎo jiě, tā shì shéi ? Tā hěn shuài !
Miss Lee, who is that? He is very handsome!
(Pointing)

他是 Terry。他是英国人。
Tā shì Terry. Tā shì Yīng guó rén.
That is Terry. He is English.

他是你的先生吗?
Tā shí nǐ de xiān shēng ma ?
Is he your husband?

是的,他是我先生。
Shí de, tā shí wǒ xiān shēng.
Yes, he is my husband.

This is a dialog between two coworkers who meet at a work function. Both are curious about the other. The mood is still polite.

Dialog Vocabulary

谁	shéi	who/ whom
他	tā	he/ him
帅	shuài	handsome
英国	Yīng guó	England
英国人	Yīng guó rén	Englishman
先生	xiān shēng	husband
你的	nǐ de	your/ yours

Useful Vocabulary

我的	wǒ de	my/ mine
他的	tā de	his
她的	tā de	her/ hers
德国	Dé guó	Germany
泰国	Tài guó	Thailand

Revision Vocabulary

他	tā	he/him
美	měi	to be pretty
人	rén	person/ people
的	de	possessive particle

Lesson Breakdown

他是我先生。

Tā shí wǒ xiān shēng.

He is my husband.

Note that in this sentence the speaker did not use the possessive particle 的 again.

She did not say: 我的先生。

In certain situations we can omit this particle. The reason is that once the Object is understood by both parties, it is acceptable to omit the possessive particle (的).

Let's look at the different situations that we can distinguish.

When two Nouns have a certain *closeness*, due to family or other personal relationships, we can omit the possessive particle.

The first example of closeness in relationship is the **relationship between family members and very close friends**. These are special relationships and the need to indicate possession through the use of 的 is not necessary.

A second example is where the speaker has a **professional connection** with an institution, like a school or company, where he/she spends the majority of their time. In a situation such as this, indicating possession with particle 的 is not necessary.

(As mentioned before, 先生 [xiān shēng] can mean Mister or husband.)

> 李 小姐, 他 是 谁?
> Lǐ xiǎo jiě, tā shì shéi ?
> Miss Lee, who is that?

> 谁　　　shéi　　　who?

You will notice that in the example sentence provided, the question particle (-吗) has been omitted.

We can omit the question particles, because the word 谁 is already a Question Word that means: who?

The rule is, that if the sentence has a **Question Word, there is no need for a question particle** -吗.

We only use the question particle for sentences where a Yes/ No answer is expected.

This is a very important aspect which should be kept in mind when forming question-type sentences.

Typical QWs you should focus on:

> Why/ When/ Where/ Who/ What/ How?

We will continue to point them out as we move along.

> Supplementary

Basic Country List of countries with character 国:

中国	zhōng guó	China
美国	měi guó	USA
英国	yīng guó	England
法国	fǎ guó	France
泰国	tài guó	Thailand
韩国	hán guó	South Korea
德国	dé guó	Germany

Similar to our explanation in Unit 8, it is interesting to note that every country name has a neutral and positive meaning:

England (brave/ outstanding), France (law/ method), Germany (virtue), Thailand (peaceful/ most), etc.

These country names should be memorized.

> Download The Bonus Audio Files To Practice Your Pronunciation

My Progress

Words	QW's	MW's	TW's	Total
Count	2	0	1	45

Hint

When using QWs we can omit the question particles. We omit 的 when 2 Nouns have a relationship.

Self-Practice

Connect and match:

谁	• shuài •	• husband
他	• shéi •	• who
的	• tā •	• Englishman
帅	• de •	• he/ him
英国	• yīng guó rén •	• England
你的	• xiān shēng •	• your
英国人	• nǐ de •	• to be handsome
先生	• yīng guó •	• possessive

Translate the following sentences into English:

1. Shí de, tā shí wǒ xiān shēng.
   _____

2. Lǐ xiǎo jiě, tā shì shéi ?
   _____

3. Tā shí nǐ de xiān shēng ma ?
   _____

4. Tā hěn shuài !
   _____

Arrange the words into sentences:

1. 是   他   Terry。

2. 先生   我   是   他。

3. 很   他   帅。

4. 谁   他   是?

● Radical Stroke Order   Character Stroke Order ●

木	央	巾	也	隹
李	英	帅	他	谁

Trace the following characters

木									
央									
巾									
也									
隹									
李									
英									
帅									
他									
谁									

Unit 9

Self-Practice

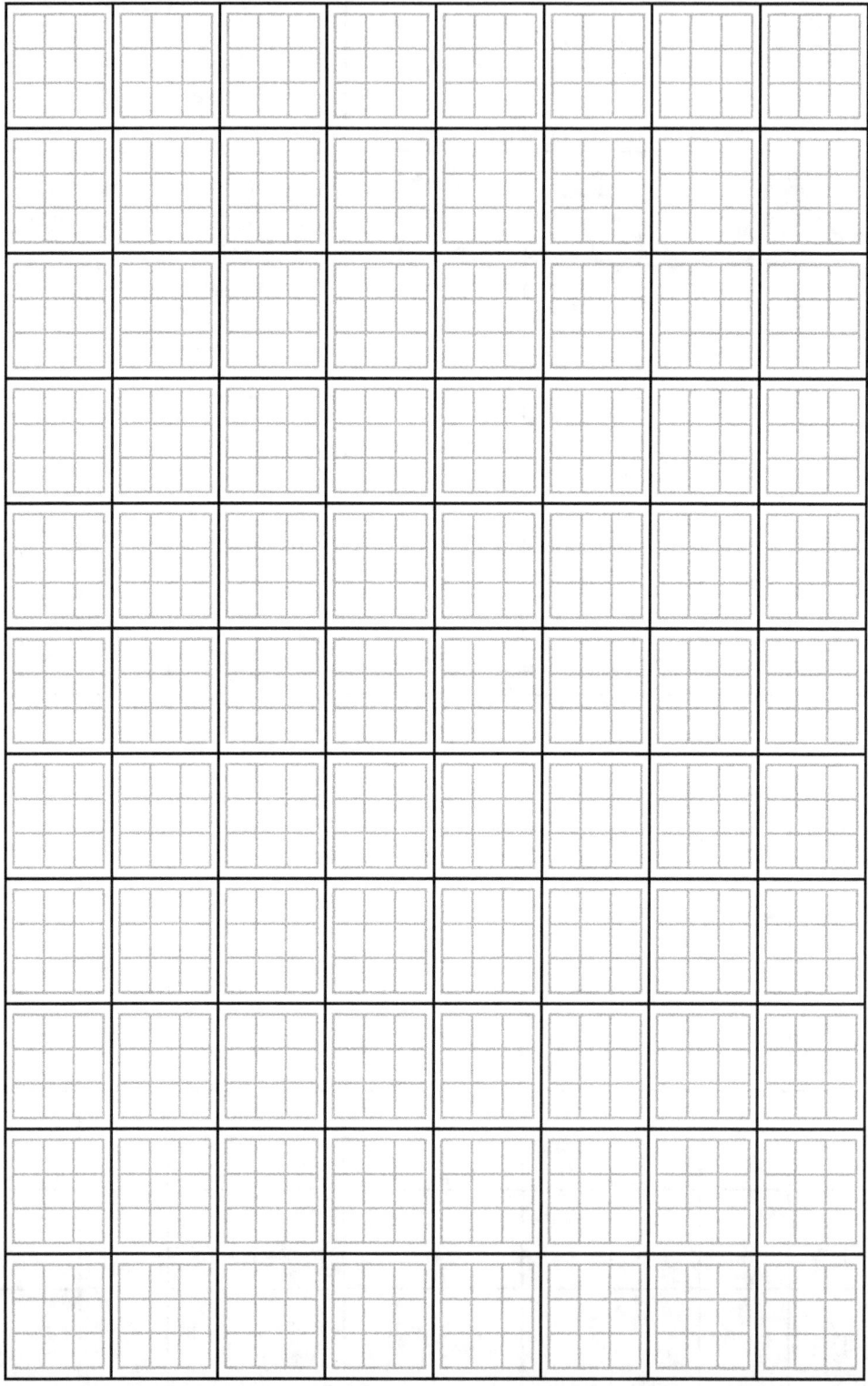

第十课 Unit 10

那是 Jenny 吗? 她很美。

Nà shí Jenny ma ? Tā hěn měi.

Is that Jenny? She is very pretty.

她不叫 Jenny。她的 中国 名字 叫 文美。

Tā bú jiào Jenny. Tā de Zhōng guó míng zi jiào Wén měi.

She is not Jenny. Her Chinese name is Wenmei.

她是 哪国人?

Tā shí něi guó rén ?

Which country is she from?

她是 德国人。

Tā shí Dé guó rén.

She is from Germany.

This is a dialog between two students who meet at the Language Institute in China. The mood is relaxed and casual.

Dialog Vocabulary

德国人	Dé guó rén	German (person)
美	měi	pretty
不叫	bú jiào	not to be called
文美	Wén Měi	Wenmei (name)
中国	Zhōng Guó	China (country)
那	nà/ nèi	that
哪	nǎ/ něi	which/ where

Useful Vocabulary

帅	shuài	handsome
可爱	kě ài	cute
丑	chǒu	ugly
高	gāo	tall
矮	ǎi	short
中文	Zhōng wén	Chinese (written)

Revision Vocabulary

她	tā	she/ her
人	rén	person/ people
国	guó	country/ nation

Lesson Breakdown

> 那 是 Jenny 吗?
> Nà shí Jenny ma ?
> Is that Jenny?

| 那 | nà/nèi | that |

This is a Place-word (PW) and it is pronounced in the 4th tone as either [nà] or [nèi].

The example sentence literally means: "**That**, is Jenny?"

Note that this is not a Question Word and it should not be confused with 哪 which has a completely different meaning.

> 她是哪国人?
> Tā shí něi guó rén ?
> Which country is she from?

哪　　nǎ/něi　which?

This is a Question Word and it is pronounced in the 3rd tone as both [nǎ] or [něi]. The example sentence literally means: "She is **which** country person?"

We use the following structure:

Noun + Verb + 哪

Example:
他要哪一个?
[tā yào nǎ yī gè]
Which one does he want?

QWs are used to form questions. They allow us to express the sentence in question form, and therefore we do not need to add the question particle 吗 at the end of the sentence.

> 她的 中国 名字 叫 文美。
> Tā de Zhōng guó míng zi jiào Wén měi.
> Her Chinese name is WenMei.

Chinese names and English names are common in China.

A Chinese name starts with the family name first, followed by the given name consisting of two characters.

Example:
王 (family name) 文美 (given name)

Supplementary

Writing: Radicals

Note the difference in character and tone (3rd/4th) between:

那 [nà] and 哪 [nǎ/ něi]

哪 might seem similar to 那, but if you look closely you will see that it is different.

哪 has the 口 radical in front which means *mouth*. This implies that it is a *spoken* question or expression.

口 + 那 = 哪

Tones:

Rule: [bù] changes to [bú] when followed by a 4th tone:

他 不 叫 Jenny。

[Tā bú jiào Jenny]

She is not (called) Jenny.

In this case [bú] is pronounced in the 2nd tone because it is followed by 叫 [jiào] which is in the 4th tone.

Explanation:

We already know that in the normal usage [bù] is pronounced in the 4th tone.

Example:

我 不 好。[wǒ bù hǎo], where [bù] is 4th tone.

BUT, when 不 is followed by another 4th tone, we change it to a 2nd tone! An example will clarify things:

不 叫 [bú jiào], where [bú] is 2nd tone.

This change in tone applies only to 不 followed by a **4th tone**.

Download The Bonus Audio Files To Practice Your Pronunciation

My Progress					Hint
Words	QW's	MW's	TW's	Total	Break characters down into their individual radicals and learn the meaning of the radical.
Count	3	0	1	52	

Self-Practice

Connect and match:

那 •	• zhōng guó •	• that
美 •	• dé guó •	• Germany
哪 •	• nà •	• which
可爱 •	• nǎ •	• Chinese
中文 •	• ǎi •	• China
德国 •	• kě ài •	• pretty
矮 •	• zhōng wén •	• cute
中国 •	• měi •	• to be short

Rewrite the following sentences into Pinyin:

1. She is Jenny. _____
2. She is not Mary. _____
3. Which country is she from? _____
4. She is from Germany. _____
5. Is that May? _____
6. She is very cute. _____

Circle the correct character in every line:

1. 中 , 口 , 甲 , 由 , 巾
2. 耶 , 那 , 邦 , 绑 , 邢
3. 聽 , 悪 , 德 , 徳 , 得
4. 丈 , 叉 , 夂 , 又 , 文

● Radical Stroke Order　　Character Stroke Order ●

四	亠	口	月	阝
德	文	中	那	哪

Trace the following characters

四									
亠									
口									
月									
阝									
德									
文									
中									
那									
哪									

Self-Practice

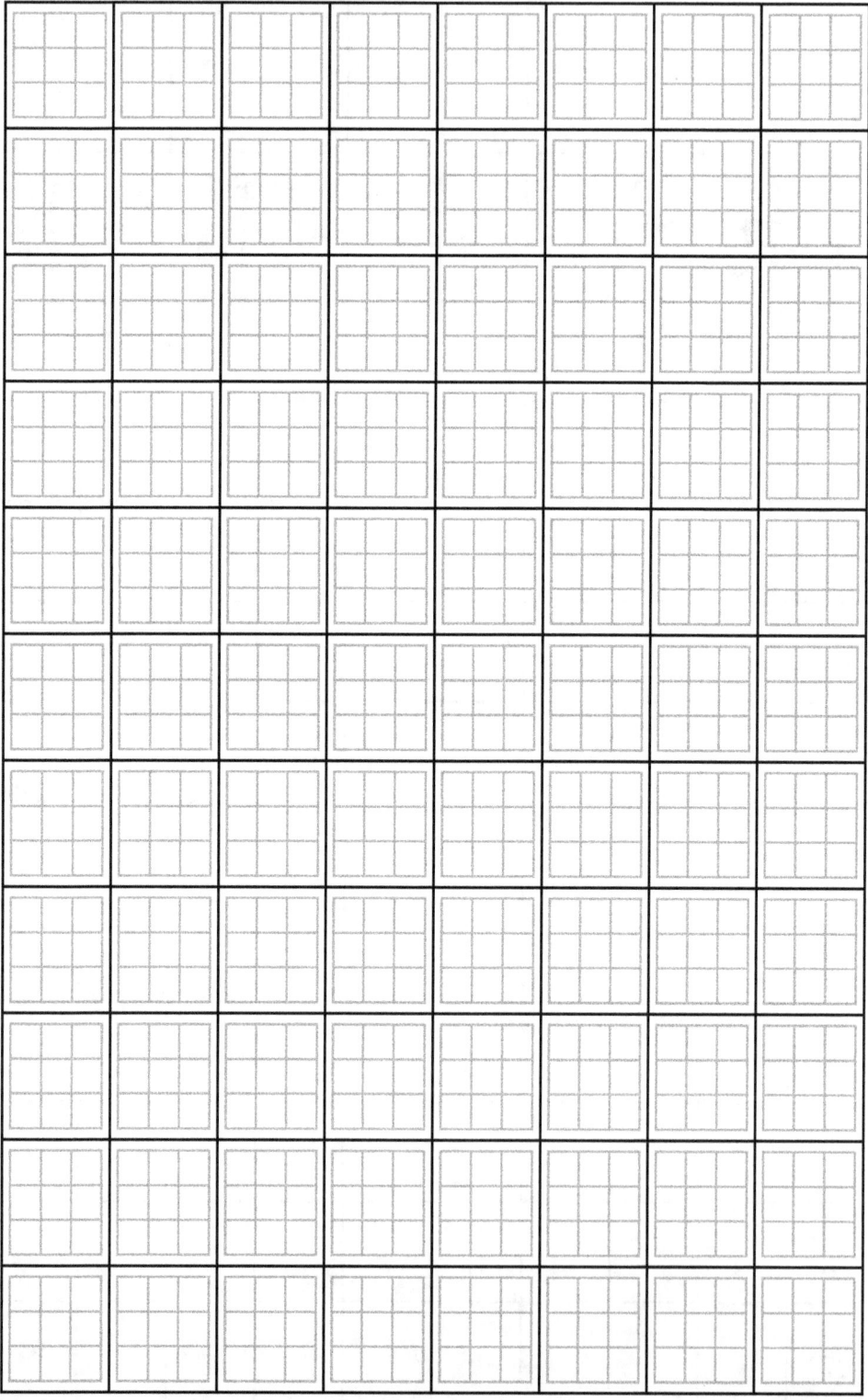

第十一课　　Unit 11

你看！他在 中国 很有名！
Nǐ kàn! Tā zài Zhōng guó hěn yǒu míng!
Look! He is very famous in China!

他的 英文 名字 是 Jimmy Decaprio。
Tā de Yīng wén míng zi shí Jimmy Decaprio.
His English name is Jimmy Decaprio.

他是 哪 国人？意大利 吗？
Tā shí něi guó rén? Yì dà lì ma?
Which country is he from? Italy?

对, 他是 意大利 人。
Duì, tā shí Yì dà lì rén.
Yes, he is Italian.

This is a dialog between two friends who are outside a convention center. Both are trying to get a peek at some celebrities present.

Dialog Vocabulary

看	kàn	to look
有名	yǒu míng	to be famous
对	duì	yes/ correct
意大利	Yì dà lì	Italy
英文	Yīng wén	English (language)
在	zài	to be on,-in, -at,

Useful Vocabulary

日本	Rì bén	Japan
法国	Fǎ guó	France
法文	Fǎ wén	French (language)
名人	míng rén	celebrity
不知名	bù zhī míng	unknown
看见	kàn jiàn	to see

Revision Vocabulary

哪	nǎ/ něi	which
他	tā	he/ him
他的	tā de	his
中国	Zhōng guó	China

Lesson Breakdown

你看!他在 中国 很有名!

Nǐ kàn ! Tā zài Zhōng guó hěn yǒu míng !

Look! He is very famous in China!

看   kàn   look

This is a Verb.
As used in the example sentence, it literally means: "You look!"
Note that, in the example provided, that the Verb 看 means *to look*.
It can however, also be used to indicate:
to watch, to read, to look and *to see*.

Unit 11

Examples:

我看书。　　[wǒ **kàn shū**]　　　I read a book.
我看电视。　[wǒ **kàn** diàn shì]　I watch TV.
我看到他。　[wǒ **kàn** daò tā]　　I see him.

> 在　　　　zài　　　　in/at/on

This is a very important Verb that acts as a **Place Word** (PW) or Preposition and it expresses place or position.

We use the following structure:

(Subject)　+　在　+　Place

Example:

我 在 这里。

[**wǒ** zài zhè lǐ]

I am over here.

This Verb acts as a **Preposition**, telling us *where* someone or something is *located*.

```
对, 他是 意大利人。
Duì, tā shí Yìdàlì rén.
Yes, he is Italian.
```

> 对　　　　dui　　　　yes/correct

This is another way to say yes or correct.

It is often used as: 对 不 对 ? meaning: correct or not correct?

This is an important word that is used very often and it also has other applications which we will learn about in later lessons.

意大利   Yì dà lì   Italy

Note the word for Italy. Not all countries have 国 in their names.

In this case the Chinese name sounds similar to the English in pronunciation.

You should know as many countries as you can for it is a great conversation topic and it's bound to come up when meeting native speakers.

Try to memorize as many individual countries as you can.

Supplementary

英文 vs 英国

Look at the following two suffixes:

文 [wén] refers to the *language* and *culture*.

国 [guó] refers to the physical *country*.

This applies to almost all countries and languages.

Chinese names:

Interesting to note, that all famous people from outside of China, are given Chinese names to be used in China. Actors and singers, whether from Japan, Europe, USA, etc. are all known by their Chinese names, given to them by the media.

As a student of Mandarin you should get your own, unique Chinese name as well.

Download The Bonus Audio Files To Practice Your Pronunciation

My Progress

Words	QW's	MW's	TW's	Total
Count	3	0	1	58

Hint

Remember that a PW is followed by the actual place. It acts as a Preposition.

Self-Practice

Connect and match:

在 •   • yīng wén •   • yes
看 •   • fǎ wén •   • English
英文 •   • kàn •   • French
有名 •   • rì běn •   • famous
名字 •   • duì •   • Japan
日本 •   • yǒu míng •   • in, on, at
对 •   • míng zi •   • name
法文 •   • zài •   • to look

Translate the following sentences into English:

1. Tā de Yīng wén míng zi shí Jimmy
   _____

2. Tā shí něi guó rén ?
   _____

3. Nǐ kàn !
   _____

4. Duì, tā shí rì běn rén.
   _____

Arrange the words into sentences:

1. 英国   是   他   人。
   _____

2. 有名   很   他。
   _____

3. 他   对   是   中国人。
   _____

4. 哪   你   是   国   人?
   _____

● Radical Stroke Order　　Character Stroke Order ●

人	目	寸	月	土
大	看	对	有	在

Trace the following characters

人	人	人	人	人	人	人	人	人
目	目	目	目	目	目	目	目	目
寸	寸	寸	寸	寸	寸	寸	寸	寸
月	月	月	月	月	月	月	月	月
土	土	土	土	土	土	土	土	土
大	大	大	大	大	大	大	大	大
看	看	看	看	看	看	看	看	看
对	对	对	对	对	对	对	对	对
有	有	有	有	有	有	有	有	有
在	在	在	在	在	在	在	在	在

Self-Practice

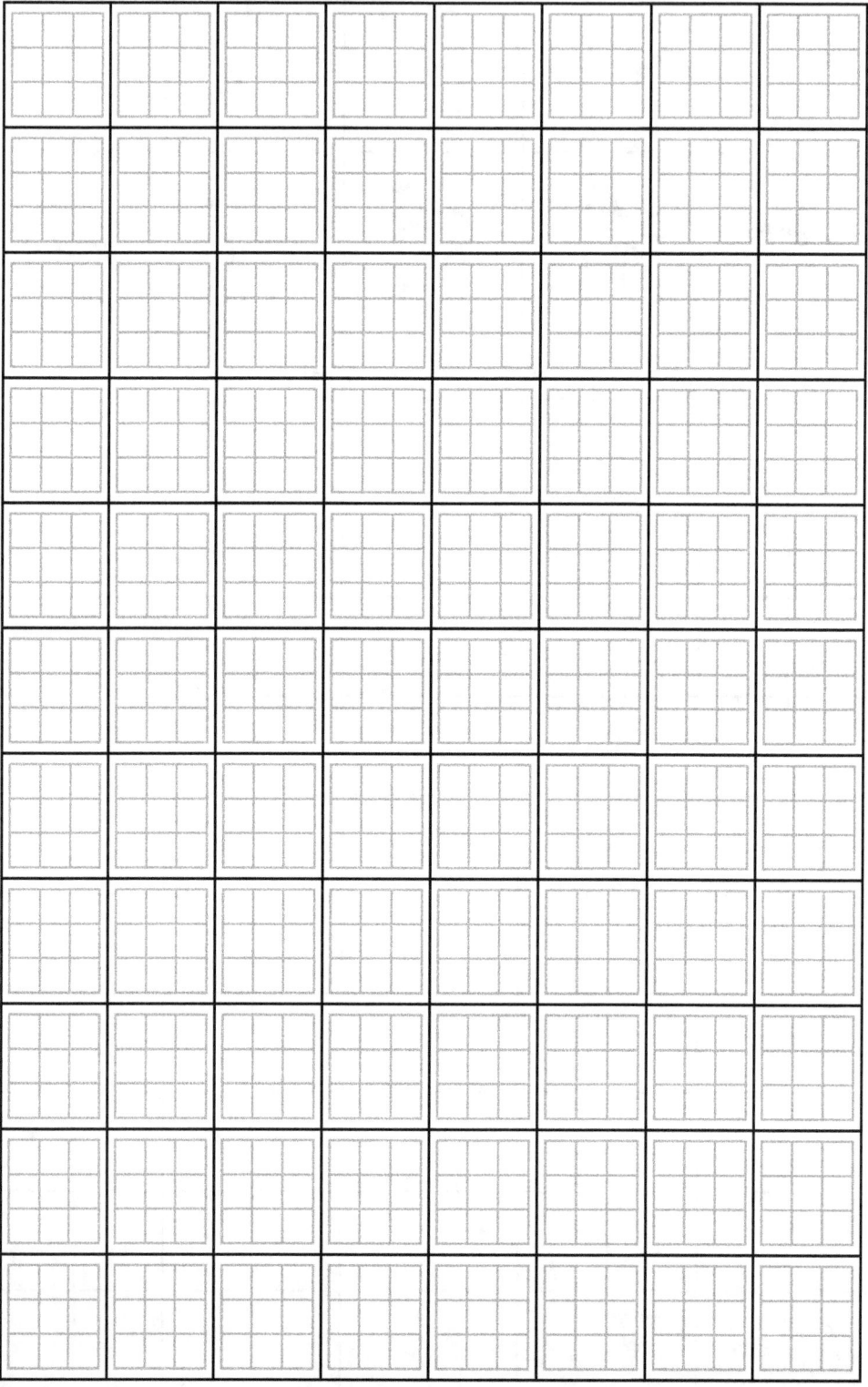

第十二课　　Unit 12

早安, 吴先生, 好久不见!
Zǎo ān, Wú xiān sheng. Hǎo jiǔ bù jiàn!
Good morning, Mr. Wu. Long time no see!

早安, 林先生! 是的, 好久不见!
Zǎo ān, Lín xiān sheng! Shì de, hǎo jiǔ bù jiàn!
Good morning, Mr. Lin! Yes, long time no see!

今天, 你好吗?
Jǐn tiān, nǐ hǎo mǎ?
How are you today?

我不好, 今天 很冷!
Wǒ bù hǎo. Jǐn tiān hěn lěng!
I am not well. It's very cold today!

This is a dialog between two old friends who bump into each other. They are glad for this opportunity to exchange pleasantries.

Dialog Vocabulary

好	hǎo	very/ quite
久	jiǔ	long time
好久	hǎo jiǔ	quite a while
冷	lěng	cold
吴	Wú	Wu
林	Lín	Lin

Useful Vocabulary

天	tiān	sky/ heaven
天气	tiān qì	weather
冬天	dōng tiān	winter
夏天	xià tiān	summer
热	rè	heat/ hot

Revision Vocabulary

今天	jīn tiān	today
是的	shì de	yes/ correct
很	hěn	very
见	jiàn	to see/ to meet

Lesson Breakdown

好久不见!

Hǎo jiǔ bù jiàn!

Long time no see!

This is a very common phrase that is used as a *greeting*.

This sentence literally means: "Very long time no see."

It is quite normal to use this expression if you haven't seen someone in quite a while.

The mood is polite and friendly. It is used in exactly the same manner as used in the English language.

好　　　hǎo　　　very

This is an Adverb that means *very*. It acts as a "joining word" between the Noun and the Adjective to describe the Adjective.

It tells us "how long ago".

In an earlier lesson we also learned that 好 can act as an Adjective to mean *good*.

Thus this word has two meanings and two functions:

As an Adverb it means **very**, and as an Adjective it means **good**.

今天 很冷！
Jǐn tiān hěn lěng！
It's very cold today!

很　　　hěn　　　quite

As mentioned before, this word has multiple functions. As an Adverb it acts as a "joining word" to join the Noun and the Adjective together.

今天 is the Noun in the above sentence.

冷　is the Adjective in the sentence.

The Adjective (cold) describe the Noun (today).

很 is used as a joining word between the Noun and the Adjective.

It indicates the *degree* of "how cold" it is.

We cannot omit the joining word:

今天 冷　[Jǐn tiān lěng] This is **not** correct.

We need a joining word like 很 to connect the Noun and the Adjective and also to indicate the **degree of the Adjective**.

Other indicators of degree is:

很	[hěn]	quite
好	[hǎo]	very
真	[zhēn]	really
非常	[fēi cháng]	extremely

Thus both 好 and 很 can act as *joining words* and they are indicators of different *degrees for the adjective*.

(Note that an Adjective is called a Stative Verb in Chinese.)

Supplementary

List of common Chinese Surnames:

王	**Wáng**	Wang
李	**Lǐ**	Li
陈	**Chén**	Chen
杨	**Yáng**	Yang
赵	**Zhào**	Zhao
吴	**Wú**	Wu
马	**Mǎ**	Ma

Download The Bonus Audio Files To Practice Your Pronunciation

My Progress

Words	QW's	MW's	TW's	Total
Count	3	0	1	64

Hint

Remember that "joining words" are essential and cannot be omitted. They show **degree**.

Self-Practice

Connect and match:

天 • • tiān qì • • very
冷 • • hǎo • • sky
好 • • dōng tiān • • weather
天气 • • jiǔ • • long time
吴 • • lín • • Wu
冬天 • • tiān • • Lin
久 • • wú • • cold
林 • • lěng • • winter

Rewrite the following sentences into Pinyin:

1. Morning Mr. Lin. _____
2. The winter is very cold. _____
3. I am not well. _____
4. It's very cold today. _____
5. How are you today? _____
6. Long time no see. _____

Circle the correct character in every line:

1. 冷 , 今 , 念 , 会 , 全
2. 欠 , 久 , 夂 , 无 , 攵
3. 王 , 天 , 天 , 无 , 夫
4. 乞 , 气 , 氕 , 吃 , 汽

94

● Radical Stroke Order　　Character Stroke Order ●

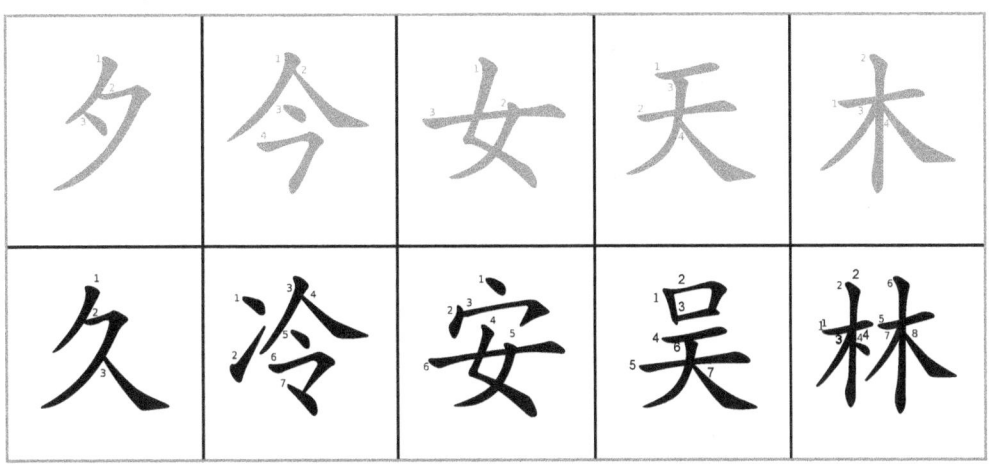

Trace the following characters

夕									
今									
女									
天									
木									
久									
冷									
安									
吴									
林									

Self-Practice

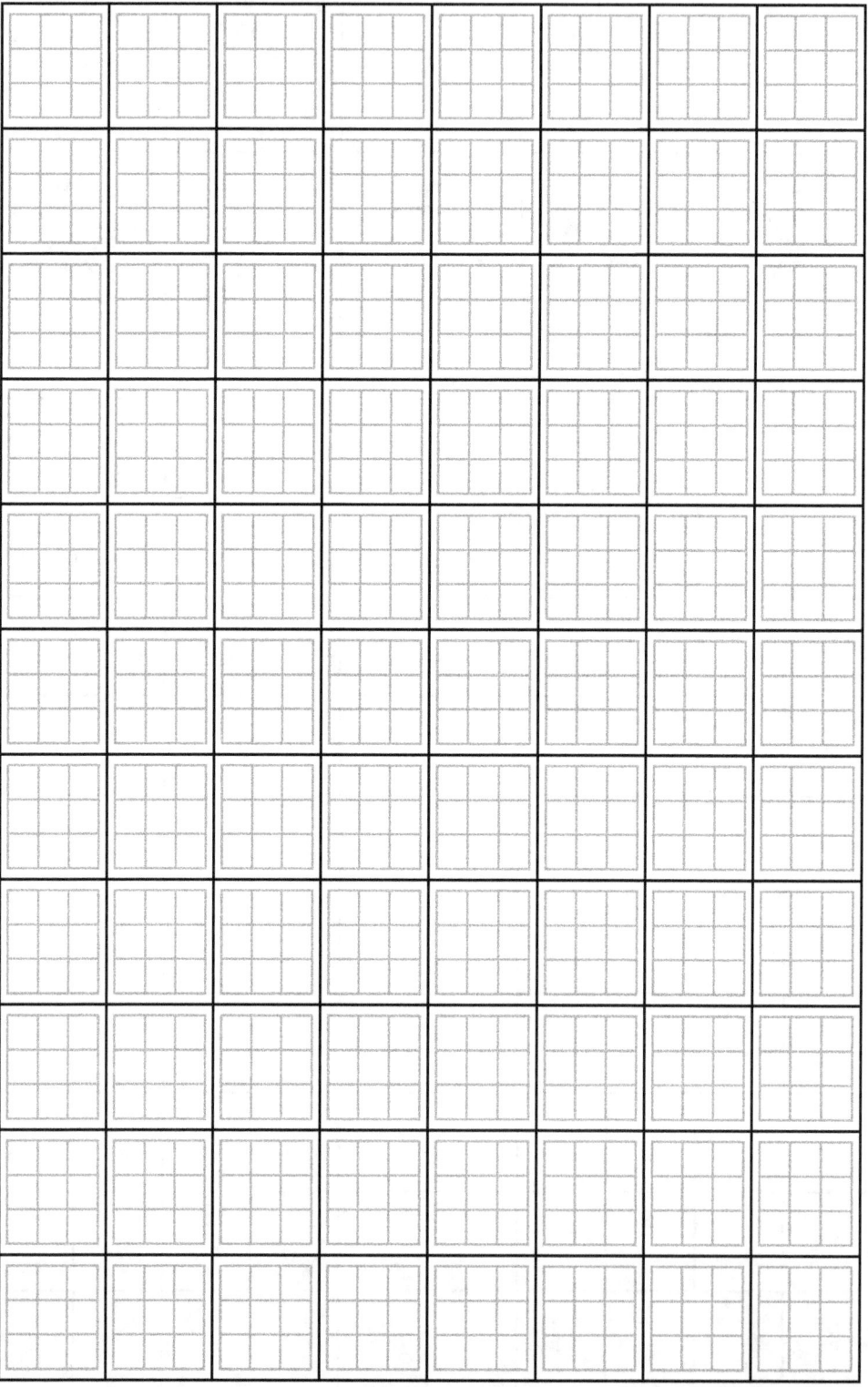

第十三课   Unit 13

林先生,我喜欢你的国家!
Lín xiān sheng, wǒ xǐ huan nǐ de guó jiā!
Mr. Lin, I like your country!

对,中国很美。
Duì, Zhong guó hěn měi.
Yes, China is very beautiful.

我太太也喜欢中国。
Wǒ tài tai yě xǐ huan Zhōng guó.
My wife also likes China.

那很好,下次再见!
Nà hěn hǎo, xià cì zài jiàn!
That is very good, see you next time!

This is a dialog between two friends from different countries. They are both visiting China and barely have time to chat.

Dialog Vocabulary

喜欢	xǐ huan	to like
也	yě	also
下次	xià cì	next time
下	xià	next (in time)
次	cì	time(s)
那	nà	then
国家	guó jiā	native country

Useful Vocabulary

我的	wǒ de	my/ mine
她的	tā de	her/ hers
他的	tā de	his
家	jiā	home
下	xià	down
上	shàng	up

Revision Vocabulary

中国	Zhōng guó	China
太太	tài tai	wife
对	duì	yes/ correct
再见	zài jiàn	see you again
你的	nǐ de	your

Lesson Breakdown

我太太 也 喜欢中国。
Wǒ tài tai yě xǐ huan Zhōng guó.
My wife also likes China.

也   yě   also

This word is an Adverb.

It is used to qualify the Verb "to like" and helps to clarify who the Subject of the sentence is and what the relationship with the Verb. Although it is used in a similar manner as we use "also" in English, we have to pay special attention to its **position** in the sentence.

It must always be placed after the Subject and before the Verb or Adjective.

We use this structure:

Subject + 也 + Verb/Adjective

Examples:
他 也 要 去。
[tā yě yaò qù]
He *also* wants (Verb) to go.

她 也 很 可爱。
[tā yě hěn kě ài]
She is also cute (Adjective).

> 那很好, 下次再见!
> Nà hěn hǎo, xià cì zài jiàn !
> That's very good, see you next time!

| 那 | nà | then |

We use this Adverb to indicate *what happens next*.

It is a response to a preceding statement and it is normally placed at the beginning of a sentence.

Pay attention to the tone: [nà]

Don't confuse it with:

那 [nà]
that / those (same character and tone, different meaning)

哪 [nǎ]
which? / where? / how?

Supplementary

When comparing the use of directions (up and down) in English and Chinese, it's obvious that there is a very big difference in usage. This can best be explained by looking at traditional Chinese script.

下 [xià] meaning: down or next.
Chinese text runs from **top to bottom**, down the page.
When looking at a character, the next character is down (below) and the previous character is up (above). Therefore, in the context of Chinese script, the character 下 means *next*.

上 [shàng] meaning: up or previously.
Using the same logic, we arrive at the conclusion that *up* or *previously* is represented with the character 上 .

次 [cì] meaning: time or times.
This word is a Measure word (MW).
It is a Verbal Measure word and it is used to describe **quantities of actions**. Basically, how many times you have done something.
It means *time/times* that something *takes place* and it normally emphasizes the frequency of a repeated action.
Example:
再说一次。
[zài shuō yí cì]
Say it again (one more time).

Download The Bonus Audio Files To Practice Your Pronunciation

My Progress

Words	QW's	MW's	TW's	Total
Count	3	1	1	71

Hint

Remember when using the Adverb 也 that it is followed by a Verb or an Adjective.

Self-Practice

Connect and match:

家	•	• xǐ huan •	• to like
那	•	• yě •	• also
上	•	• xià •	• down
也	•	• nà •	• up
国家	•	• shàng •	• home
次	•	• guó jiā •	• then
下	•	• cì •	• time(s)
喜欢	•	• jiā •	• home country

Write questions for the following answers:

1. _____?
对，我 喜欢 中国。

2. _____?
我 不好。

3. _____?
他 是 美国人。

4. _____?
她 是 Jenny。

Arrange the words into sentences:

1. 那   好   很。
_____

2. 下   见   次   再。
_____

3. 你的   我   喜欢   国家。
_____

4. 美   中国   很。
_____

● Radical Stroke Order   Character Stroke Order ●

豆	欠	豕	冫	乜
喜	欢	家	次	也

Trace the following characters

豆									
欠									
豕									
冫									
乜									
喜									
欢									
家									
次									
也									

Unit 13

Self-Practice

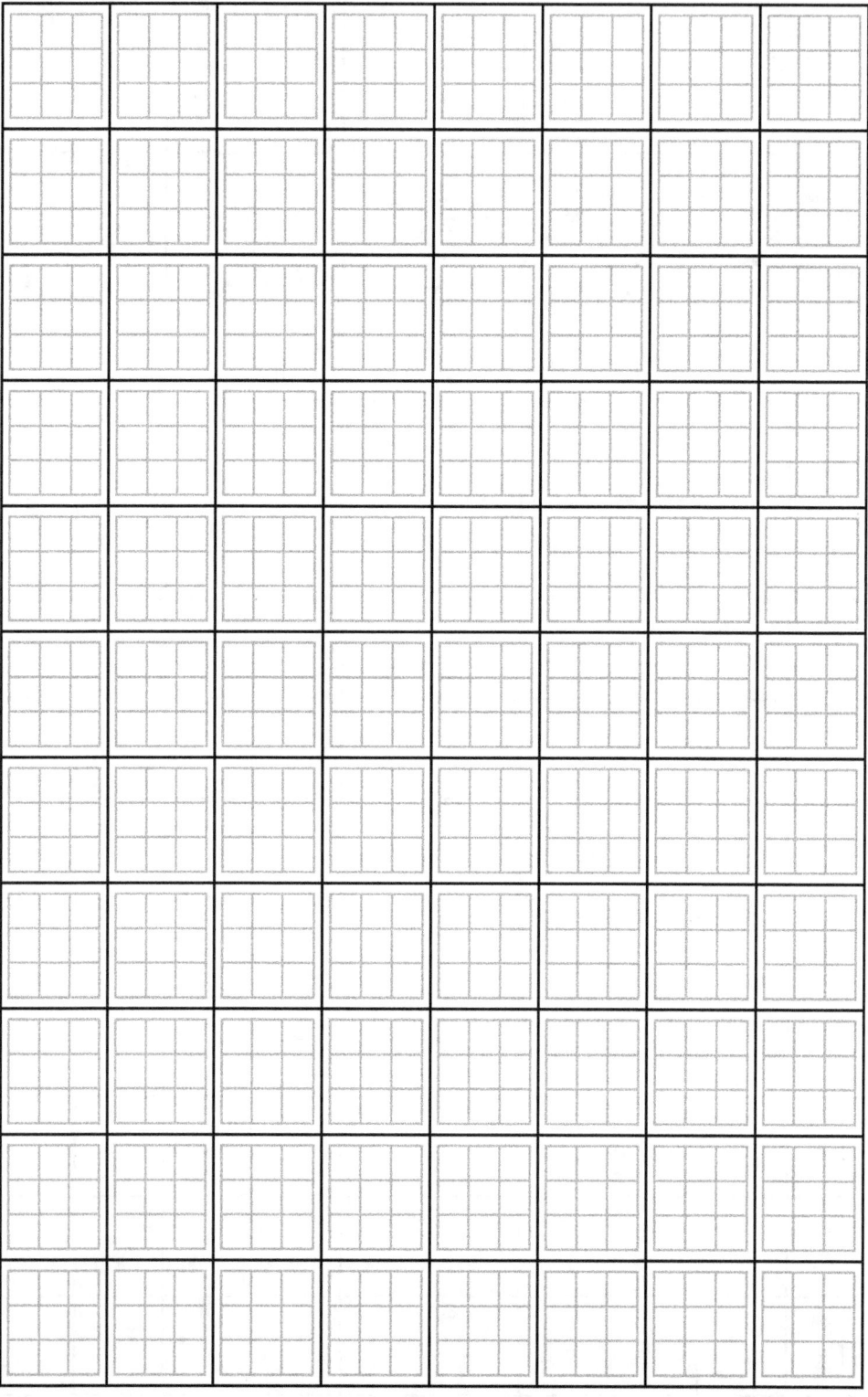

第十四课   Unit 14

Jeff, 好久不见!
Jeff, hǎo jiǔ bù jiàn!
Jeff, long time no see!

是的, 真的 好久不见! 你去 哪里?
Shì de, zhēn de hǎo jiǔ bù jiàn! Nǐ qù nǎ lǐ?
Yes, really long time no see! Where are you going?

我去 上课, 明天见。
Wǒ qù shàng kè, míng tiān jiàn.
I am going to class, see you tomorrow.

好, 明天见。
Hǎo, míng tiān jiàn.
OK, see you tomorrow.

This is a dialog between two friends who bump into each other at school. Both are in a hurry and there is no time for pleasantries.

Dialog Vocabulary

去	qù	to go
课	kè	class/ lesson
上课	shàng kè	to attend class
明天	míng tiān	tomorrow
真的	zhēn de	really
哪里	nǎ lǐ	where

Useful Vocabulary

哪儿	nǎ er (nǎr)	where
那儿	nà er (nàr)	there
那里	nà lǐ	there
上班	shàng bān	to work
班	bān	work shift/ duty

Revision Vocabulary

不见	bù jiàn	not to see
见	jiàn	to meet
好久	hǎo jiǔ	a very long time

Lesson Breakdown

我去 上课。

Wǒ qù shàng kè.

I am going to class。

| 上课 | shàng kè | to attend class |

In this phrase, the word 上 [shàng] acts as the Verb and the word 课 [kè] is the Object of the sentence.

It means "to go into". This implies *to attend* a class or a lesson.

This is understandably an expression that all students of Mandarin should know.

It is of course no surprise that the opposite of attending class, *to get out of class*, is represented with the Verb 下 [xià] :

下课 [xià kè]

> 上班   shàng bān   to go to work

In this phrase, 上 also means *to go into*.

This implies "to go to" or "to start" work.

The opposite of starting work, *to finish or leave work*, is also represented with the Verb 下 .

下班 [xià bān]

> 好, 明天见。
> Hǎo, míng tiān jiàn.
> OK, see you tomorrow.

> 见   jiàn   to see/meet

We already know that we can use this Verb to say "see you again" (再见). In our example sentence, the Subject is taking leave of someone, but he is saying "see you tomorrow".

This expression is just another way to *take leave of somebody,* but the speaker is being specific about when the next meeting will take place.

In this case, the meeting will take place on the following day and therefore, 明天 is a Time Word (TW).

(Remember that this Verb can mean *to see* or *to meet somebody*, depending on the context of the sentence.)

> 你去 哪里?
>
> Nǐ qù nǎ lǐ?
>
> Where are you going?

哪里　　　nǎ lǐ　　　where

This QW means "where" and is quite simple to use. We follow this structure:

Subject + Verb + 哪里

When looking at the above structure, we can see that the QW is used as the Object of the sentence: You *are going* **where**?

In English we would have said: **Where** are you going?

Supplementary

Tones:

nǎ

There is a difference in tone in the following two words:
哪儿 [nǎ er] or 哪里 [nǎ lǐ] means: where? (QW)
Note the 3rd tone in [nǎ].
You can use 哪儿 or 哪里, since they share the same meaning.

nà

那儿 [nà er] or 那里 [nà lǐ] means: there (PW)
Note the 4th tone in [nà].
You can use either 那儿 or 那里, since they share the same meaning.

Download The Bonus Audio Files To Practice Your Pronunciation

My Progress

Words	QW's	MW's	TW's	Total
Count	4	1	2	77

Hint

With similar looking and sounding characters, make sure you pronounce them correctly.

Self-Practice

Connect and match:

明天 •	• qù •	• tomorrow
课 •	• nǎ lǐ •	• to leave class
上课 •	• míng tiān •	• to go
那里 •	• shàng kè •	• class
哪里 •	• xià kè •	• where
真的 •	• nà lǐ •	• there
去 •	• kè •	• really
下课 •	• zhěn de •	• to attend class

Rewrite the following sentences into Pinyin:

1. Where are you going? _____
2. I am going to class. _____
3. Long time no see. _____
4. Hello Mr. Wang. _____
5. I really like going to class. _____
6. See you tomorrow. _____

Circle the correct character in every line:

1. 杲 , 凍 , 東 , 果 , 课
2. 苴 , 且 , 直 , 真 , 具
3. 娌 , 俚 , 里 , 哩 , 理
4. 法 , 丢 , 宪 , 赱 , 去

● Radical Stroke Order   Character Stroke Order ●

厶	果	月	直	甲
去	课	明	真	里

Trace the following characters

厶									
果									
月									
直									
甲									
去									
课									
明									
真									
里									

Self-Practice

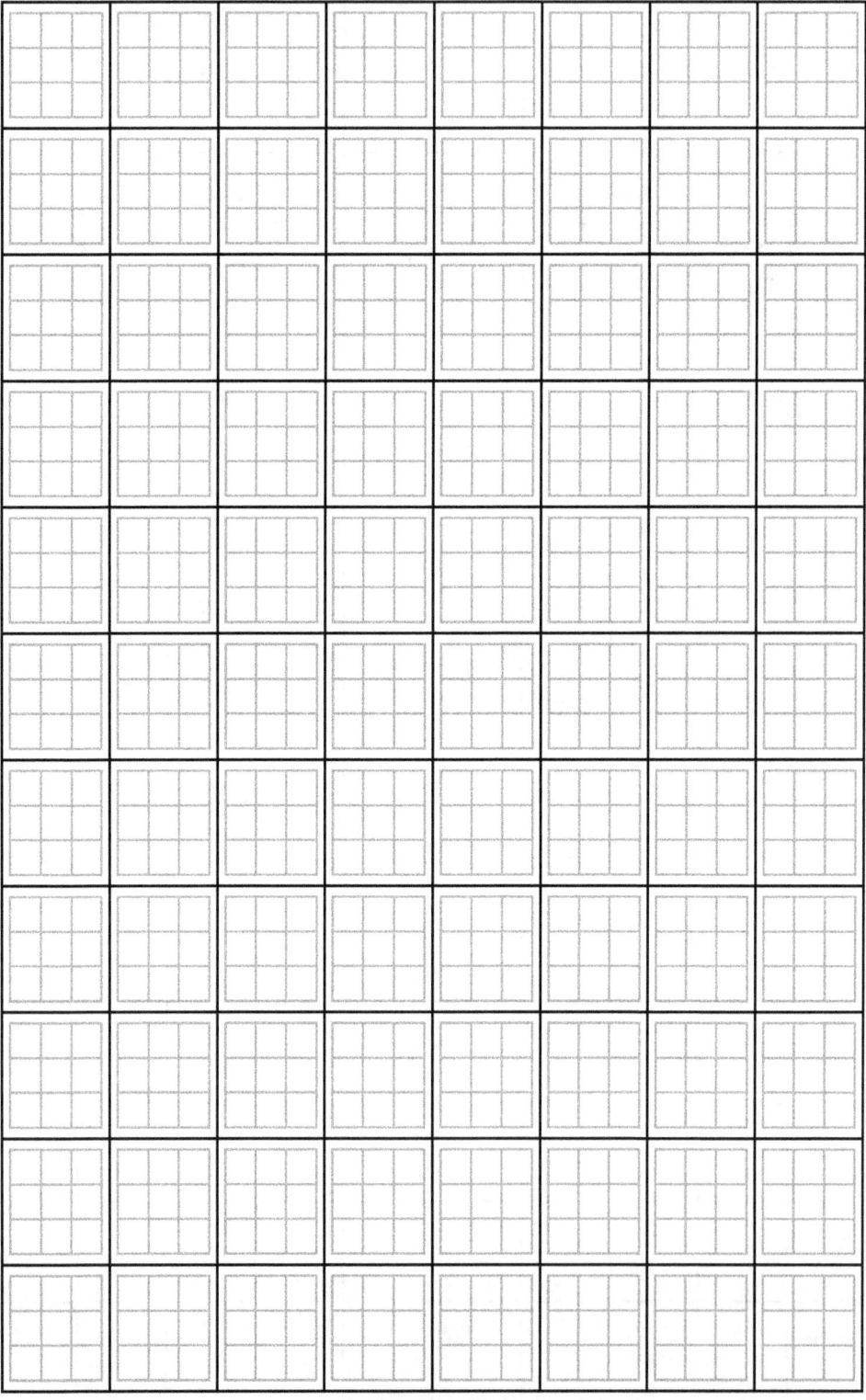

第十五课   Unit 15

他们 是谁?

Tā mén shì shéi ?

Who are they?

他们 是 韩先生的 家人。

Tā mén shì Hán xiān shēng de jiā rén.

They are Mr. Han's family.

他们 人 很多, 他们 今天 去 美国吗?

Tā mén rén hěn duō, tā mén jīn tiān qù měi guó mǎ ?

That is a large family! Are they going to America today?

不是, 他们 明天 去。

Bú shì, tā mén míng tiān qù.

No, they will go tomorrow.

This is a dialog between two family members sitting in the lobby of a hotel. They are discussing the people coming and leaving.

Dialog Vocabulary

他们	tā mén	they
多	duō	many
家人	jiā rén	family member
韩	Hán	Han (Surname)
不是	bú shì	no/not right

Useful Vocabulary

我们	wǒ mén	we
我们的	wǒ mén de	our/ ours
她们	tā mén	they (female)
他们的	tā mén de	their/ theirs
韩国	Hán guó	Korea
回家	huí jiā	return home

Revision Vocabulary

去	qù	to go
很	hěn	very/ quite
今天	jīn tiān	today
明天	míng tiān	tomorrow
谁	shéi	who/ whom

Lesson Breakdown

他们 是谁?

Tā mén shì shéi ?

Who are they?

谁   shéi   who?

As mentioned in Unit 9, 谁 is a Question-word, and therefore no particle - 吗 is needed at the end of the sentence.

Similar to the example given, it is often used when inquiring after someone.

Let's take a closer look at this QW.

We use this structure:

Subject + 是 + 谁

In this structure, 谁 is used as the Object of the sentence. This means that the QW is put in the place of the Subject or Object that you are asking about.

Explanation, literally translated:

"They are **who**?"

They are the **Han family**.

You can see that the **QW is put in the place of the Subject** that you are asking about.

Example:

你 是 谁?

[nǐ shì **shéi**]

Who are you?

我 是 你的 同学。

[wǒ shì nǐ de **tóng xúe**]

I am your classmate.

> 他们 今天 去 美国 吗?
>
> Tā mén jīn tiān qù měi guó ma ?
>
> Are they going to America today?

今天   jīn tiān   today

Time Words (TWs) are words that are used to indicate the *time* or the *date*. They are placed towards the **beginning of a sentence**. You can place the Subject or the TW first, depending on which one needs more emphasis. When dealing with TWs we typically use the following structure:

TW + Subject + Verb + Object

or

Subject + TW +Verb +Object

(Both are perfectly fine to use, it just depends on whether the speaker wants to put the emphasis on the TW or on the Subject.)

These TWs indicate "when" an action takes place. They are very important in that the tense is indicated through the use of TWs, instead of using the form of the Verb, as we do in English.

Simply put, TWs indicate "when" an action takes place.

Supplementary

他们　tā men　they (male)

Let's separate this word into its two separate characters.

他 + 们 = 他们

The Pronoun 他 means *he* or *him*.

The suffix -们 [men] indicates the *plural form* of the Pronoun.

Other plurals include:

我们　[wǒmen]　we
她们　[tāmen]　they (female)
你们　[nǐmen]　you
它们　[tāmen]　they (inanimate objects)

Tones:

不是　bú shì　no/not so

Again, let's take note of the tone: Note the 2nd tone of [bú].

It is pronounced in the 2nd tone, because it is followed by 是 [shì] which is 4th tone. (See Unit 10)

Download The Bonus Audio Files To Practice Your Pronunciation

My Progress

Words	QW's	MW's	TW's	Total
Count	4	1	2	82

Hint

Remember that the QW is put in the place of the Subject. It's the opposite of English patterns.

Self-Practice

Connect and match:

他们 •   • hán •   • Han
韩 •   • huí jiā •   • they
多 •   • duō •   • us
你们 •   • nǐ mén •   • you
韩国 •   • tā mén •   • many
不是 •   • wǒ mén •   • no/ not right
我们 •   • bú shì •   • return home
回家 •   • hán guó •   • Korea

Translate the following sentences into English:

1. Tā mén shì shéi ?
   _____

2. Tā mén jīn tiān qù měi guó mǎ?
   _____

3. Bú shì, tā mén míng tiān qù?
   _____

4. Tā mén shì Hán xiān shēng de jiā rén.
   _____

Arrange the words into sentences:

1. 谁   是   他们？
   _____

2. 明天   他们   不是   去。
   _____

3. 去   今天   她   美国   吗？
   _____

4. 家人   先生   韩   的。
   _____

● Radical Stroke Order　　　Character Stroke Order ●

门	夕	韦	豕	走
们	多	韩	家	是

Trace the following characters

门	门	门	门	门	门	门	门	门
夕	夕	夕	夕	夕	夕	夕	夕	夕
韦	韦	韦	韦	韦	韦	韦	韦	韦
豕	豕	豕	豕	豕	豕	豕	豕	豕
是	是	是	是	是	是	是	是	是
们	们	们	们	们	们	们	们	们
多	多	多	多	多	多	多	多	多
韩	韩	韩	韩	韩	韩	韩	韩	韩
家	家	家	家	家	家	家	家	家
是	是	是	是	是	是	是	是	是

Self-Practice

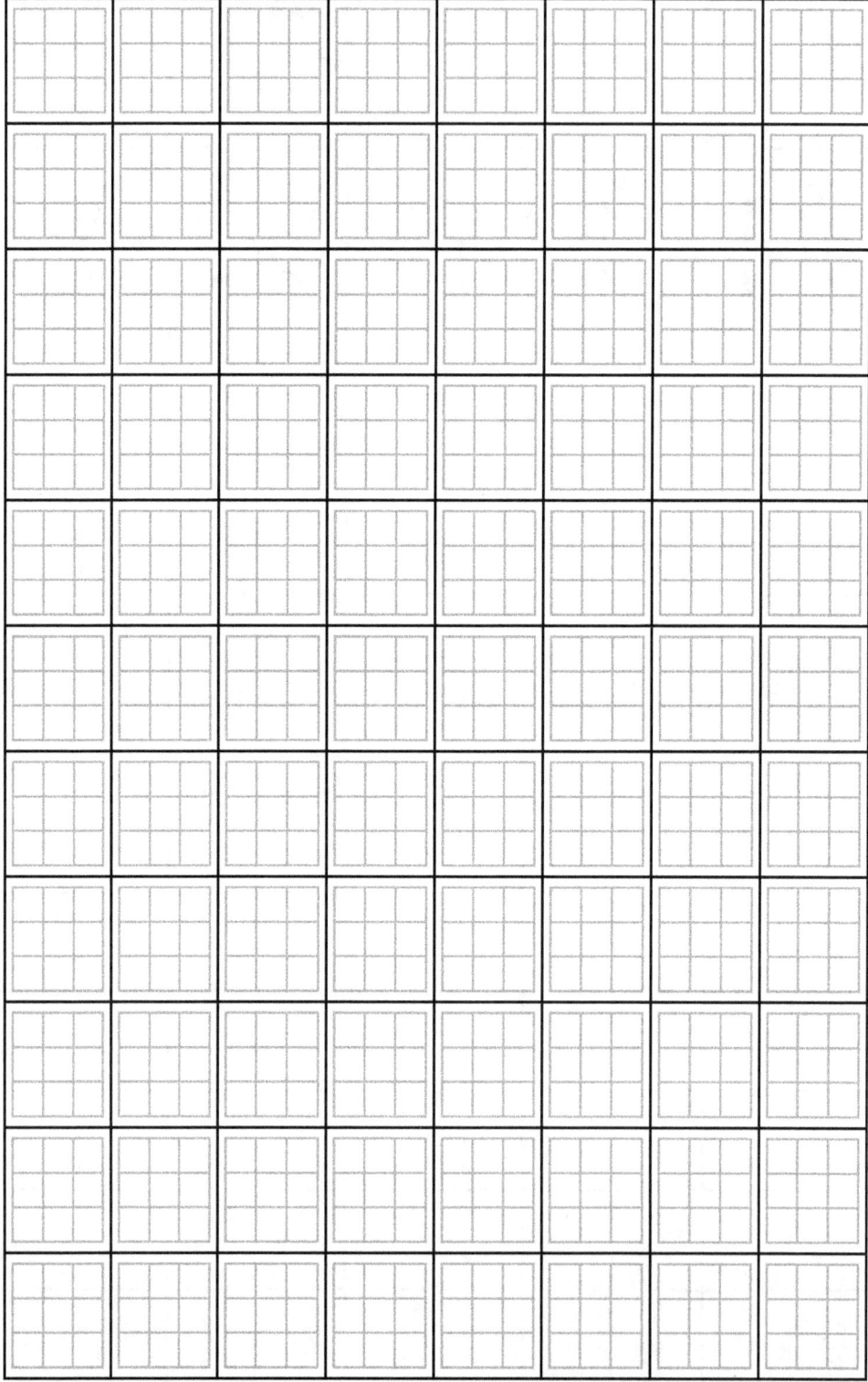

第十六课   Unit 16

我很累,我要 回家。
Wǒ hěn lèi, wǒ yào huí jiā.
I am really very tired. I want to go home.

你 为什么 很累?
Nǐ wéi shén me hěn lèi ?
Why are you so tired?

今天 真的 太热!
Jīn tiān zhēn de tài rè !
It is really too hot today!

对,今天 真的 太热!
Duì, jīn tiān zhēn de tài rè !
Yes, it is too hot today!

This is a dialog between two classmates.
They are sitting in the library, doing their homework.

Dialog Vocabulary

累	lèi	tired
回	huí	go back
家	jiā	home
为什么	wéi shén me	why?
要	yào	to want
热	rè	hot

Useful Vocabulary

白天	bái tiān	daytime
回来	huí lái	return back
房子	fáng zi	house
烫	tàng	hot (food)
走	zǒu	to walk

Revision Vocabulary

真的	zhēn de	really
对	duì	yes/ correct
太	tài	too/ extremely

Lesson Breakdown

你 为什么 很累?

Nǐ wéi shén me hěn lèi?

Why are you so tired?

为什么   wéi shén me   why?

This is a Question-word that literally means: "Why is it that?"
As is typical when asking a question, we normally place this QW towards the front of the sentence.
(Note that three characters combined, form one word.)

We use the following structure:
Subject + 为什么 + Predicate* ?
Example:
你 为什么 要回去?
[nǐ **wèi shén me** yào húi qù]
Why do you want to go home?

Always remember, that when using QW's we do not need to add question particle 吗 at the end of the sentence.
(*Predicate=The part of the sentence that expresses what is said about the subject.)

> 对, 今天 真的 太热!
> Duì, jīn tiān zhēn de tài rè !
> Yes, it's really too hot today!

| 真的 | zhēn de | really |

This is an Adverb and it is used to *indicate degree*. These words are important because they **describe the degree of the Adjective** and they act as "joining words".
In our example they describe "how hot it is".

Other similar Adverbs are 很 , 好 , 真 , 非常 .
很 热　　[hěn rè]　　　　It's quite hot.
好 热　　[hǎo rè]　　　　It's very hot.
真 热　　[zhēn rè]　　　　It's really hot!
非常 热　[feī cháng rè]　　It's extremely hot!
More about these Adverbs in later lessons.

> 我要 回家。
> Wǒ yào huí jiā.
> I want to go home.

This literally means: "to return home".

This phrase is a Verb + Object (VO) agreement.

The Verb 回 [huí] means "to return" and it is often used together with:

来　[lái]　meaning: to come

去　[qù]　meaning: to go

Example:

回来
[huí lái]
to come back

他 快 回来。
[tā kuài huí lái]
He will be back soon.

回去
[huí qù]
to go back

我 是 走 回去 的。
[wǒ shì zǒu huí qù de]
I went back on foot.

The usage depends on the speaker's position and if the Subject is *coming* or *going*.

Download The Bonus Audio Files To Practice Your Pronunciation

My Progress					Hint
Words	QW's	MW's	TW's	Total	Remember to practice tones as often as possible and to get yourself a relevant Chinese name.
Count	5	1	2	88	

Self-Practice

Connect and match:

累 •	• zǒu •	• to be tired
回 •	• wéi shén me •	• hot
热 •	• huí •	• why
家 •	• yào •	• daytime
为什么 •	• bái tiān •	• to want
白天 •	• jiā •	• to walk
要 •	• rè •	• go back
走 •	• lèi •	• home

Rewrite the following sentences into Pinyin:

1. Why are you so tired? _____
2. Why are you (feeling) so hot? _____
3. Yes, I am too hot. _____
4. It is really too hot today. _____
5. I want to go home. _____
6. I am really tired. _____

Circle the correct character in every line:

1. 嫁，稼，象，家，豕
2. 僦，就，九，丸，热
3. 妾，要，受，雯，耍
4. 累，糹，系，界，等

● Radical Stroke Order   Character Stroke Order ●

力	丸	西	口	糸
为	热	要	回	累

Trace the following characters

力	力	力	力	力	力	力	力	力
丸	丸	丸	丸	丸	丸	丸	丸	丸
西	西	西	西	西	西	西	西	西
口	口	口	口	口	口	口	口	口
糸	糸	糸	糸	糸	糸	糸	糸	糸
为	为	为	为	为	为	为	为	为
热	热	热	热	热	热	热	热	热
要	要	要	要	要	要	要	要	要
回	回	回	回	回	回	回	回	回
累	累	累	累	累	累	累	累	累

Self-Practice

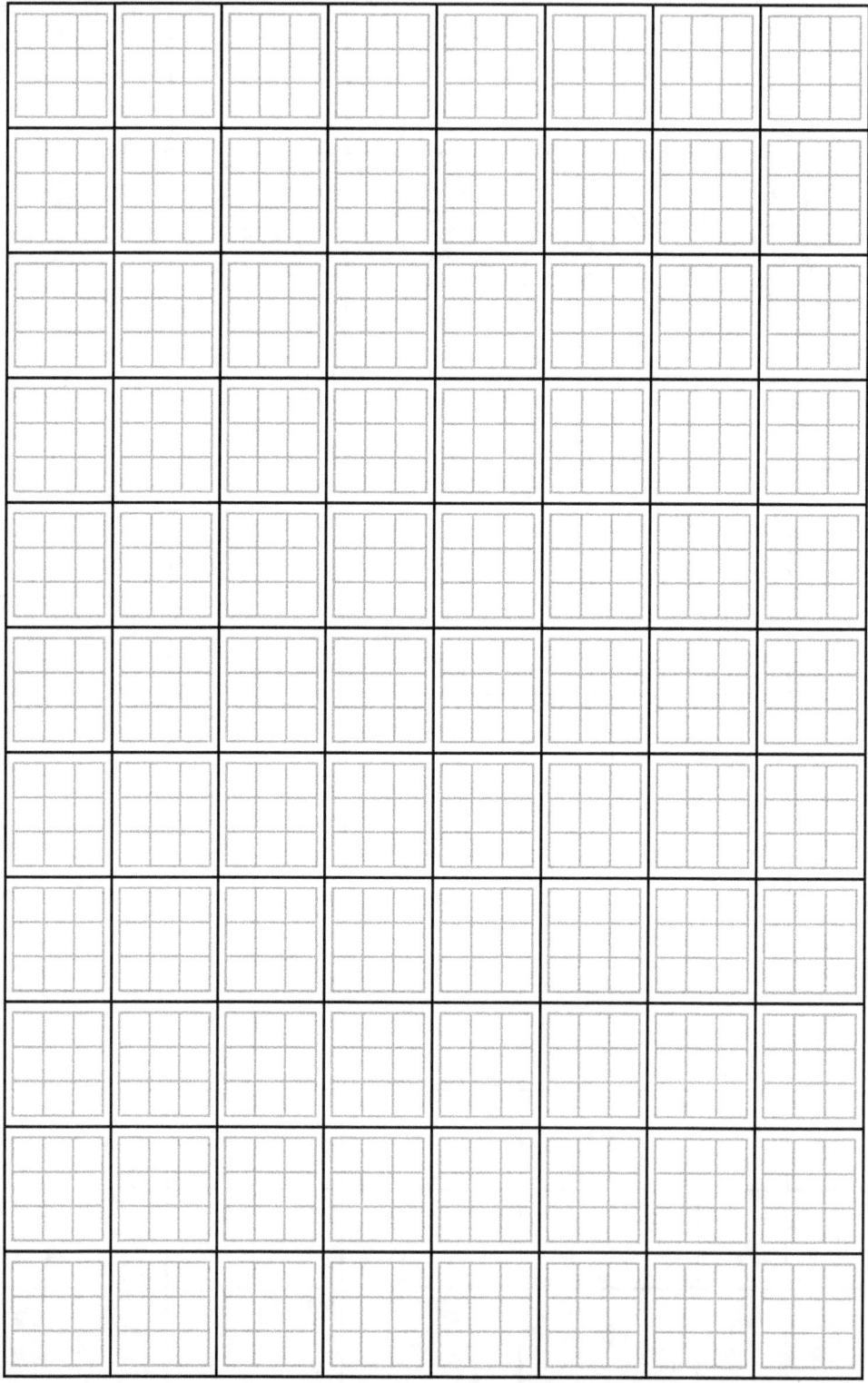

第十七课　　Unit 17

林先生, 你 不 舒服 吗?
Lín xiān shēng, nǐ bù shū fú mǎ?
Mr. Lin, are you not feeling well?

不是, 我好渴。
Bú shì, wǒ hǎo kě.
No, I am very thirsty.

喝水, 今天 天气 真的 很热!
Hē shuǐ, jīn tiān tiān qì zhēn de hěn rè!
Drink some water. The weather is very hot today!

谢谢你!
Xiè xiè nǐ!
Thank you!

This is a dialog between employer and employee.
They are doing construction work outside. The mood is polite.

Dialog Vocabulary

渴	kě	to be thirsty
喝	hē	to drink
水	shuǐ	water
天气	tiān qì	weather
谢谢	xiè xiè	thank you
不舒服	bù shū fú	uncomfortable

Useful Vocabulary

饿	è	to be hungry
吃	chī	to eat
生病	shēng bìng	to be sick
舒服	shū fu	comfortable
不客气	bù kè qi	you're welcome (polite)

Revision Vocabulary

热	rè	hot
不是	bú shì	not right
好	hǎo	very/ quite

Lesson Breakdown

> 谢谢你!
> Xiè xiè nǐ !
> Thank you!

When you add the Pronoun 你 [nǐ], to say "thank you", it means that you are being *extra polite*.

You recognize the other party and say *thank you* specifically to that individual.

This is a very common occurrence, since the act of being polite is held in high regard in traditional Chinese culture.

> 你 不 舒服 吗?
> Nǐ bù shū fú mǎ ?
> Are you not feeling well?

| 不舒服 | bù shū fú | to be not well |

Literally: "not comfortable."

This is a very common expression.

The use of 不 is to indicate a negative and thus to negate the Adjective or the Verb.

Examples:

我 不 饿。 [wǒ bú è]   I'm not hungry.
我 不 累。 [wǒ bú lèi]   I'm not tired.
我 不 要。 [wǒ bú yào]   I do not want.
我 不 去。 [wǒ bú qù]   I'm not going.
我 不 懂。 [wǒ bù dǒng]   I do not understand.

Of major importance is the fact that we can also use 不 to ask a more specific question:

你不饿 吗? [nǐ bú è mǎ ?]   Are you not hungry?
你不累 吗? [nǐ bú lèi mǎ ?]   Are you not tired?
你不要 吗? [nǐ bú yào mǎ ?]   Don't you want?
你不懂 吗? [nǐ bú dǒng mǎ ?]   Don't you understand?

Take note that it is the intention of the speaker to put emphasis on the question.

Supplementary

Writing: Radicals

渴 vs. 喝

These two characters might seem similar and this can lead to confusion. Let's break them down into their individual radicals.

渴   kě   thirsty

The character 渴 represents an Adjective and has a 氵 - radical in front. This radical means water and describes anything related to water like *being thirsty*.

喝   hē   to drink

The character 喝 is a Verb and it has a 口 - radical in front. This radical means *mouth* for *drinking*.

Pay attention to radicals.

They are crucial for determining which is the appropriate character to use.

Start to make these connections with the characters and that will enable you to recognize and memorize them when needed.

Download The Bonus Audio Files To Practice Your Pronunciation

My Progress

Words	QW's	MW's	TW's	Total
Count	5	1	2	94

Hint

Remember that 不 is used to negate Verbs and Adjectives. Don't confuse it with 没有.

Self-Practice

Connect and match:

谢谢	kě	comfortable
渴	shū fú	very
喝	hěn	thank you
很	xiè xiè	no/ not
天气	bù	to be thirsty
舒服	shuǐ	to drink
水	tiān qì	weather
不	hē	water

Write questions for the following answers:

1. _____?
对, 我 不 舒服。

2. _____?
我 去上课。

3. _____?
他们 是 我 家人。

4. _____?
对, 他们 今天 去 美国。

Arrange the words into sentences:

1. 你   吗   不舒服？
_____

2. 太   我   今天   热。
_____

3. 喝   我   要   水。
_____

4. 渴   我   好。
_____

● Radical Stroke Order   Character Stroke Order ●

人	勹	乚	身	乞
水	渴	喝	谢	气

Trace the following characters

人									
勹									
乚									
身									
乞									
水									
渴									
喝									
谢									
气									

Self-Practice

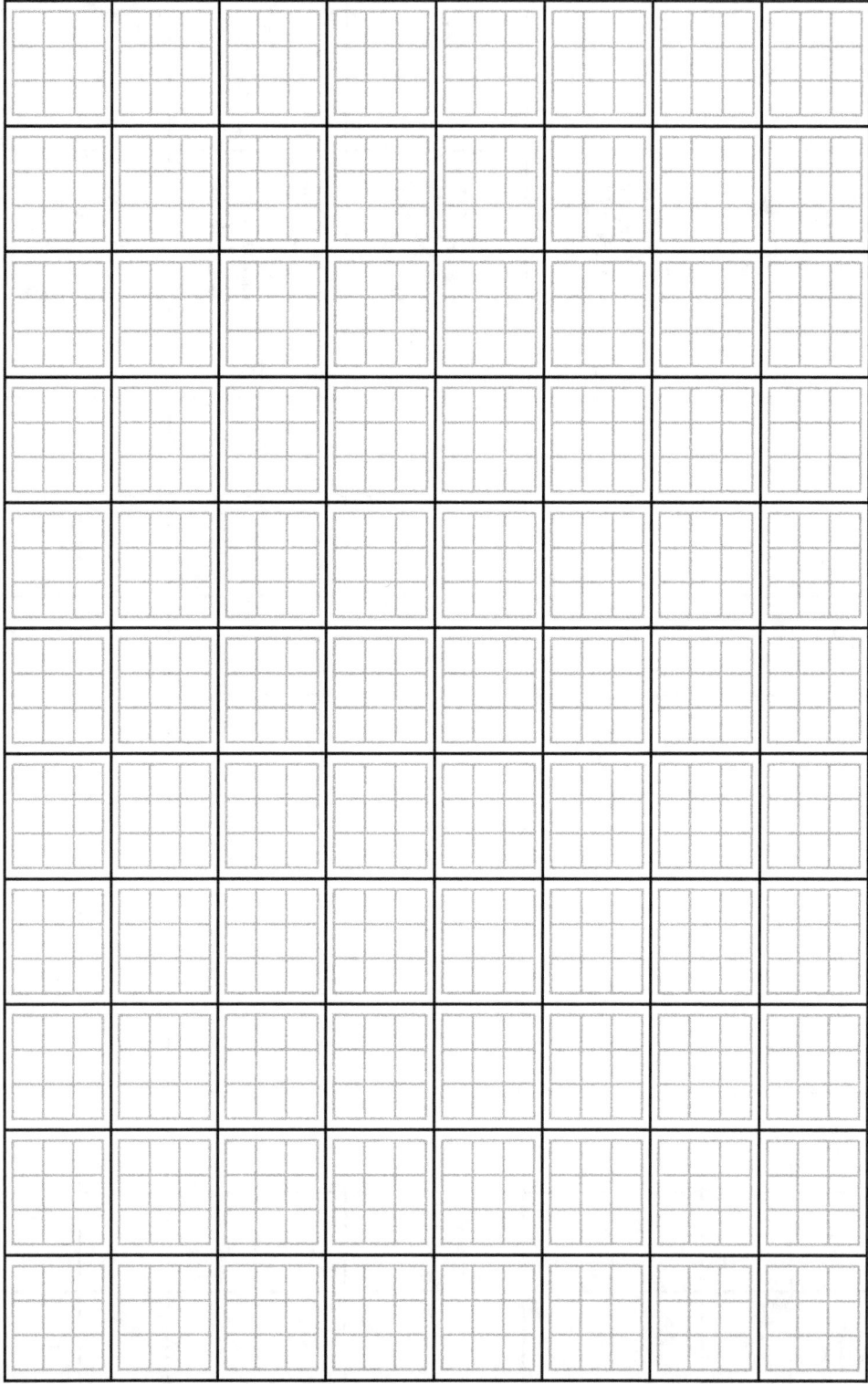

第十八课　　Unit 18

你们 昨天 不在 家 吗?
Nǐ mén zuó tiān bù zài jiā mǎ?
You (plural) were not at home yesterday?

不在, 我们 很早 去上课。
Bù zài, wǒ mén hěn zǎo qù shàng kè.
No, we went to class very early.

今天 呢?
Jīn tiān nē?
What about today?

一样!
Yī yàng!
The same again!

This is a dialog between two friends.
The one party is hoping to visit the other when time allows.

Dialog Vocabulary

你们	nǐ mén	you (plural)
我们	wǒ mén	we
昨天	zuó tiān	yesterday
早	zǎo	to be early
一样	yī yàng	same
呢	nē	-and today?

Useful Vocabulary

晚	wǎn	to be late
工人	gōng rèn	worker
作	zuò	to do
不一样	bù yī yàng	different
放假	fàng jià	have a day off

Revision Vocabulary

家	jiā	home
上课	shàng kè	go to class
在	zài	at/ in/ on
去	qù	to go to

Lesson Breakdown

你们 昨天 不在 家 吗?
Nǐ mén zuó tiān bù zài jiā mǎ ?
You (plural) were not at home yesterday?

This sentence literal translation is: "You, yesterday, not at home?"
Note the word placement and sentence structure.
It has a distinct order that is very different from English. This is where you develop a "feel" for the language, by getting used to the Chinese sentence structure.
Let's take a closer look at the components at work.

> 在   zài   at/in/on

In Unit 11 we were introduced to this Place Word (PW) which indicates *where* the action takes place.

Example:

我在家。[wǒ zài jiā]   I am at home.

Remember that PWs are placed before Nouns or Pronouns.

When necessary, we also have to negate this PW. We can add the word 不 [bù] meaning *not*, in front of the PW. This changes the meaning to: *not* at home.

Example:

我不在家。 [wǒ bù zài jiā]

I am not at home.

> 昨天   zuó tiān   yesterday

This is a Time Word (TW) and it is an indicator of the *past tense*. It tells us *when* an action is taking place. Mandarin is very different from other languages in that there are no Verb tenses.

The Time-words will indicate when something occurs and the Verbs need not change.

> 今天 呢?
>
> Jīn tiān nē ?
>
> What about today?

This is a very short sentence and we notice that it ends with a question mark, but that there is no question particle (吗) present. It is basically a **statement** followed by particle 呢 .

> 呢   nē   ...and today?

In our example sentence we use 呢, to ask "...and today?". In a previous example (Unit 7) we used the same particle, to ask "...and you?". This is a modal or question particle with many uses, but it is mostly placed at the end of a sentence to make a suggestion.

It can mean: ....*and you?* ....*and today?*

We follow a simple structure:

Statement + 呢

It can be connected to a Pronoun to ask a related question: I am hungry, ...**and you**?

It can also inquire about a time: Today is not convenient,....**and tomorrow**?

> 一样!
> Yī yàng!
> The same again!

> 一样   yī yàng   the same

The opposite of "same" is "different". In this case, an opposite can be created by simply adding 不 [bù] which means *not*. This means that it becomes a negative.

不一样 [bù yī yàng] means: *not the same* or *different*.

This is very common in the Chinese language.

Instead of creating a new word, we just add the negative particle 不 to indicate a new word with opposite meaning.

Download The Bonus Audio Files To Practice Your Pronunciation

My Progress

Words	QW's	MW's	TW's	Total
Count	5	1	3	100

Hint

呢 redirects the question back at the asker, by making a statement followed by a suggestion.

Self-Practice

Connect and match:

你们 •	• wǒ mén •	• and today?
今天 呢? •	• wǎn •	• same
不一样 •	• zuó tiān •	• to be early
晚 •	• bù yī yàng •	• you (plural)
我们 •	• nǐ mén •	• we
昨天 •	• zǎo •	• to be late
早 •	• yī yàng •	• different
一样 •	• Jīn tiān nē? •	• yesterday

Rewrite the following sentences into Pinyin:

1. We went to class very early. _____
2. The same. _____
3. What about today? _____
4. Were you not at home yesterday? _____
5. Today is different. _____
6. Were you not at home this morning? _____

Circle the correct character in every line:

1. 昵 , 妮 , 泥 , 尼 , 呢
2. 佯 , 洋 , 羊 , 样 , 姅
3. 柞 , 祚 , 昨 , 做 , 作
4. 晚 , 免 , 挽 , 娩 , 脘

● Radical Stroke Order　　Character Stroke Order ●

昨	天	我	你	们
早	一	样	呢	工

Trace the following characters

昨	昨	昨	昨	昨	昨	昨	昨	昨	昨
天	天	天	天	天	天	天	天	天	天
我	我	我	我	我	我	我	我	我	我
你	你	你	你	你	你	你	你	你	你
们	们	们	们	们	们	们	们	们	们
早	早	早	早	早	早	早	早	早	早
一	一	一	一	一	一	一	一	一	一
样	样	样	样	样	样	样	样	样	样
呢	呢	呢	呢	呢	呢	呢	呢	呢	呢
工	工	工	工	工	工	工	工	工	工

Self-Practice

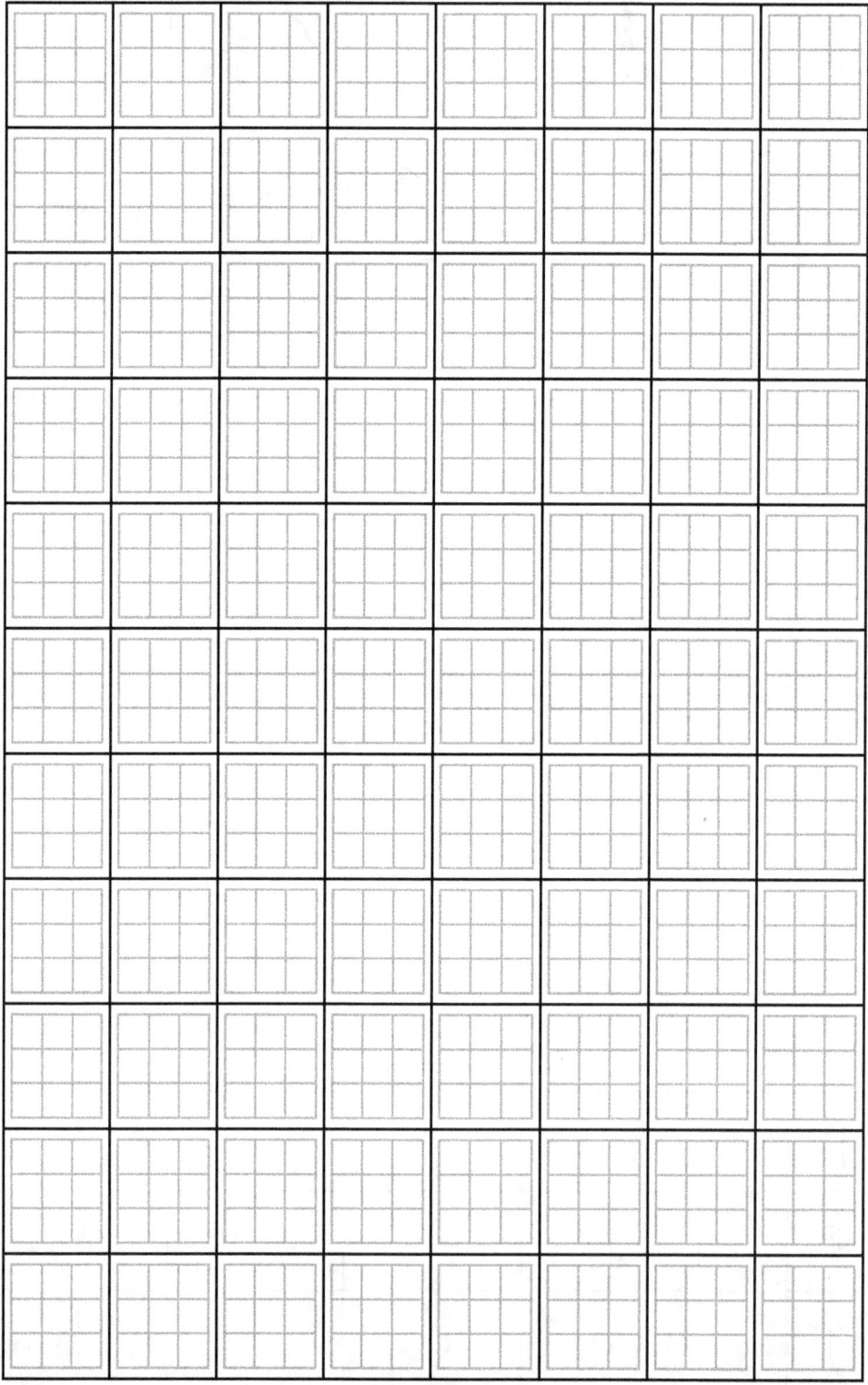

第十九课　　　Unit 19

高小姐 很 高 吗?
Gāo xiǎo jiě hěn gāo mǎ?
Is Miss Gao very tall?

对, 她 又 高 又 可爱。
Duì, tā yòu gāo yòu kě ài.
Yes, she is both tall and cute!

可是 杨小姐 不高。
Kě shì Yáng xiǎo jiě bù gāo.
But, Miss Yang is not tall.

是的, 你 是 对的。
Shì de, nǐ shì duì de.
Yes, you are right.

This is a dialog between two coworkers who are discussing the other employees at work. The mood is relaxed, but a bit cheeky.

Dialog Vocabulary

高	gāo	to be tall
可爱	kě ài	to be cute
可是	kě shì	but
又...	yòu	both...and...
高	Gāo	Gao
杨	Yáng	Yang

Useful Vocabulary

矮	ǎi	to be short
胖	pàng	to be fat
瘦	shòu	to be skinny
可以	kě yǐ	can/ may
爱	ài	to love

Revision Vocabulary

她	tā	she/ her
是的	shì de	yes
对	duì	right/ correct
吗	ma	question particle

Lesson Breakdown

> 对, 她 又高 又可爱。
> Duì, tā yòu gāo yòu kě ài.
> Yes, she is both tall and cute!

In this sentence we notice that the Pronoun (she) is described with the help of two Adjectives (*tall* and *cute*).

Descriptions are very important in any language.

Simple descriptions tend to be straight-forward, but using multiple Adjectives can lead to confusion.

In Mandarin, we use a particular word order to deal with multiple Adjectives in a sentence.

When using Adjectives, it is fortunately very easy to describe someone with multiple features in Mandarin.

We use the following words:

又 ... 又 ... [yòu]

both ... and ...

They are used in the following sentence pattern:

Noun + 又 + Adjective 1 + 又 + Adjective 2

Following each 又 is an Adjective that describes one person or thing, as viewed by the speaker.

Example 1:

她 先生 又 高 又 帅。

[tā xiān sheng yòu gāo yòu shuài]

Her husband is both **tall** and **handsome**. (Adjectives highlighted)

Both Adjectives are *positive in mood* since being tall and handsome are good or positive attributes in this sentence.

Example 2:

他 又 矮 又 胖。

[tā yòu ǎi yòu pàng]

He is both **short** and **fat**. (Adjectives highlighted)

Both Adjectives are *negative in mood*.

Note!

Do not use one positive and one negative indicator (Adj) in the same sentence.

e.g. You cannot say a person is handsome (positive) and fat (negative) when using the 又 pattern.

> 是的, 你是 对的。
>
> Shì de, nǐ shì duì de.
>
> Yes, you are right.

是的 vs. 对的 vs. 好的

At times it may seem that certain words have exactly the same meaning. This might lead to confusion or frustration. In Chinese, the differences between words can be subtle at times, but with a little bit of patience, you will find a logical explanation just around the corner.

The following words can all be translated to have a meaning of: "yes".

When we take a closer look, we notice that there are actually small and clear differences.

• On its own, 是 is a Verb and it means: "to be" (am/ is/ are).

Thus, 是的 [shì de] means: **Yes, it is**.

• On its own, 对 is an Adjective and it means: "yes".

对的 [duì de] is used where you have to confirm something or indicate that you *agree*.

Thus, 对的 [duì de] means: **Yes, correct**.

• On its own, 好 is an Adjective and it means: "good".

好的 [hǎo de] is used where someone suggests something or if they need your *permission*.

Thus, 好的 [hǎo de] means: **Okay or alright.**

Download The Bonus Audio Files To Practice Your Pronunciation

My Progress

Words	QW's	MW's	TW's	Total
Count	5	1	3	106

Hint

We can describe the Noun with two Adjectives that are **similar in mood**.

Self-Practice

Connect and match:

高	• kě shì	• to be tall
又…	• Yáng	• to be cute
可爱	• Gāo	• but
胖	• pàng	• to be fat
可是	• ǎi	• Gao
高	• kě ài	• Yang
杨	• yòu	• to be short
矮	• gāo	• both…and

Translate the following sentences into English:

1. Duì, tā yòu gāo yòu kě ài.
   _____

2. Shì de, nǐ shì duì de.
   _____

3. Kě shì Yáng xiǎo jiě bù gāo.
   _____

4. Gāo xiǎo jiě hěn gāo mǎ?
   _____

Arrange the words into sentences:

1. 又   她   又   高   可爱。
   _____

2. 不高   杨   小姐。
   _____

3. 好   小姐   杨   可爱。
   _____

4. 小姐   高   可是   也   好   可爱。
   _____

● Radical Stroke Order   Character Stroke Order ●

问	丁	友	爫	勿
高	可	爱	又	杨

Trace the following characters

问	问	问	问	问	问	问	问	问	问
丁	丁	丁	丁	丁	丁	丁	丁	丁	丁
友	友	友	友	友	友	友	友	友	友
爫	爫	爫	爫	爫	爫	爫	爫	爫	爫
勿	勿	勿	勿	勿	勿	勿	勿	勿	勿
高	高	高	高	高	高	高	高	高	高
可	可	可	可	可	可	可	可	可	可
爱	爱	爱	爱	爱	爱	爱	爱	爱	爱
又	又	又	又	又	又	又	又	又	又
杨	杨	杨	杨	杨	杨	杨	杨	杨	杨

Self-Practice

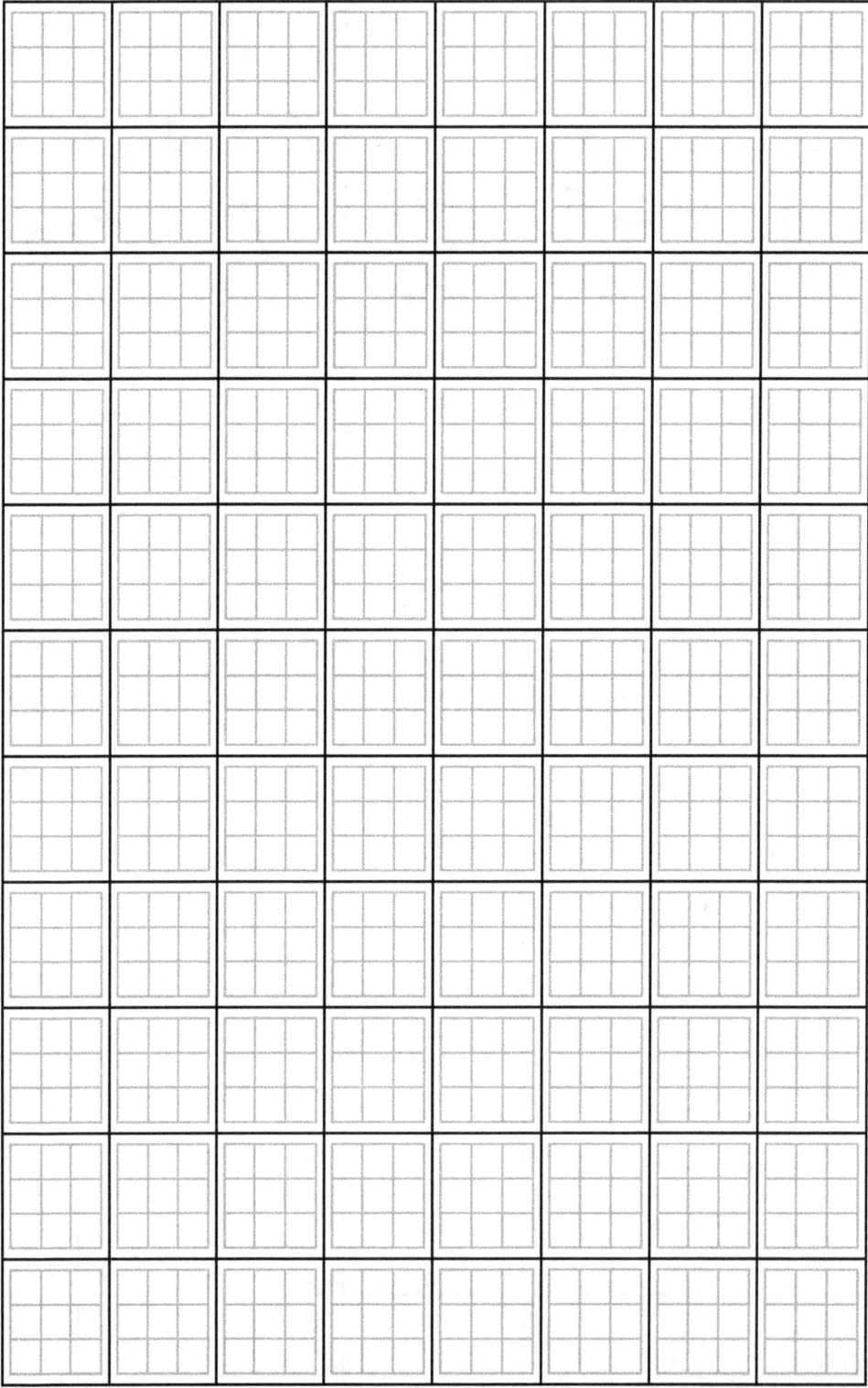

第二十课   Unit 20

你冷不冷？你的外套在哪儿？

Nǐ lěng bù lěng ? Nǐ de wài tào zài nǎr ?

Are you cold? Where is your overcoat?
(Looking for something.)

当然我很冷，可是我的外套不在那儿。

Dāng rán wǒ hěn lěng, kě shì wǒ de wài tào bú zài nàr.

Of course I'm cold, but my overcoat is not over there.

今天不冷，可是前天很冷。

Jīn tiān bù lěng, kě shì qián tiān hěn lěng.

Today, I am not cold, but the day before yesterday was quite cold.

白天太冷，我待在家。

Bái tiān tài lěng, wǒ dāi zài jiā.

The daytime is too cold, and I stay at home.

This is a dialog between two friends who are having a casual chat. Both are a bit depressed about the cold weather.

Dialog Vocabulary

白天	bái tiān	daytime
待	dāi	stay (informal)
那儿	nàr	there
哪儿	nǎr	where
外套	wài tào	overcoat
当然	dāng rán	of course
前天	qián tiān	day before yesterday

Useful Vocabulary

雨天	yǔ tiān	rainy day
雪	xuě	snow
冰	bīng	ice
冷气	lěng qì	air conditioning
后天	hòu tiān	day after tomorrow

Revision Vocabulary

可是	kě shì	but
在	zài	at, in, on
昨天	zuó tiān	yesterday

Lesson Breakdown

你的 外套 在 哪儿?

Nǐ de wài tào zài nǎr?

Where is your overcoat?

| 哪儿 | nǎr | where? |

This sentence uses a QW to form a question.

Of importance to the student, is the position of the QW in the sentence.

Let's take a closer look at **where** to place QWs in a sentence and also how this compares to the use of QWs in English.

Earlier we mentioned that QWs, as used in Mandarin, are quite similar to the QWs we use in English. This statement is true if we compare the usage and meaning of the individual words. There is however, a big difference in their placement in the sentence.

Let's look at an example:

In **English** we place our QWs at the beginning of the sentence:

Where is your jacket?

In **Chinese** we put it in the place of the Subject/ Object that you are asking about. We literally ask:

Your jacket is **where**?
你的外套在 哪儿?
[nǐ de wài tào zài **nǎr**]

Pay attention to the position of the QW in the sentence. We will continue to point this out as we move along.

> 白天 太冷。
> Bái tiān tài lěng.
> The daytime is too cold.

白天　　　　bái tiān　　　day time

Literally: *white day*, implying when it's bright outside.

The visual aspect, of what every word or character represent, is something that is inherent about the Chinese language.

晴 天 [qíng tiān]　means: clear skies/ sunny day
天 黑 [tiān hēi]　means: to get dark/ dusk/ rain is coming
蓝 天 [lán tiān]　means: blue skies

A sequence of days (TWs) and their specific order:

今天 [jīn tiān] means: today
昨天 [zuó tiān] means: yesterday
前天 [qián tiān] means: the day before yesterday
(前 means: front or before)

明天 [míng tiān] means: tomorrow
后天 [hòu tiān] means: the day after tomorrow
(后 means: after or behind)

> 你 冷不冷?
>
> Nǐ lěng bù lěng ?
>
> Are you not cold?

A revision reminder!

Pay attention to the use of the Adjective.

As we saw in Unit 7, one way to ask a question in Chinese, is to place emphasis on the Adjective through the use of the negative 不 meaning *not*.

We do this by asking a **question with alternatives**.

At first this might seem unnecessary, but remember that the intention is to put emphasis on the Adjective, which acts as the main topic of the sentence.

(Download The Bonus Audio Files To Practice Your Pronunciation)

My Progress

Words	QW's	MW's	TW's	Total
Count	6	1	4	113

Hint

The word 天 has many applications and you should be comfortable with using most of them.

Self-Practice

Connect and match:

待 • • bái tiān • • to stay
外套 • • dāi • • overcoat
白天 • • nàr • • of course
当然 • • nǎr • • day before yesterday
前天 • • wài tào • • day after tomorrow
后天 • • dāng rán • • where
那儿 • • qián tiān • • there
哪儿 • • hòu tiān • • daytime

Rewrite the following sentences into Pinyin:

1. Are you cold? _____
2. Where is your overcoat? _____
3. Of course I am cold. _____
4. I stay at home. _____
5. The daytime is too cold. _____
6. I am not cold today. _____

Circle the correct character in every line:

1. 侍，得，时，带，待
2. 前，消，削，逍，硝
3. 久，外，卜，补，卟
4. 薹，雲，芸，云，套

● Useful Words Stroke Order   Character Stroke Order ●

后	雨	白	儿	待
前	当	然	外	套

Trace the following characters

后	后	后	后	后	后	后	后	后
雨	雨	雨	雨	雨	雨	雨	雨	雨
白	白	白	白	白	白	白	白	白
儿	儿	儿	儿	儿	儿	儿	儿	儿
待	待	待	待	待	待	待	待	待
前	前	前	前	前	前	前	前	前
当	当	当	当	当	当	当	当	当
然	然	然	然	然	然	然	然	然
外	外	外	外	外	外	外	外	外
套	套	套	套	套	套	套	套	套

Self-Practice

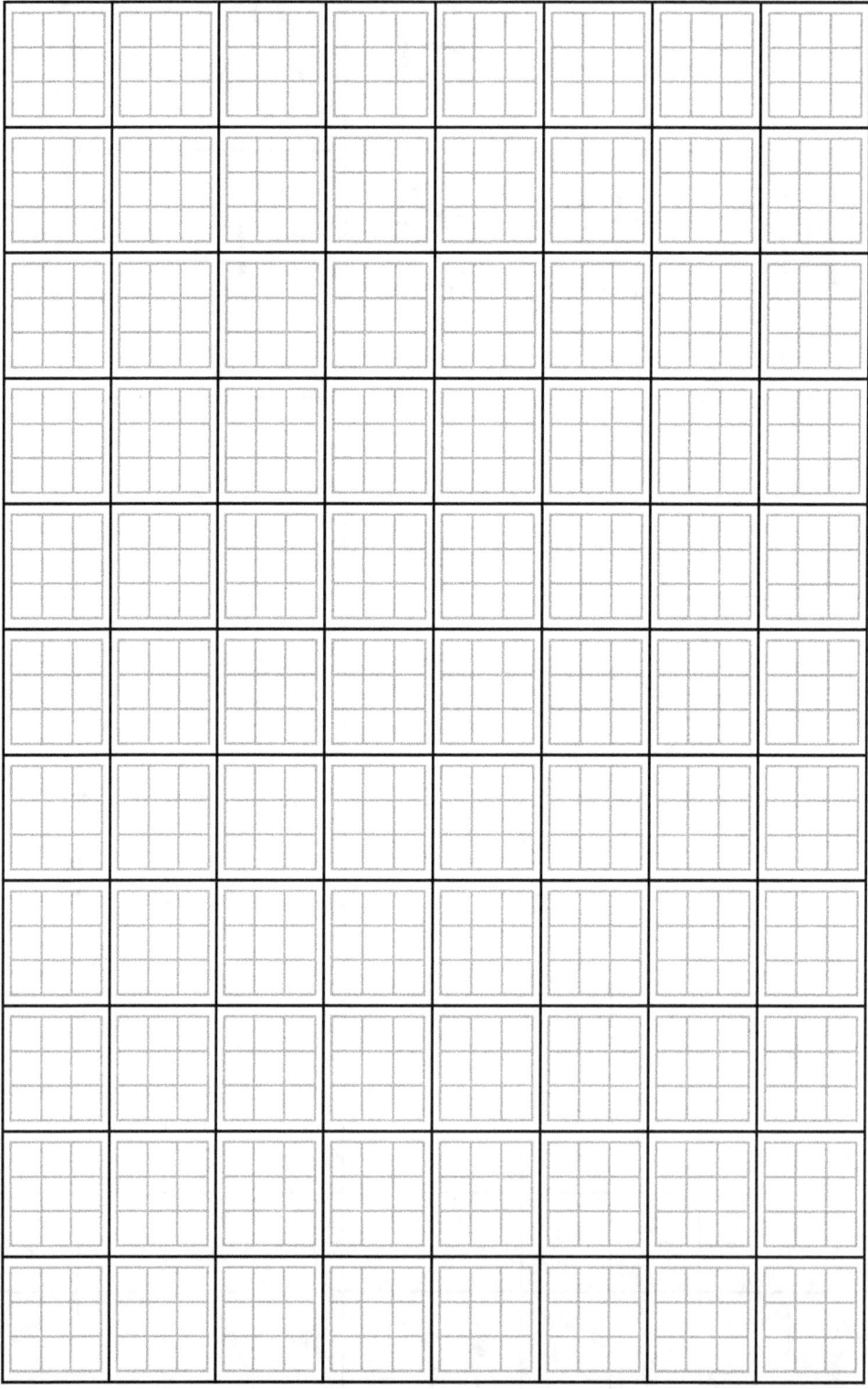

Unit 21

第二十一课　　　　Unit 21

今天, 我不是 很高兴。
Jīn tiān, wǒ bù shì hěn gāo xìng.
I am not very happy, today.

为什么? 你 怎么了?
Wéi shén me ? Nǐ zěn me le ?
Why? What's wrong with you?

我 太矮又胖。
Wǒ tài ǎi yòu pàng !
I am too short and fat!

你 不胖! 你 很瘦!
Nǐ bù pàng. Nǐ hěn shòu !
You are not fat! You are very thin!

This is a dialog between two friends who are confiding in each other.
The mood is serious and the one is comforting the other.

Dialog Vocabulary

高兴	gāo xìng	to be happy
矮	ǎi	to be short
胖	pàng	to be fat
瘦	shòu	to be thin
又	yòu	furthermore
怎么了	zěn me le	what's wrong?

Useful Vocabulary

生气	shēng qì	to be angry
哭	kū	to cry
好看	hǎo kàn	good-looking
开心	kāi xīn	to be happy
外表	wài biǎo	appearance

Revision Vocabulary

为什么	wéi shén me	why?
太	tài	too
很	hěn	very

Lesson Breakdown

> 你 怎么 了?
> Nǐ zěn me le ?
> What's wrong with you?

This sentence literally means: "What's the matter with you?".

This is a very common expression and it's good to memorize it early on.

We use this expression when the other party *does not look like before*.

Something has changed, and the speaker wants to know "What's the matter?" or "What's up?" with him or her.

怎么 is a Question Word and on its own it means "how" or "what".
Note!
怎么 is pronounced as [zěn me]
how? / what is?
什么 is also a QW and is pronounced as [shén me]
what?
Don't confuse these two words (especially their pronunciations) with each other.

> 我 太矮 又胖。
> Wǒ tài ǎi yòu pàng !
> I am too short and fat!

太   tài   too

This Adverb is used in the above sentence to indicate that something is **excessive**.
It indicates a degree of excessiveness that is unwanted.
You will notice that we use a very simple structure:
太 + Adjective

Example:
今天 太 冷。
[jīn tiān tài lěng]
It's too cold today.

太 is tied to the Adjective, in that it describes the *degree* of the Adjective. In our example the speaker is indicating that it is **too cold** (in his opinion), to a degree that he feels it is **unwanted**.
Fortunately, this Adverb can also be used to lift the mood. Besides indicating that something is negative (excessive), it can also show that something is positive (admiration).

Examples:

我 太 饿 了。
[wǒ tài è le]
I'm too hungry. (excess)

他 太 好 了。
[tā tài hǎo le]
He is too good. (admiration)

Note that the tone is 4th tone and that it puts emphasis on the "condition", whether positive or negative.

> 今天, 我 不是 很高兴。
> Jīn tiān, wǒ bù shì hěn gāo xìng.
> I am not very happy, today.

Take note of the word order used in this sentence.

The speaker or Subject did not say: "I'm unhappy today."

They chose to say: "I am **not** very happy today."

A specific word order is used to convey a specific message. The message is that the situation is not this way, but it is actually a completely different way.

We use the following structure:

Subject + 不是 + Adjective/ Verb/ Noun

Example:

他 不是 日本人。
[tā bú shì rì běn rén]
He is not Japanese.

The use of this structure is for **emphasis**.

Download The Bonus Audio Files To Practice Your Pronunciation

My Progress

Words	QW's	MW's	TW's	Total
Count	7	1	4	119

Hint

Many words are used simply for emphasis. You should identify them and their functions.

Self-Practice

Connect and match:

高兴 •	• hǎo kàn •	• good-looking
好看 •	• ǎi •	• to cry
哭 •	• shēng qì •	• to be angry
生气 •	• kū •	• to be thin
瘦 •	• zěn me le •	• furthermore
怎么了 •	• shòu •	• what's wrong?
又 •	• yòu •	• to be short
矮 •	• gāo xìng •	• to be happy

Write questions for the following answers:

1. _____?
我 不舒服。
2. _____?
我 外套 不在 那儿。
3. _____?
我 不冷。
4. _____?
高小姐 不高。

Arrange the words into sentences:

1. 怎么　了　你？
_____
2. 她　瘦　好。
_____
3. 很　我　不是　高兴。
_____
4. 矮　我　太　又　胖。
_____

● Useful Words Stroke Order   Character Stroke Order ●

很	心	开	哭	表
怎	胖	瘦	矮	兴

Trace the following characters

很	很	很	很	很	很	很	很	很
心	心	心	心	心	心	心	心	心
开	开	开	开	开	开	开	开	开
哭	哭	哭	哭	哭	哭	哭	哭	哭
表	表	表	表	表	表	表	表	表
怎	怎	怎	怎	怎	怎	怎	怎	怎
胖	胖	胖	胖	胖	胖	胖	胖	胖
瘦	瘦	瘦	瘦	瘦	瘦	瘦	瘦	瘦
矮	矮	矮	矮	矮	矮	矮	矮	矮
兴	兴	兴	兴	兴	兴	兴	兴	兴

Self-Practice

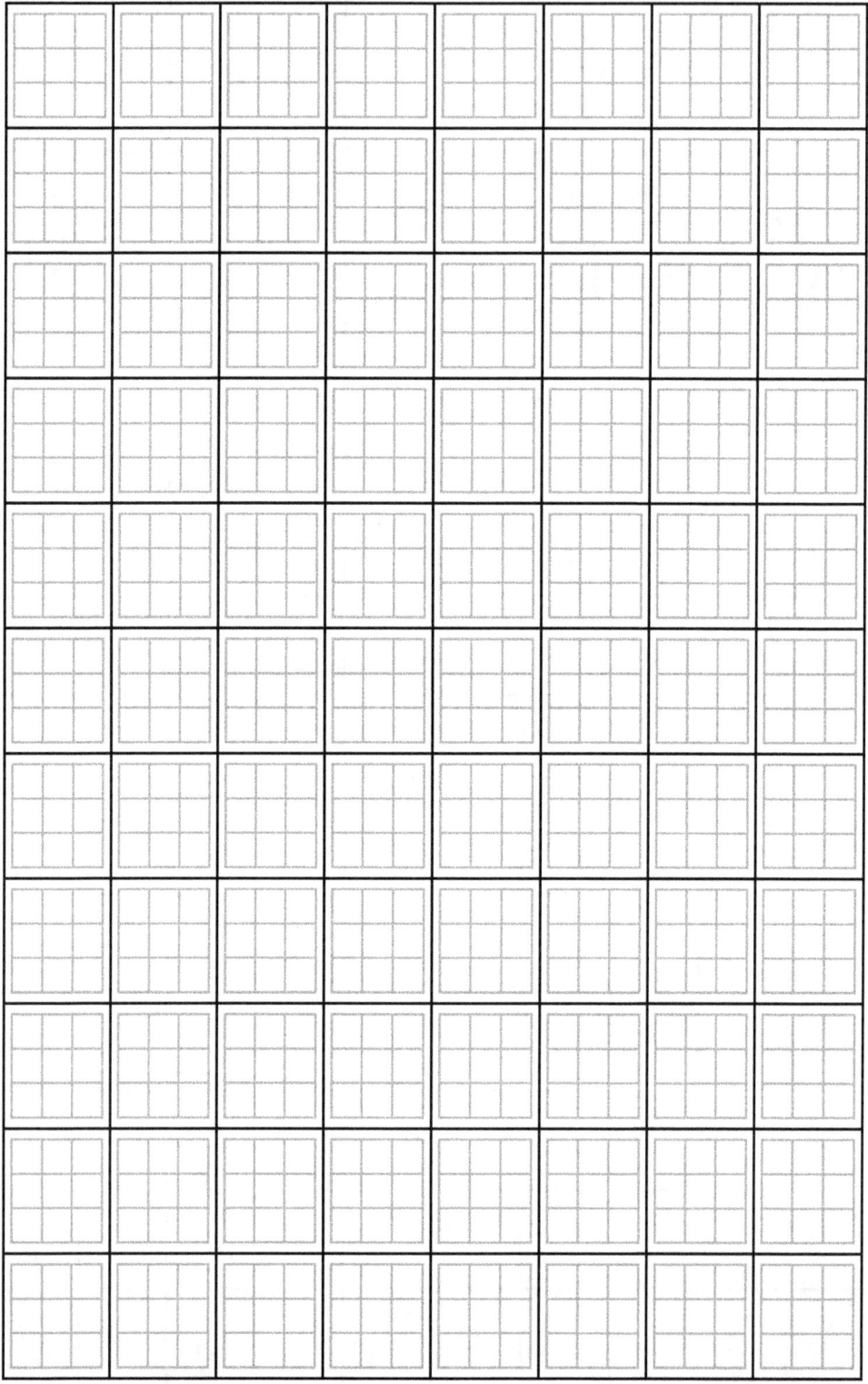

第二十二课 Unit 22

她 好瘦, 她是 你的 新朋友 吗?
Tā hǎo shòu, tā shì nǐ de xīn péng you ma?
She is very skinny, is she your new friend?

当然 不是, 她是 我太太。
Dāng rán bù shì, tā shì wǒ tài tai.
Of course not, she is my wife.

她是 南非人 吗?
Tā shì nán fēi rén ma?
Is she South African?

不, 她是 澳洲人。
Bù, tā shì Ào zhōu rén.
No, she is Australian.

This is a dialog between two friends who haven't seen each other for quite a while. The mood is relaxed and informal.

Dialog Vocabulary

朋友	péng you	friend
新	xīn	new
澳洲	ào zhōu	Australia
南非	nán fēi	South Africa
南	nán	south

Useful Vocabulary

女朋友	nǔ péng yǒu	girlfriend
男朋友	nán péng yǒu	boyfriend
老朋友	lǎo péng yǒu	old friend
好朋友	hǎo péng yǒu	good friend
非洲	Fēi zhōu	Africa
欧洲	Ōu zhōu	Europe

Revision Vocabulary

当然	dāng rán	of course
你的	nǐ de	your/ yours
不是	bù shì	not
瘦	shòu	skinny/ thin
好	hǎo	very

Lesson Breakdown

她 好瘦。
Tā hǎo shòu.
She is very skinny.

Remember (as mentioned earlier) that in this case 好 acts as an Adverb and it does not mean *good*, it means *very*.

It is used for emphasis and to indicate the *degree of the Adjective*. (Telling us *how thin* she is.)

It is similar to the use of 很 [hěn] meaning *quite*.

Note!
好 can only mean *good or very*.
The context of the sentence will determine the usage.
Examples of the difference in usage:
今天好热!
[jīn tiān hǎo rè]
Today it is very hot! (**very**)

我很好。
[wǒ hěn hǎo]
I'm doing good. (**good**)
(Remember that Adjectives are called Stative Verbs in Chinese.)

> 她是你的新朋友吗?
> Tā shì nǐ de xīn péng you ma ?
> Is she your new friend?

新　　　xīn　　　new

This is an Adjective and it describes the Noun (friend).
When something is new, we can say:
我的新车。
[wǒ de xīn chē]
My new car.
or
我的车是新的。
[wǒ de chē shì xīn de]
My car is a new car.
The second example is used for **emphasis**. It states that "my car is new, not old or used".

Supplementary

Writing:

When looking at the country of Australia [澳洲], we can see the character for continent 洲. This character is of course present in the list of continents:

澳洲	ào zhōu	Australia
亚洲	yà zhōu	Asia
欧洲	ōu zhōu	Europe
南美洲	nán měi zhōu	South America
北美洲	běi měi zhōu	North America
非洲	fēi zhōu	Africa
南极洲	nán jí zhōu	Antarctica

Make sure to memorize the names of as many countries and continents possible, since these words often pop up during conversations with native Mandarin speakers, especially when meeting someone for the first time.

Download The Bonus Audio Files To Practice Your Pronunciation

My Progress

Words	QW's	MW's	TW's	Total
Count	7	1	4	124

Hint

We can utilize Adjectives to show emphasis. Sentence structure indicates where the emphasis lies.

Self-Practice

Connect and match:

南 • • lǎo péng yǒu • • south
新 • • nán péng yǒu • • Australia
朋友 • • nǚ péng yǒu • • new
南非 • • nán • • friend
澳洲 • • péng yǒu • • South Africa
男朋友 • • xīn • • girlfriend
女朋友 • • nán fēi • • boyfriend
老朋友 • • ào zhōu • • old friend

Rewrite the following sentences into Pinyin:

1. Of course not. _____
2. No, she is Australian. _____
3. Is she French? _____
4. She is my wife. _____
5. She is very skinny. _____
6. She is an old friend. _____

Circle the correct character in every line:

1. 滴 , 腩 , 南 , 楠 , 喃
2. 诉 , 所 , 新 , 薪 , 莘
3. 倗 , 硼 , 月 , 朋 , 堋
4. 佑 , 右 , 又 , 有 , 友

● Useful Words Stroke Order　　Character Stroke Order ●

欧	洲	老	男	女
新	朋	友	非	南

Trace the following characters

欧	欧	欧	欧	欧	欧	欧	欧	欧	欧
洲	洲	洲	洲	洲	洲	洲	洲	洲	洲
老	老	老	老	老	老	老	老	老	老
男	男	男	男	男	男	男	男	男	男
女	女	女	女	女	女	女	女	女	女
新	新	新	新	新	新	新	新	新	新
朋	朋	朋	朋	朋	朋	朋	朋	朋	朋
友	友	友	友	友	友	友	友	友	友
非	非	非	非	非	非	非	非	非	非
南	南	南	南	南	南	南	南	南	南

Self-Practice

第二十三课 Unit 23

我 要 去 上班。
Wǒ yào qù shàng bān.
I want to go to work.

小美, 你 怎么 去 上班?
Xiǎo Měi, nǐ zěn me qù shàng bān?
Little Mei, how do you go to work?

我 走路, 很 好 玩。
Wǒ zǒu lù, hěn hǎo wán.
I walk to work; it is fun.

我也 喜欢 走路。
Wǒ yě xǐ huān zǒu lù.
I also like to walk (to work).

This is a dialog between two friends who meet at the market. Both are in a hurry and they have to get to work.

Dialog Vocabulary

上班	shàng bān	go to work
玩	wán	to enjoy (fun)
走路	zǒu lù	to walk (on road)
走	zǒu	to walk/ to go
路	lù	road
怎么	zěn me	how?
小美	Xiǎo Měi	Little Mei

Useful Vocabulary

玩	wán	to play
学	xué	to study
学校	xué xiào	school
大学	dà xué	university
上课	shàng kè	go to class

Revision Vocabulary

喜欢	xǐ huān	to like
去	qù	to go
要	yào	to want
也	yě	also

Lesson Breakdown

> 你 怎么 去 上班?
> Nǐ zěn me qù shàng bān?
> How do you go to work?

This sentence literally means: "You, how to go, to work?"

We already know that simple questions require a Yes/No answer. They all end with a question particle 吗.

When we want to ask a more specific question, i.e. make an inquiry into *how* somebody does *something*, we need to use a Question-word to inquire about the specific Verb *to do*.

> 怎么　　zěn me　　how to?

This Question-word describes and inquires about the Verb.

It asks *how* some action is performed.

We use the following structure:

(Subject) + 怎么 + Verb

The Subject can be a person or topic that's related to the Verb that's doing something. This action (Verb) can be any of the simple Verbs we use on a daily basis like write, study, say, do, cook, use, go, etc.

Thus, the QW allows us to ask **how to do** something.

Example:

蛋糕 怎么 做?

[dàn gāo zěn me zuò]

How to bake a cake?

Note!

Question Words are very important to Mandarin speakers and are used in various grammar patterns.

> 我 走路。
> Wǒ zǒu lù.
> I walk (to work).

> 走路　　zǒu lù　　to walk (VO)

Certain Verbs are unique in that they can be separated into two parts. These Verbs consist of two characters and they can be separated into a Verb component and an Object component. (We call them the VO compound or agreement.)

Try not to over-think this concept. Mandarin has many unique qualities and this is just one of them. Just focus on the fact that the **Verb** has its own function and that the **Object** has its own function and that **they are closely related** to each other.

走 [zǒu] means: to walk (Verb)

路 [lù] means road (Object)

We combine these two characters to form a new word which means: "to walk on the road".

This VO compound is used often in Mandarin and you can use it for walking on any terrain.

For the Verb-Object (VO) agreement to exist, **the two words must have the ability to function individually on their own**.

Pay attention to these Verb-Object agreements for they are used in various sentence patterns. We will continue to point them out in the upcoming Units.

Typical VO compounds:

吃饭 [chī fàn]   to eat

睡觉 [shuì jiào]   to sleep

见面 [jiàn miàn] to meet

Supplementary

Writing: Radicals

Let's look at the character 路 and the radical used.

⻊ represents the "foot" radical.

Characters that use this radical are connected to the "foot" in some way or another. Examples:

跑 [páo] meaning: to run

跌 [diē] meaning: to fall down

Download The Bonus Audio Files To Practice Your Pronunciation

My Progress

Words	QW's	MW's	TW's	Total
Count	7	1	4	131

Hint

Remember that VO compounds can be separated into two words that have a relationship.

Self-Practice

Connect and match:

玩 •	• shàng bān •	• to walk
走 •	• wán •	• to enjoy
路 •	• zǒu lù •	• walk (on road)
上班 •	• lù •	• how?
怎么 •	• zěn me •	• to study
走路 •	• zǒu •	• school
学 •	• xué •	• road
学校 •	• xué xiào •	• go to work

Translate the following sentences into English:

1. Wǒ yě xǐ huān zǒu lù.
   _____

2. Nǐ zěn me qù shàng bān?
   _____

3. Wǒ zǒu lù, hěn hǎo wán.
   _____

4. Wǒ yào qù shàng bān.
   _____

Arrange the words into sentences:

1. 我　　去　　上班　　要。
   _____

2. 怎么　　上班　　去　　你？
   _____

3. 我　　喜欢　　也　　走路。
   _____

4. 学校　　你　　怎么　　去？
   _____

● Useful Words Stroke Order   Character Stroke Order ●

大	上	学	校	课
走	路	美	玩	班

Trace the following characters

大	大	大	大	大	大	大	大	大
上	上	上	上	上	上	上	上	上
学	学	学	学	学	学	学	学	学
校	校	校	校	校	校	校	校	校
课	课	课	课	课	课	课	课	课
走	走	走	走	走	走	走	走	走
路	路	路	路	路	路	路	路	路
美	美	美	美	美	美	美	美	美
玩	玩	玩	玩	玩	玩	玩	玩	玩
班	班	班	班	班	班	班	班	班

Self-Practice

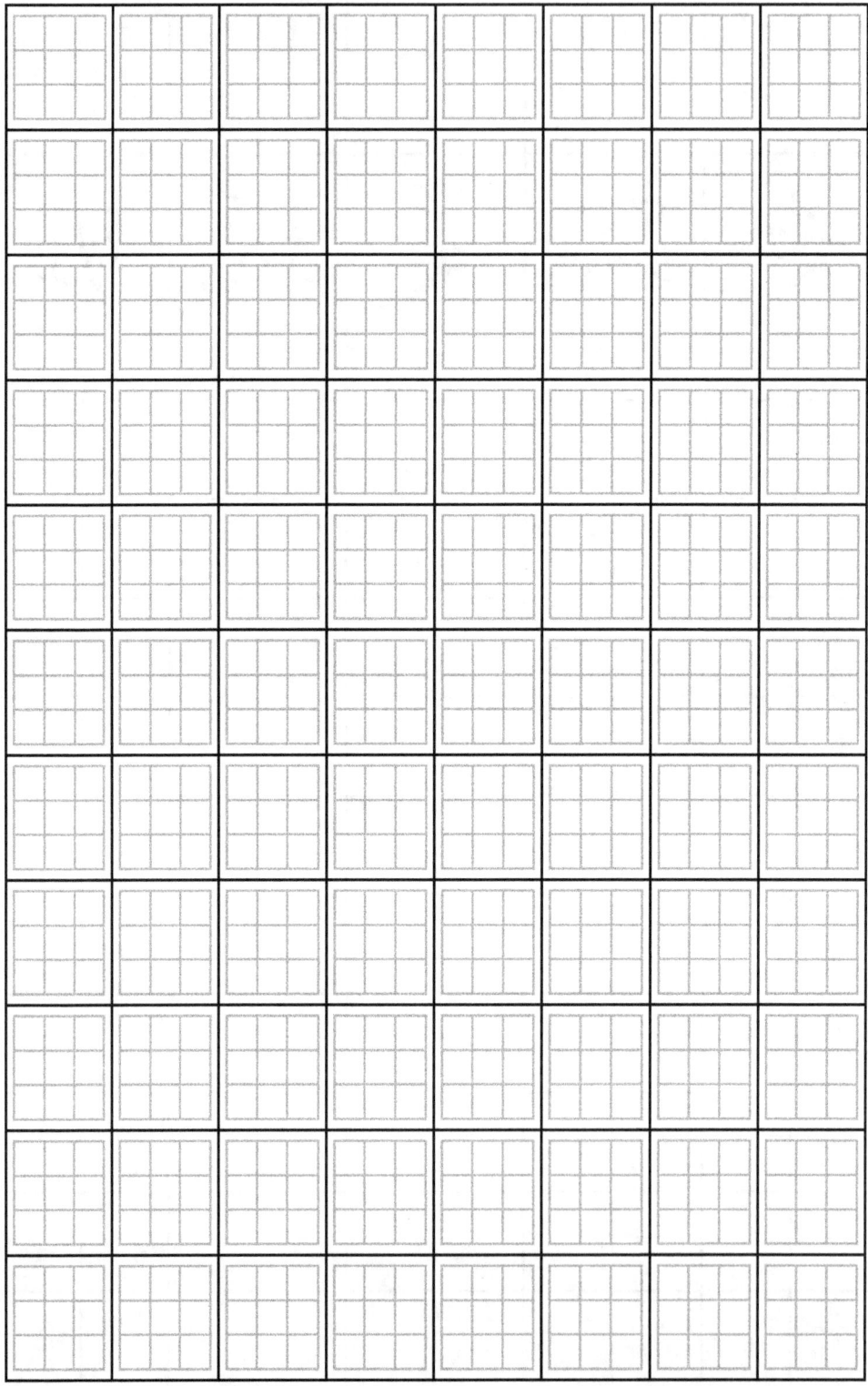

第二十四课   Unit 24

今天 晚上 你 忙不忙?
Jīn tiān wǎn shàng nǐ máng bù máng ?
Are you busy tonight?

为什么?
Wéi shén me ?
Why?

我要 去看 一部 电影。不要 一个人去。
Wǒ yào qù kàn yí bù diàn yǐng. Bù yào yí gè rén qù.
I want to go to watch a movie. Don't want to go alone.

好的, 我不忙。
Hǎo de, wǒ bù máng.
OK. I am not busy.

This is a dialog between two friends. The mood is relaxed and friendly. It is not a romantic affair.

Dialog Vocabulary

电影	diàn yǐng	movie
晚上	wǎn shàng	tonight/evening
看	kàn	to watch
部	bù	MW for films
好的	hǎo de	good
一	yī	one
个	gè	general MW

Useful Vocabulary

早上	zǎo shàng	morning
下午	xià wǔ	afternoon
晚	wǎn	late
二	èr	two
三	sān	three
四	sì	four
五	wǔ	five

Revision Vocabulary

忙	máng	to be busy
为什么	wéi shén me	why?
要	yào	to want

Lesson Breakdown

> 我要 去看 一部 电影。不要 一个人去。
> Wǒ yào qù kàn yí bù diàn yǐng. Bù yào yí gè rén qù.
> I want to go to watch a movie. Don't want to go alone.

| 部 | bù | MW (movies) |

This is a Specific Measure Word (MW) used for **movies**.

Measure words are placed after numbers and Question Words (QW). They express *frequency of actions* and *also units for people and things*.

A specific measure word is used for a **specific object**.

个 ge general MW

To remember all the MWs used for specific objects is no easy task. Fortunately, help is at hand in the form of a "generic" MW that can be used for all Nouns.

个 is a general or common MW that is used before Nouns that do not have their own special MWs.

When unsure about which MW to choose, you can use 个.

Examples:
我 有 一 个。 [wǒ yǒu yí gè]   I have one.
我 要 这 个。 [wǒ yào zhè gè] I want this one.
一 个 人。   [yí gè rén]   One person.

Examples of Specific MWs:
一 辆 车   [yí liàng chē] one car
一 个 车   [yí gè chē]   one car
一 位 先生 [yí weì xiān shēng]   one gentleman
一 个 先生 [yí gè xiān shēng]   one gentleman
一 台 电脑 [yī tái diàn nǎo]   one computer
一 个 电脑 [yí gè diàn nǎo]   one computer

一个 yí gè one (MW)

Tones:
一 [yī] means: one

This number is pronounced in the 1st tone when used as part of a number sequence:
一, 二, 三
[yī, èr, sān]
1, 2, 3

But!

When [yī] is followed by a 4th tone, we change and pronounce it in a 2nd tone as [yí].

Explanation:

一个 [yí gè], where [yí] is 2nd tone.

The reason is, because it is followed by a fourth tone 个 [gè].

This normally happens where it is followed by a Measure Word (MW).

This change in tone applies only to [yī] followed by a **4th** tone.

Supplementary

Numbers:

一	yī	one	十一	shí yī	eleven
二	èr	two	十二	shí èr	twelve
三	sān	three	十三	shí sān	thirteen
四	sì	four	十四	shí sì	fourteen
五	wǔ	five	十五	shí wǔ	fifteen
六	liù	six	十六	shí liù	sixteen
七	qī	seven	十七	shí qī	seventeen
八	bā	eight	十八	shí bā	eighteen
九	jiǔ	nine	十九	shí jiǔ	nineteen
十	shí	ten	二十	èr shí	twenty
零	líng	zero	二十一	èr shí yī	twenty one

Download The Bonus Audio Files To Practice Your Pronunciation

My Progress

Words	QW's	MW's	TW's	Total
Count	7	3	4	138

Hint

Initially you can use the general MW 个, and gradually over time you can introduce specific MWs.

Self-Practice

Connect and match:

电影 •   • bù •   • movie
看 •   • wǎn shàng •   • to watch
部 •   • hǎo de •   • good
晚上 •   • yī •   • one
好的 •   • gè •   • two
一 •   • èr •   • general MW
个 •   • diàn yǐng •   • tonight
二 •   • kàn •   • MW films

Rewrite the following sentences into Pinyin:

1. Are you busy tonight? _____
2. Don't want to go alone. _____
3. Why? _____
4. I want to go watch a movie. _____
5. I'm not busy. _____
6. I like to watch movies. _____

Circle the correct character in every line:

1. 者 , 着 , 春 , 舂 , 看
2. 个 , 人 , 亻 , 仒 , 八
3. 都 , 部 , 邜 , 培 , 始
4. 虫 , 屯 , 电 , 申 , 中

Useful Words Stroke Order   Character Stroke Order

一	二	三	四	五
电	影	晚	部	个

Trace the following characters

一	一	一	一	一	一	一	一	一
二	二	二	二	二	二	二	二	二
三	三	三	三	三	三	三	三	三
四	四	四	四	四	四	四	四	四
五	五	五	五	五	五	五	五	五
电	电	电	电	电	电	电	电	电
影	影	影	影	影	影	影	影	影
晚	晚	晚	晚	晚	晚	晚	晚	晚
部	部	部	部	部	部	部	部	部
个	个	个	个	个	个	个	个	个

Self-Practice

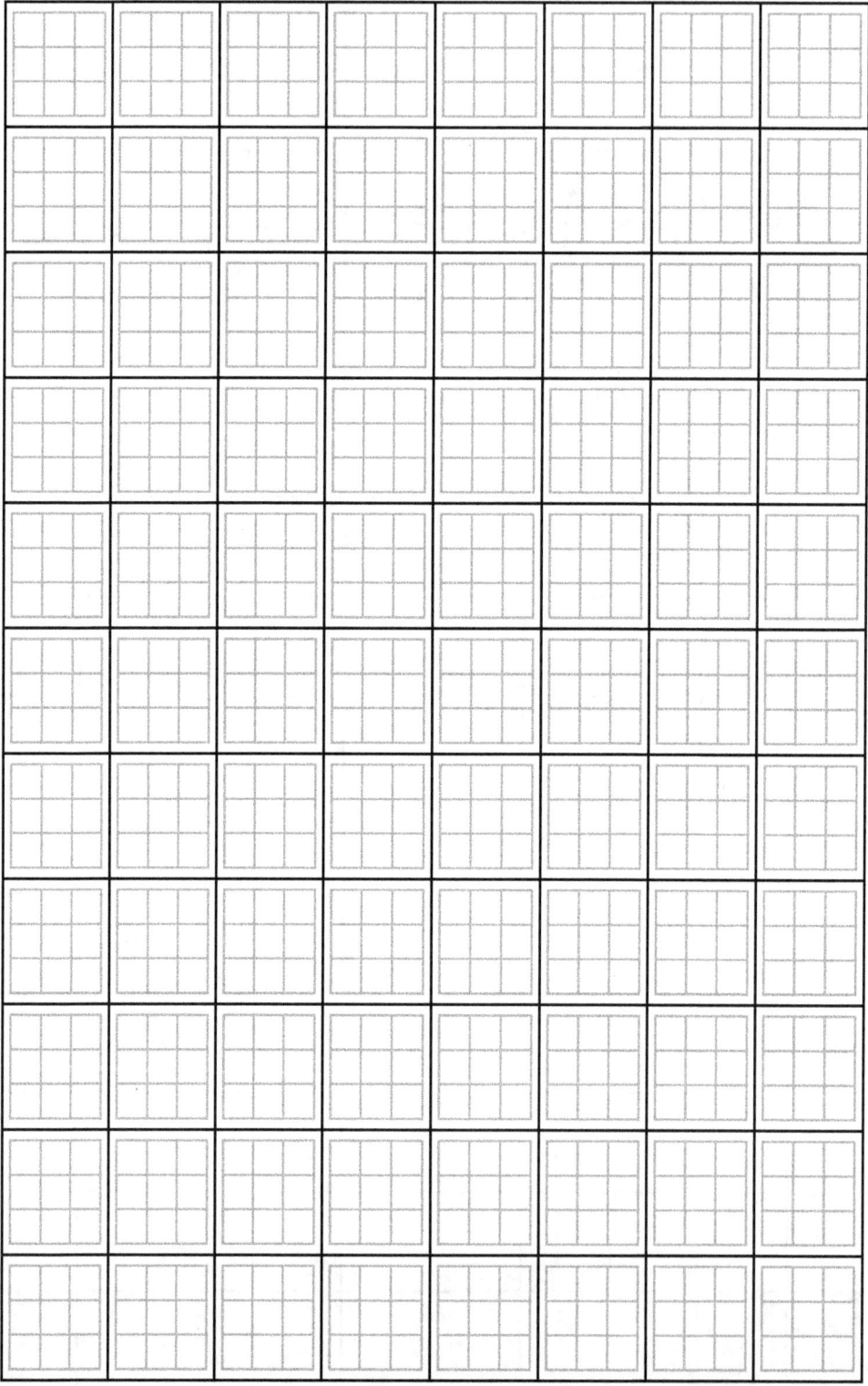

第二十五课 Unit 25

你 有 电视 吗?
Nǐ yǒu diàn shì ma ?
Do you have a TV?

不, 我 没有 电视, 我朋友 有 一台。
Bù, wǒ méi yǒu diàn shì, wǒ péng you yǒu yī tái.
No, I don't have a TV. My friend has one.

但是, 我要 看 电视!
Dàn shì, wǒ yào kàn diàn shì !
But, I want to watch TV!

我也 想要 看 电视!
Wǒ yě xiǎng yào kàn diàn shì !
I also want to watch TV!

This is a dialog between two friends who are discussing televisions. Both are big fans of watching TV.

Dialog Vocabulary

电视	diàn shì	television
有	yǒu	to have
没有	méi yǒu	not to have
但是	dàn shì	but
想要	xiǎng yào	to want to
台	tái	MW for machinery

Useful Vocabulary

电	diàn	electricity
电话	diàn huà	telephone
电脑	diàn nǎo	computer
电灯	diàn dēng	light
电冰箱	diàn bīng xiāng	refrigerator

Revision Vocabulary

也	yě	also
要	yào	to want
看	kàn	to watch
一	yī	one

Lesson Breakdown

> 不, 我 没有 电视, 我朋友 有 一台。
> Bù, wǒ méi yǒu diàn shì, wǒ péng you yǒu yī tái.
> No, I do not have a TV. My friend has one.

一台   yī tái   MW (machines)

This is a specific Measure Word that is used for all *machinery and instruments*.

This includes TVs, computers, radios, etc.

In the modern age of technology, this is a MW that is used often in written and spoken Chinese.

电视　　diàn shì　　Television

The root of this word is 电 [diàn], which means "electricity" (N).
You will find that it is present in all forms of technology that utilizes *electricity* to function.

电视 [diàn shì]　　TV
电脑 [diàn nǎo]　　computer
电话 [diàn huà]　　telephone
电灯 [diàn dēng]　　light

You will notice that the character for electricity, 电 is present in all of the above mentioned electric appliances.

有　　yǒu　　to have

This Verb is used to indicate that somebody *has/ have* something.

It can be used for having physical objects like money, things, people, properties, etc. It can also be used for more abstract things like jobs, time, patience and manners.

When using this Verb, we follow a specific structure:

Subject + 有 + Object

Example:
我 有 钱。
[wǒ yǒu qián]
I do have money.

Let's take a look at how to negate this Verb.

没有　　　méi yǒu　　　not to have

We use the negative prefix 没 [méi] which means "have not", together with the Verb 有 "to have". It is placed before the Verb (有) and means: *not to have*.

It can be used to indicate that the speaker does not have money, things, people, jobs, time, etc.

Example:
我 没有 钱。
[wǒ méi yǒu qián]
I do not have money.

(Remember that 不 can never be used for the negative form of this Verb.)

> 我也 想要 看 电视!
> Wǒ yě xiǎng yào kàn diàn shì !
> I also want to watch TV!

想要　　　xiǎng yào　　to feel like

This is a Verb and if we dissect it, we see that it literally means: "to think and to want".

Let's look at the individual words:

On its own 想　[xiǎng] means: *to think or to want*.

On its own 要　[yào] means: *to want*.

想要 puts more emphasis on the "thinking" part and therefore it could best be translated as: *to feel like*.

Download The Bonus Audio Files To Practice Your Pronunciation

My Progress

Words	QW's	MW's	TW's	Total
Count	7	4	4	144

Hint

Remember when using the Verb 有 that it is always followed by an Object.

Self-Practice

Connect and match:

电视 •	• dàn shì •	• MW machinery
有 •	• méi yǒu •	• television
没有 •	• xiǎng yào •	• to have
但是 •	• yǒu •	• to want to
想要 •	• diàn shì •	• not to have
台 •	• diàn •	• electricity
电 •	• diàn huà •	• telephone
电话 •	• tái •	• but

Write questions for the following answers:

1. _____?

我 没有 电视。

2. _____?

对,我 要 看 电视。

3. _____?

我朋友没有电视。

4. _____?

我 没有 电话。

Arrange the words into sentences:

1. 有   你   吗   电视?

_____

2. 但是   要   我   看   电视。

_____

3. 也   我   看   想要   电视。

_____

4. 朋友   我   有   一台   电视。

_____

● Useful Words Stroke Order   Character Stroke Order ●

电	话	脑	灯	箱
视	没	但	想	台

Trace the following characters

电	电	电	电	电	电	电	电	电
话	话	话	话	话	话	话	话	话
脑	脑	脑	脑	脑	脑	脑	脑	脑
灯	灯	灯	灯	灯	灯	灯	灯	灯
箱	箱	箱	箱	箱	箱	箱	箱	箱
视	视	视	视	视	视	视	视	视
没	没	没	没	没	没	没	没	没
但	但	但	但	但	但	但	但	但
想	想	想	想	想	想	想	想	想
台	台	台	台	台	台	台	台	台

Self-Practice

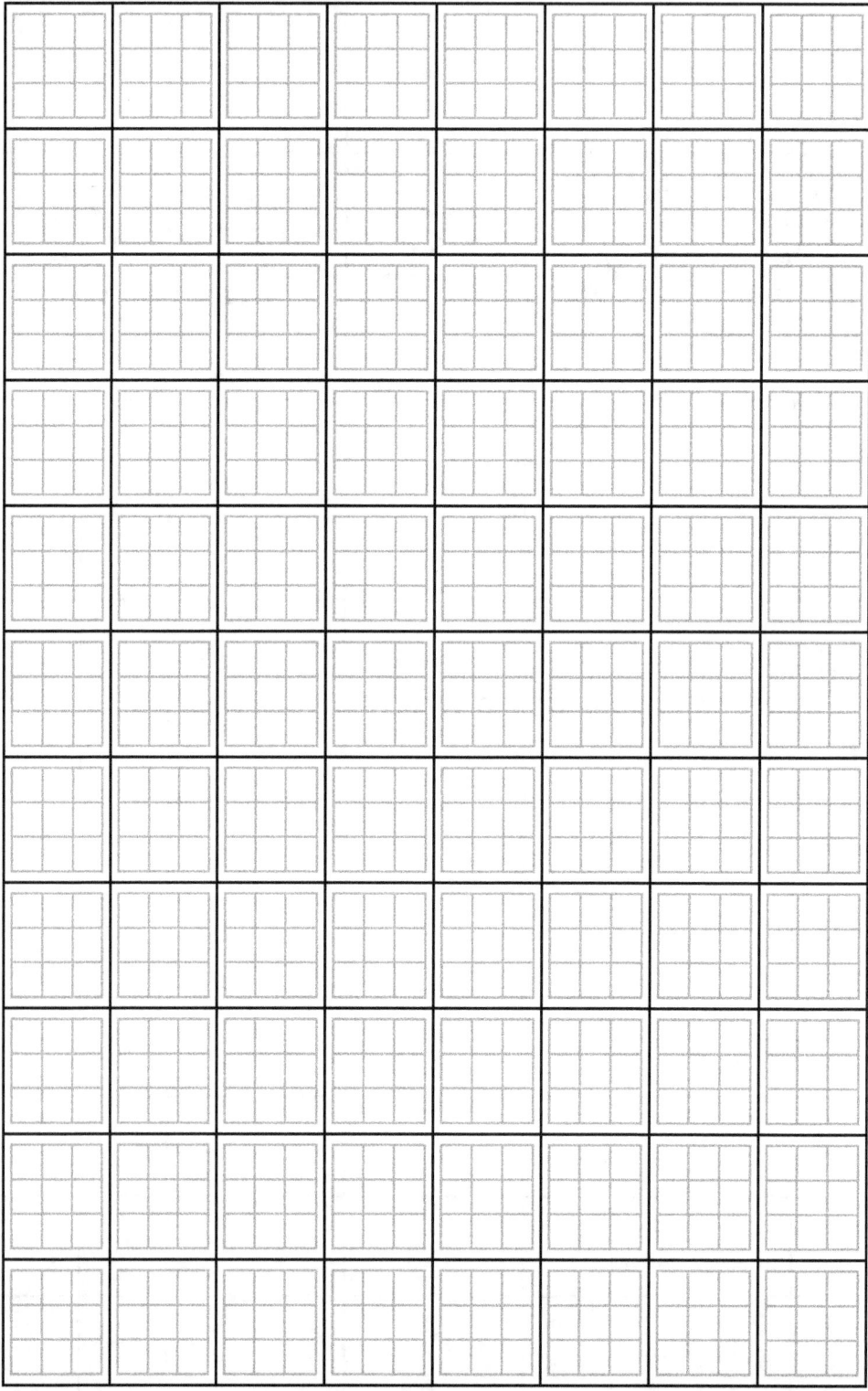

第二十六课 Unit 26

林小姐,你的 车子 很漂亮!
Lín xiǎo jiě, nǐ de chē zǐ hěn piāo liàng!
Miss Lin, your car is very beautiful!

谢谢你!
Xiè xiè nǐ!
Thank you.

告诉 我,这是 新的 吗?
Gào sù wǒ, zhè shì xīn de ma?
Tell me, is it new?

对,它是。
Duì, tā shì.
Yes, it is.

This is a dialog between two coworkers. Both are outside admiring a new car. The mood is polite and slightly formal.

Dialog Vocabulary

车子	chē zǐ	car
漂亮	piāo liàng	beautiful
告诉	gào sù	to tell
这	zhè	this
它	tā	it (things)

Useful Vocabulary

开车	kāi chē	to drive
火车	huǒ chē	train
摩托车	mó tuō chē	motorcycle
脚踏车	jiǎo tà chē	bicycle

Revision Vocabulary

你的	nǐ de	your/ yours
谢谢	xiè xie	thank you
新	xīn	new

Lesson Breakdown

对,它是。
Duì, tā shì.
Yes, it is.

| 它 | tā | it |

This word is a Pronoun and it is used for **inanimate objects** and sometimes for animals.

Don't confuse it with the other Pronouns sharing the same pronunciation.

Generally it is not used for people, but in rare instances, it can be used for a group of people like a political party.

Take note of the different characters used for *he*, *she* and *it*:

他 [tā] he
她 [tā] she
它 [tā] it

All three words share the same pronunciation.

> 告诉 我, 这是 新的 吗?
> Gào sù wǒ, zhè shì xīn de ma ?
> Tell me, is it new?

告诉我   gào sù wǒ   tell me

This expression means: "Tell me".
The Pronoun 我 does not change whether it is the Object or the Subject of the sentence.
It differs from English where " I " becomes "me":
In the English language you will refrain from saying:
Give it to **I**. (Incorrect)
You will instead say:
Give it to **me**. (Correct)
In Mandarin this is not necessary. A Pronoun like 我 does not change, whether it is the Subject or the Object of the sentence. It remains in its original form and can be placed anywhere in the sentence, as the Object or the Subject.
This goes for all Pronouns like 我, 他, 她, 你, 你们, etc.

This is one of the less-complicated areas of learning Mandarin. We use particles to show possession and plurals of Pronouns.

Supplementary

Writing: Character

车   chē   car

In Mandarin the character for car 车 is present and functions as the root in all traditional vehicles:

Let's look at the following word:
火车 [huǒ chē] which means: train
火 [huǒ] means: fire
This word literally means: "fire car".

Other examples include:
脚踏车   [jiǎo tà chē] meaning: bicycle
摩托车   [mó tuō chē] meaning: motorcycle
计程车   [jì chéng chē] meaning: taxi

Pay attention to these subtle differences and they will help you to recognize the individual characters.

Download The Bonus Audio Files To Practice Your Pronunciation

My Progress

Words	QW's	MW's	TW's	Total
Count	7	4	4	149

Hint

Dissect every new character and identify relevant radicals and character components.

Self-Practice

Connect and match:

这 •	• huǒ chē •	• it (things)
它 •	• gào sù •	• car
车子 •	• kāi chē •	• beautiful
告诉 •	• piāo liàng •	• to tell
漂亮 •	• chē zǐ •	• this
开车 •	• tā •	• to drive
火车 •	• zhè •	• train
她 •	• tā •	• she

Rewrite the following sentences into Pinyin:

1. Miss Lin, you are very beautiful. _____
2. Miss Wang, your car is very beautiful. _____
3. Tell me. _____
4. Is it new? _____
5. Thank you very much. _____
6. Yes, it is. _____

Circle the correct character in every line:

1. 过，迢，边，送，这
2. 宁，宅，字，它，方
3. 耳，车，本，東，东
4. 丼，卉，共，井，开

Useful Words Stroke Order   Character Stroke Order

开	火	告	诉	这
车	子	票	亮	它

Trace the following characters

开									
火									
告									
诉									
这									
车									
子									
票									
亮									
它									

Unit 26

Self-Practice

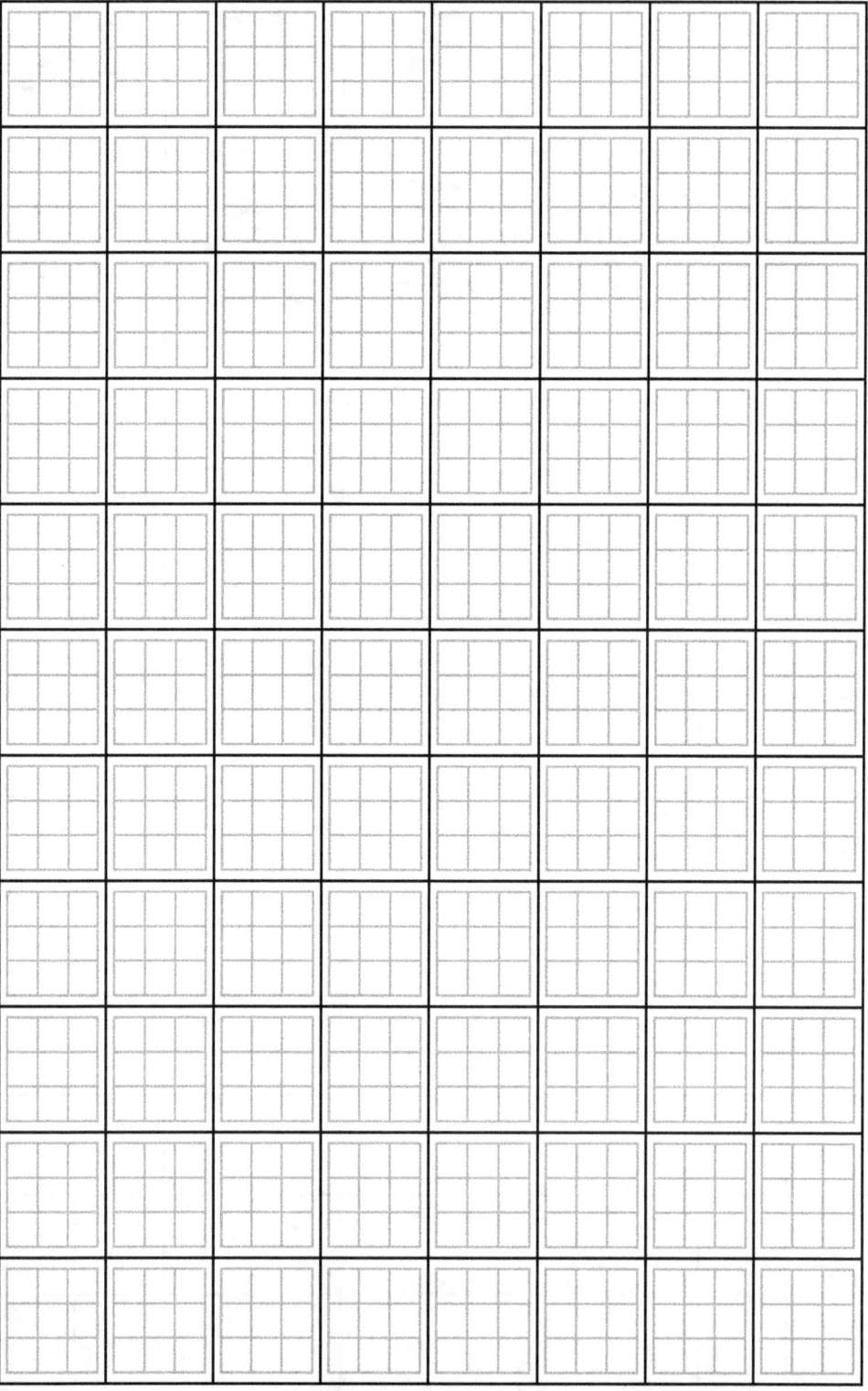

第二十七课　　Unit 27

不好 意思, 你要 这本书 吗?
Bù hǎo yì sī, nǐ yào zhè běn shū ma ?
Excuse me, do you want this book?

我要, 可是它太贵。
Wǒ yào, kě shì tā tài gui.
I do. But it is too expensive.

这是 一本 非常 好的书。
Zhè shì yī běn fēi cháng hǎo de shū.
This is an extremely good book.

好!
Hǎo !
OK!

This is a dialog between customer and sales clerk at a book store.
The mood is casual, but professional.

Dialog Vocabulary

不好意思	bù hǎo yì sī	excuse me
意思	yì sī	meaning
书	shū	book
贵	guì	expensive
本	běn	MW for book
非常	fēi cháng	very/ extremely

Useful Vocabulary

便宜	pián yi	cheap
报纸	bào zhǐ	newspaper
纸	zhǐ	paper
对不起	duì bu qǐ	sorry/ excuse me
书店	shū diàn	bookstore

Revision Vocabulary

这	zhè	this
它	tā	it
可是	kě shì	but

Lesson Breakdown

> 不好 意思, 你要 这本书 吗?
> Bù hǎo yì sī, nǐ yào zhè běn shū ma?
> Excuse me, do you want this book?

本　　běn　　MW (books)

This is a Measure Word (MW) specifically for *book-like objects*. This includes novels, magazines, comics, etc.

Example:
这 本 书 是 我 的。
[zhè běn shū shì wǒde]
This book is mine.

> 不好意思   bù hǎo yì sī   excuse me

Mandarin is a very polite language.
The use of this phrase indicates a polite mood and it means: *to find it embarrassing*. The speaker is basically saying, very politely, that he/she feels embarrassed to ask for assistance.

> 不好意思,你要这本书吗?
> Bù hǎo yì sī, nǐ yào zhè běn shū ma?
> Excuse me, do you want this book?

> 要   yào   to want

A Verb can be used to ask a specific question. There are two ways that this can be done:

你要这本书吗?
[nǐ yào zhè běn shū ma?]
Do you want this book?

你要不要这本书?
[nǐ yào bù yào zhè běn shū ma?]
Do you want this book or not?

The last example puts more **emphasis on the Verb**, and changes the mood. It becomes a question with options.
We use the following structure:
V + 不 + V
Example:
你要不要一个?
[nǐ yào bù yào yī gè]
Do you want one?

Supplementary

非常 VS 很

At first glance it might seem as if the two words share the same meaning. (This is a very common occurrence in the Chinese language.)

There is however a distinct difference and a few examples will clarify the matter:

非常　[fēi cháng]　means: extremely
很　　[hěn]　　means: quite

The only difference lies in the **mood**.
非常 is more serious in mood than 很 .

Example:
很 冷　　[hěn lěng] quite cold
非常 冷　[fēi cháng lěng] extremely cold

We can assume that the person using the second example is feeling considerably colder than the other.

In Mandarin Chinese, it is very normal to use Adverbs to express degree.

Download The Bonus Audio Files To Practice Your Pronunciation

My Progress					Hint
Words	QW's	MW's	TW's	Total	Words that seem similar in meaning, usually differ is mood and degree.
Count	7	5	4	155	

Self-Practice

Connect and match:

便宜 •   • fēi zháng •   • book store
非常 •   • běn •   • MW books
本 •   • guì •   • meaning
贵 •   • pián yi •   • not good
书店 •   • shū •   • book
意思 •   • yì sī •   • cheap
书 •   • bù hǎo •   • expensive
不好 •   • shū diàn •   • very

Translate the following sentences into English:

1. Bù hǎo yì sī.
   _____

2. Zhè shì yī běn fēi cháng hǎo de shū.
   _____

3. Wǒ yào, kě shì tā tài gui.
   _____

4. Nǐ yào zhè běn shū ma ?
   _____

Arrange the words into sentences:

1. 本   你   要   书   吗   这？

2. 好   意思   不。

3. 可是   我   要   它   贵   太。

4. 本   这   我   喜欢   书。

● Useful Words Stroke Order   Character Stroke Order ●

便	宜	报	纸	店
书	常	本	意	思

Trace the following characters

便	便	便	便	便	便	便	便	便
宜	宜	宜	宜	宜	宜	宜	宜	宜
报	报	报	报	报	报	报	报	报
纸	纸	纸	纸	纸	纸	纸	纸	纸
店	店	店	店	店	店	店	店	店
书	书	书	书	书	书	书	书	书
常	常	常	常	常	常	常	常	常
本	本	本	本	本	本	本	本	本
意	意	意	意	意	意	意	意	意
思	思	思	思	思	思	思	思	思

Self-Practice

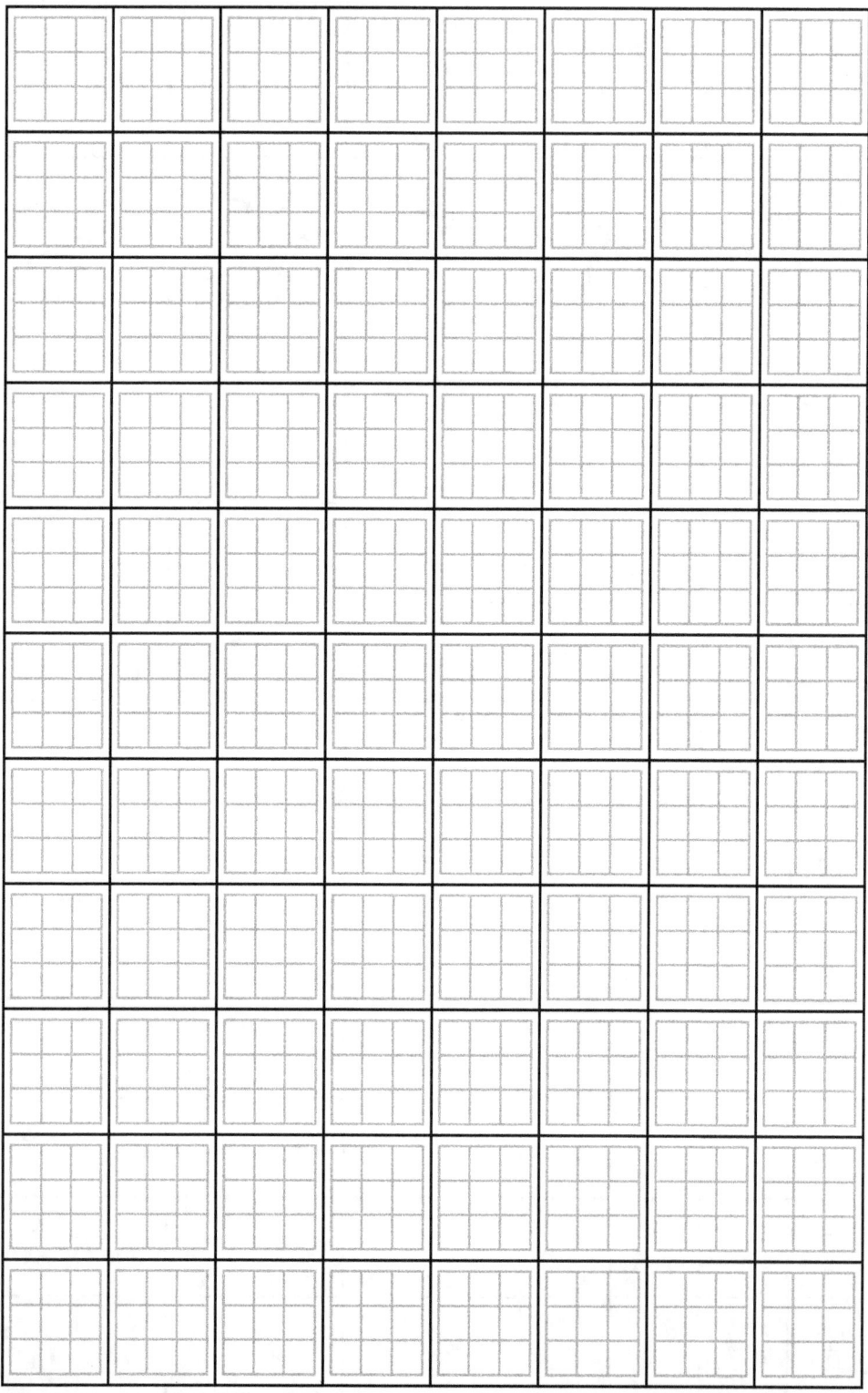

第二十八课 Unit 28

你喜欢哪一辆车?
Nǐ xǐ huān nǎ yí liàng chē?
Which car do you like?

这 两 辆车 都 非常 漂亮。
Zhè liǎng liàng ché dōu fēi cháng piāo liàng.
These two are both very beautiful.

都 是 名车。
Dōu shì míng chē.
Both are famous models.

但是, 我要 这 一辆, 我 喜欢 大车。
Dàn shì, wǒ yào zhè yí liàng. Wǒ xǐ huān dà chē.
But, I want this one. I like big cars.

This is a dialog between a car salesman and a prospective buyer. The mood is relaxed and polite.

Dialog Vocabulary

都	dōu	both/ all
大	dà	big
名车	míng chē	luxury car
两	liǎng	two (before MW)
辆	liàng	MW for vehicles

Useful Vocabulary

小	xiǎo	small
脚踏车	jiǎo tà chē	bicycle
摩托车	mó tuō chē	motorcycle
火车	huǒ chē	train
二	èr	two
三	sān	three

Revision Vocabulary

非常	fēi cháng	very/ extremely
车	chē	car
这	zhè	this
喜欢	xǐ huān	to like
哪	nǎ	which
但是	dàn shì	but

Lesson Breakdown

都是名车。

Dōu shì míng chē.

(They) both are famous models.

| 都 | dōu | both/all |

This Adverb is used to express *both* or *all*, depending on the situation.

When using this word, we have to follow a specific sentence structure:

Subject + 都 + (Verb)

We always **place this Adverb behind the Subject** of the sentence.

In our dialog example sentence the Pronoun "they" is omitted because the Subject (cars) is already understood by both parties.

We could rewrite it as:

它们 都 是 名车。/ or   都 是 名车。

They both are famous models. (same meaning)

Thus, we always place this Adverb behind the Subject (mostly a Pronoun).

Example:

它们 + 都 meaning: "them all".

Note that it is never placed in front of a Pronoun or Noun.

> 这 两 辆车 都 非常 漂亮。
> Zhè liǎng liàng chē dōu fēi cháng piāo liàng.
> These two are both very beautiful.

两   liǎng   two

In Mandarin the number 2 is written as 二 [èr], but often you will hear people refer to **two** as 两 [liǎng]. This may sound very confusing, but it is not that hard to distinguish between these two words.

二 [èr] is a number.

It represents a digit that is used for counting and also for repeating numbers like place numbers, pin numbers, floor numbers, telephone numbers, etc. It stands alone and is used without a Measure Word.

Example:

一, 二, 三, 四, 五

[yī, èr, sān, sì, wǔ]

1, 2, 3, 4, 5

However, when the number two is followed by a Measure Word, it is written as 两 [liǎng]. It is still a number, but it is bound to a Noun. It must always be used with a MW.

The structure used is:

两 + MW + Noun

Example:
两 本 书
[liǎng běn shū]
two books

Following 两 is the Measure word 本 [běn].

You cannot say: 二 本 书   [èr běn shū] ! That is incorrect !

We use this word daily when making purchases and when describing or referring to Nouns. It is also used for expressing time and quantities.

辆   liàng   MW (cars)

This is a Specific Measure word.

It is used specifically for all *vehicles on wheels*. The key ingredient is the presence of wheels.

这 辆 车 很 好。
[zhè liàng chē hěn haǒ]
This car is quite good.

Note the radical for car 车 that is present in the character 辆.

That makes it easy to distinguish it from 两 .

Download The Bonus Audio Files To Practice Your Pronunciation

My Progress

Words	QW's	MW's	TW's	Total
Count	7	6	4	160

Hint

When the number "two" is followed by a MW, then we use the word 两.

Self-Practice

Connect and match:

都	•	• èr •	• MW (cars)
两	•	• dōu •	• luxury car
大	•	• dà •	• big
辆	•	• liǎng •	• small
小	•	• míng chē •	• both/all
车	•	• liàng •	• two (MW)
名车	•	• chē •	• two
二	•	• xiǎo •	• car

Rewrite the following sentences into Pinyin:

1. Which car do you like? _____
2. I like this car. _____
3. I like big cars. _____
4. These two cars are very beautiful. _____
5. Both are famous model cars. _____
6. This car is too small. _____

Circle the correct character in every line:

1. 肉 , 辆 , 雨 , 而 , 内
2. 少 , 忄 , 必 , 心 , 小
3. 两 , 肉 , 内 , 雨 , 而
4. 都 , 培 , 部 , 瓿 , 站

● Useful Words Stroke Order   Character Stroke Order ●

小	脚	踏	摩	托
名	车	两	辆	都

Trace the following characters

小	小	小	小	小	小	小	小	小
脚	脚	脚	脚	脚	脚	脚	脚	脚
踏	踏	踏	踏	踏	踏	踏	踏	踏
摩	摩	摩	摩	摩	摩	摩	摩	摩
托	托	托	托	托	托	托	托	托
名	名	名	名	名	名	名	名	名
车	车	车	车	车	车	车	车	车
两	两	两	两	两	两	两	两	两
辆	辆	辆	辆	辆	辆	辆	辆	辆
都	都	都	都	都	都	都	都	都

Self-Practice

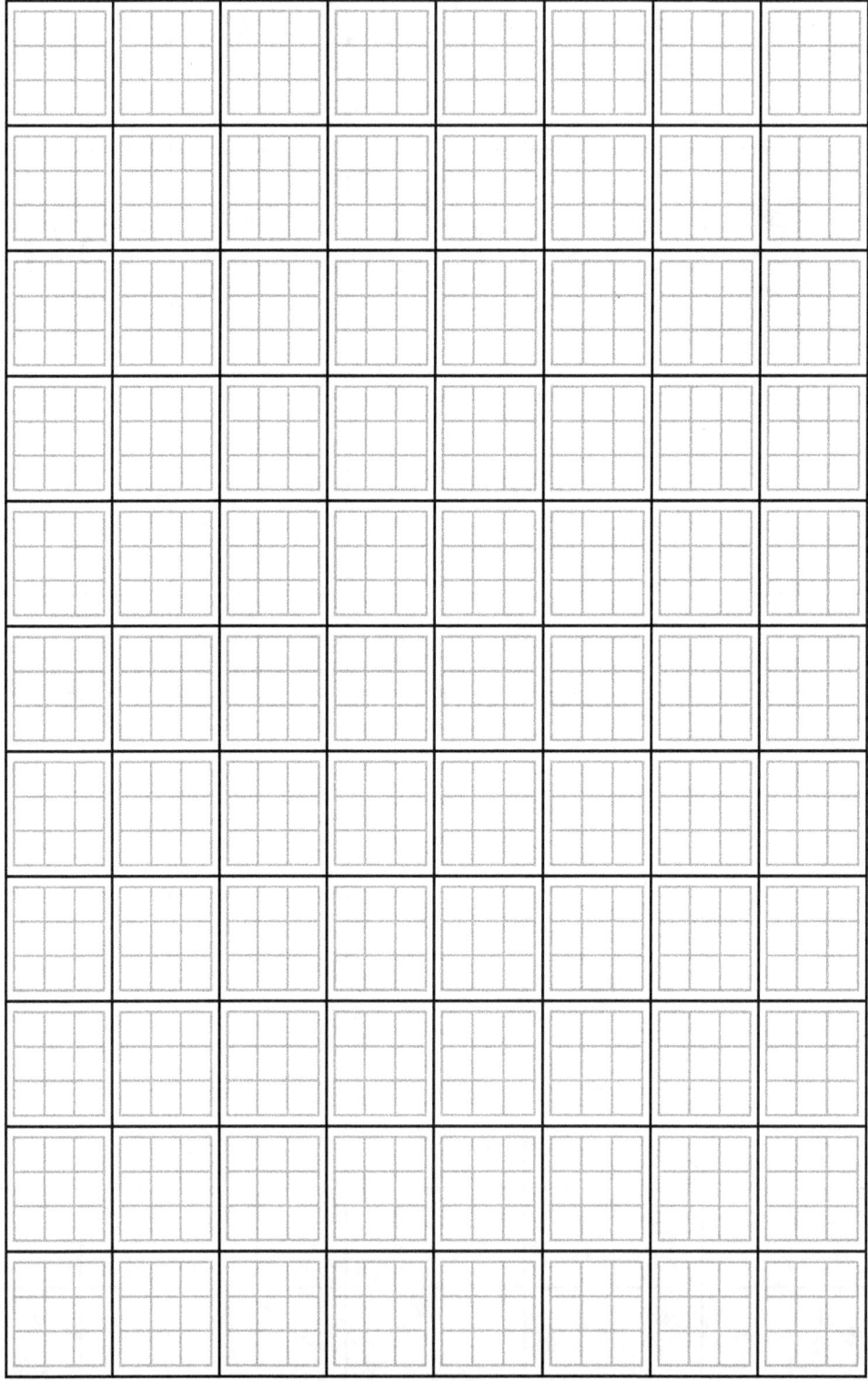

第二十九课　　Unit 29

中文 很 简单, 我 和 我妈妈 都 会 说中文!

Zhōng wén hěn jiǎn dān, wǒ hé wǒ mā ma dōu huì shuō zhōng wén!

Chinese is easy. My mother and I can both speak Chinese!

法文 很简单, 我爱 学 法文。

Fǎ wén hěn jiǎn dān, wǒ ài xué Fǎ wén.

French is easy. I love to study French.

好, 都 很 简单。

Hǎo, dōu hěn jiǎn dān.

Ok, both are quite easy.

对, 两个 都 很 简单!

Duì, liǎng ge dōu hěn jiǎn dān!

Correct, both languages are easy!

This is a dialog between two friends who are students of foreign languages. The mood is relaxed and friendly.

Dialog Vocabulary

中文	Zhōng wén	Chinese
法文	Fǎ wén	French
简单	jiǎn dān	easy
爱	ài	to love
和	hé	and
会	huì	to be able
说	shuō	to say/speak

Useful Vocabulary

英文	Yīng wén	English
日文	Rì wén	Japanese
语言	yǔ yán	language
难	nán	difficult
中	zhōng	middle/ centre
文化	wén huà	culture
容易	róng yì	easy

Revision Vocabulary

都	dōu	both
对	duì	right/ correct
两	liǎng	two (MW)
个	gè	general MW

Lesson Breakdown

好, 都 很 简单。
Hǎo, dōu hěn jiǎn dān.
Ok, both are quite easy.

This sentence can be written as :
它们 都 很 简单。
[tā men dōu hěn jiǎn dān]
They, both, are easy.
It should be pointed out that the Pronoun (they) has been omitted.
Remember that we always place 都 behind the Pronoun.
It cannot be placed before a Noun.

> 我 和 我妈妈 都 会 说中文！
> Wǒ hé wǒ mā ma dōu huì shuō zhōng wén!
> My mother and I can both speak Chinese!

会   huì   to be able to

This Verb is used to express the ability of the Subject.

What makes this ability special is that it is an **acquired skill** and not an ability that you were born with. It is usually used for **learned knowledge**.

We use the following structure:

Subject + 会 + Verb + Object

Example:
我 会 做饭。
[wǒ huì zuò fàn]
I can cook.

This Verb can be used for all kinds of abilities like driving, cooking, music, etc.

和   hé   and

This Conjunction is used to join two Nouns together. We use this structure:

Noun1 + 和 + Noun2

Example:
我 和 我妹妹 都 喜欢 吃 蛋糕。
[wǒ hé wǒ mèi mei dōu xǐ huan chī dàn gāo]
My sister and I both like to eat cake.

Often we see words that seem similar in meaning and application. One such example is 和 and 跟.
The Conjunction 和 [hé] means "and".
The Conjunction 跟 [gēn] is used to express "with".
There is a subtle difference and best to be aware of it.

说　　　shuō　　to speak/say

This Verb can be used to express the ability to **speak a language**.
我会 说 中文。
[wǒ huì shuō zhōng wén]
I can *speak* Chinese.
It can also mean **to say something**.
她 说 她 很忙。
[tā shuō tā hěn máng]
She *says* she is quite busy.

Supplementary

Take care not to confuse 会, 能, 可以 with one another.
All three words mean "can", but there is a difference in application:
- 会 [huì] is for *learned knowledge*.
"Being able to" because you **acquired** the skill.
- 能 [néng] is for *physical ability*.
"Being able to" because of natural ability.
- 可以 [kě yǐ] means *to be allowed/ permitted to*.
"To be allowed to" do something.

Download The Bonus Audio Files To Practice Your Pronunciation

My Progress

Words	QW's	MW's	TW's	Total
Count	7	6	4	167

Hint

The Verb 会 expresses ability and is used for an acquired skill and ability.

Self-Practice

Connect and match:

会	• nán •	• difficult
爱	• shuō •	• to love
说	• huì •	• easy
简单	• ài •	• to say/ speak
中文	• jiǎn dān •	• to be able
和	• zhōng wén •	• Chinese
法文	• hé •	• and
难	• fǎ wén •	• French

Write questions for the following answers:

1. _____?
对,我爱学中文。

2. _____?
对,我会说中文。

3. _____?
对,法文很简单。

4. _____?
对,中文很难学。

Arrange the words into sentences:

1. 简单　　很　　法文。
_____

2. 简单　　很　　都。
_____

3. 和　　我　　我妈妈　　都　　说　　会　　英文。
_____

4. 都　　很　　两个　　简单。
_____

● Useful Words Stroke Order   Character Stroke Order ●

Trace the following characters

语	语	语	语	语	语	语	语	语
言	言	言	言	言	言	言	言	言
日	日	日	日	日	日	日	日	日
化	化	化	化	化	化	化	化	化
难	难	难	难	难	难	难	难	难
简	简	简	简	简	简	简	简	简
单	单	单	单	单	单	单	单	单
法	法	法	法	法	法	法	法	法
会	会	会	会	会	会	会	会	会
说	说	说	说	说	说	说	说	说

Self-Practice

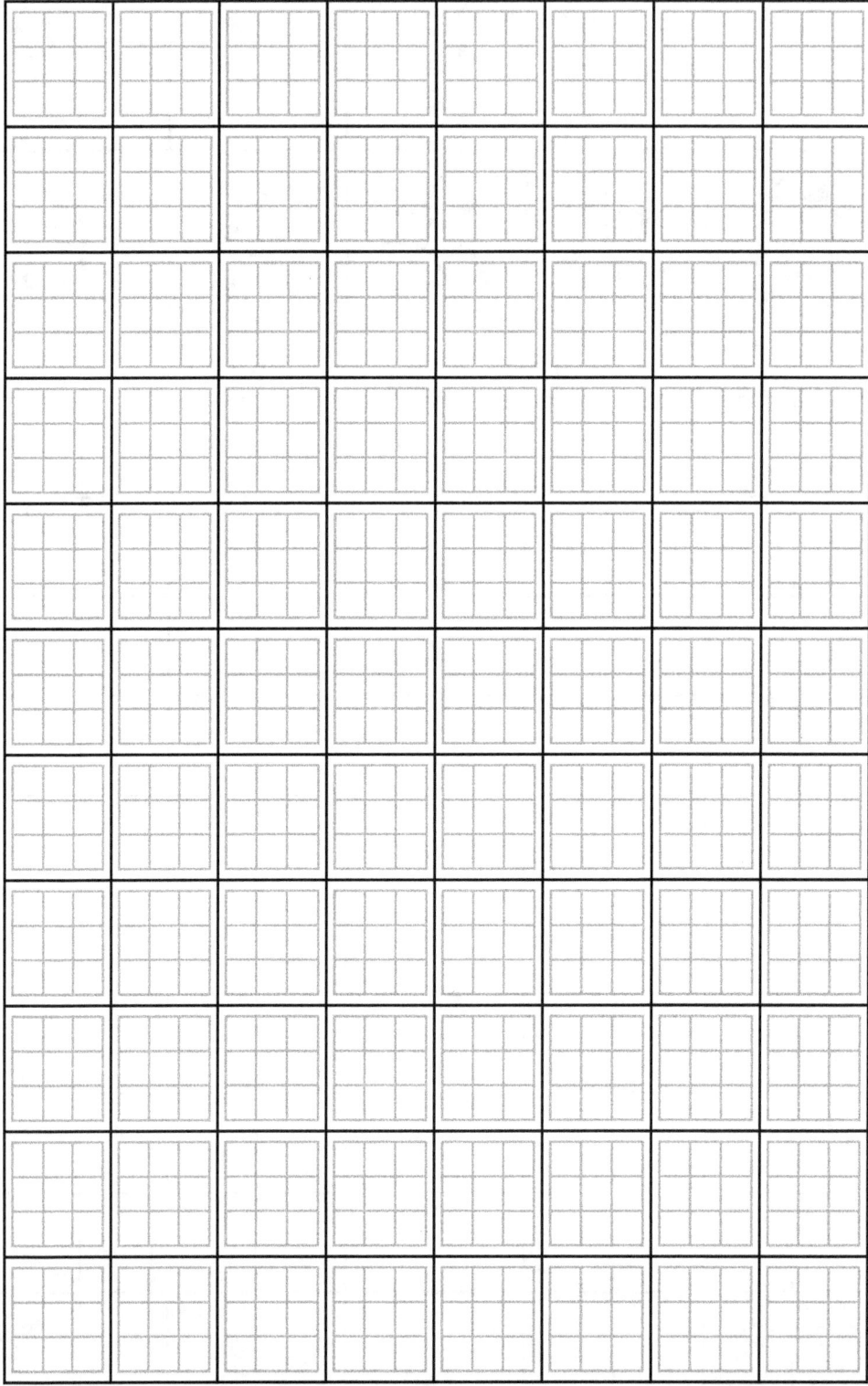

第三十课 Unit 30

德文很难学，而且我没有进步。
Dé wén hěn nán xué, ér qiě wǒ méi yǒu jìn bù.
German is hard and in addition I have not improved.

是啊，但是日文一样很难学。
Shì a, dàn shì rì wén yī yàng hěn nán xué.
Yes, but Japanese is also hard.

我喜欢学日文。
Wǒ xǐ huān xué rì wén.
I like to study Japanese.

我喜欢学德文。
Wǒ xǐ huān xué dé wén.
I like to study German.

This is a dialog between two friends who are both students of a foreign language. The mood is relaxed and friendly.

Dialog Vocabulary

难	nán	to be difficult
进步	jìn bù	to improve
学	xué	to study
而且	ér qiě	in addition
日文	rì wén	Japanese (language)
德文	dé wén	German (language)
啊	a	particle of agreement

Useful Vocabulary

写	xiě	to write
看	kàn	to read (silently)
听	tīng	to listen
意大利语	yì dà lì yǔ	Italian
说话	shuō huà	to speak/ say

Revision Vocabulary

但是	dàn shì	but
没有	méi yǒu	not have
喜欢	xǐ huān	to like
一样	yī yàng	alike/the same

Lesson Breakdown

是啊, 但是 日文 一样 很 难 学。
Shì a, dàn shì rì wén yī yàng hěn nán xué.
Yes, but Japanese is also hard.

啊	a	particle

The particle 啊 is a sound that is used when the speaker feels that the **answer is obvious or assumed**.

It's the same as exclaiming: Of course!

It is often used in conjunction with 是 as seen in the example sentence.

Let's take a closer look at the rest of the sentence and specifically how the word "hard" is used in the context of learning or studying:

> 难   nán   difficult

This word acts as an Adverb and means *hard or difficult,* as seen in the dialog sentence provided. It indicates that something is **hard to do**.

We use the following structure:

Subject + 难 + Verb

It describes and tells us more about the Verb *to study*.

Take note that the Adverb is placed directly in front of the Verb.

Examples:

难 说 [nán shuō]   hard to say
难 写 [nán xiě]   hard to write
难 做 [nán zuò]   hard to make
难 学 [nán xué]   hard to study

It can also be combined with Verbs that we use for our senses, like *smell, look, taste, etc.*

It indicates that something is **bad to our senses to do**.

We follow the exact same sentence structure:

Subject + 难 + Verb

难 听 [nán tīng]   hard to listen to
难 吃 [nán chī]   taste bad
难 喝 [nán hē]   unpleasant to drink

The emphasis is on 难 and it sets the mood of the sentence.

> 德文很难学，而且 我没有 进步。
>
> Dé wén hěn nán xué, ér qiě wǒ méi yǒu jìn bù.
>
> German is hard and in addition I have not improved.

Let's take a closer look at this sentence. It consists of two parts. The first part of this sentence makes a statement that "German is hard".

而且　　ér qiě　　furthermore

The second part of the sentence starts after 而且, and it states that the person is not improving.

The reason following 而且 is the most important one and thus the main point that the speaker wants to stress.

没有 进步　　méi yǒu jìn bù　　haven't improved

This is a very unique structure. We use 没有 [méi yǒu] to indicate that a specific **action was not completed** and that it happened in the past tense. Because we are dealing with an action, the word 没有 must be followed by a Verb.

The structure is:

Subject + 没有 + Verb

Example:

我 没有 吃。

[wǒ méi yǒu chī]

I did not eat.

The focus is on the Verb and the speaker is indicating that the action was not completed.

We can use 没 [méi] or 没有 [méi yǒu].

Download The Bonus Audio Files To Practice Your Pronunciation

My Progress

Words	QW's	MW's	TW's	Total
Count	7	6	4	174

Hint

To indicate that an action was not completed, we use 没有 followed by the action (Verb).

Self-Practice

Connect and match:

难 •	• ér qiě •	• difficult
进步 •	• jìn bù •	• German
学 •	• xué •	• to write
而且 •	• nán •	• agreement
啊 •	• a •	• Japanese
写 •	• rì wén •	• to study
日文 •	• xiě •	• to improve
德文 •	• dé wén •	• in addition

Rewrite the following sentences into Pinyin:

1. German is hard. _____
2. I like to study German. _____
3. Japanese is hard. _____
4. I like to study Japanese. _____
5. I have not improved. _____
6. English is easy. _____

Circle the correct character in every line:

1. 且，苴，真，苴，姐
2. 雪，辆，两，雨，而
3. 党，常，学，子，字
4. 喹，堆，佳，谁，难

Useful Words Stroke Order   Character Stroke Order

德	文	日	啊	难
学	进	步	而	且

Trace the following characters

德	德	德	德	德	德	德	德	德
文	文	文	文	文	文	文	文	文
日	日	日	日	日	日	日	日	日
啊	啊	啊	啊	啊	啊	啊	啊	啊
难	难	难	难	难	难	难	难	难
学	学	学	学	学	学	学	学	学
进	进	进	进	进	进	进	进	进
步	步	步	步	步	步	步	步	步
而	而	而	而	而	而	而	而	而
且	且	且	且	且	且	且	且	且

Self-Practice

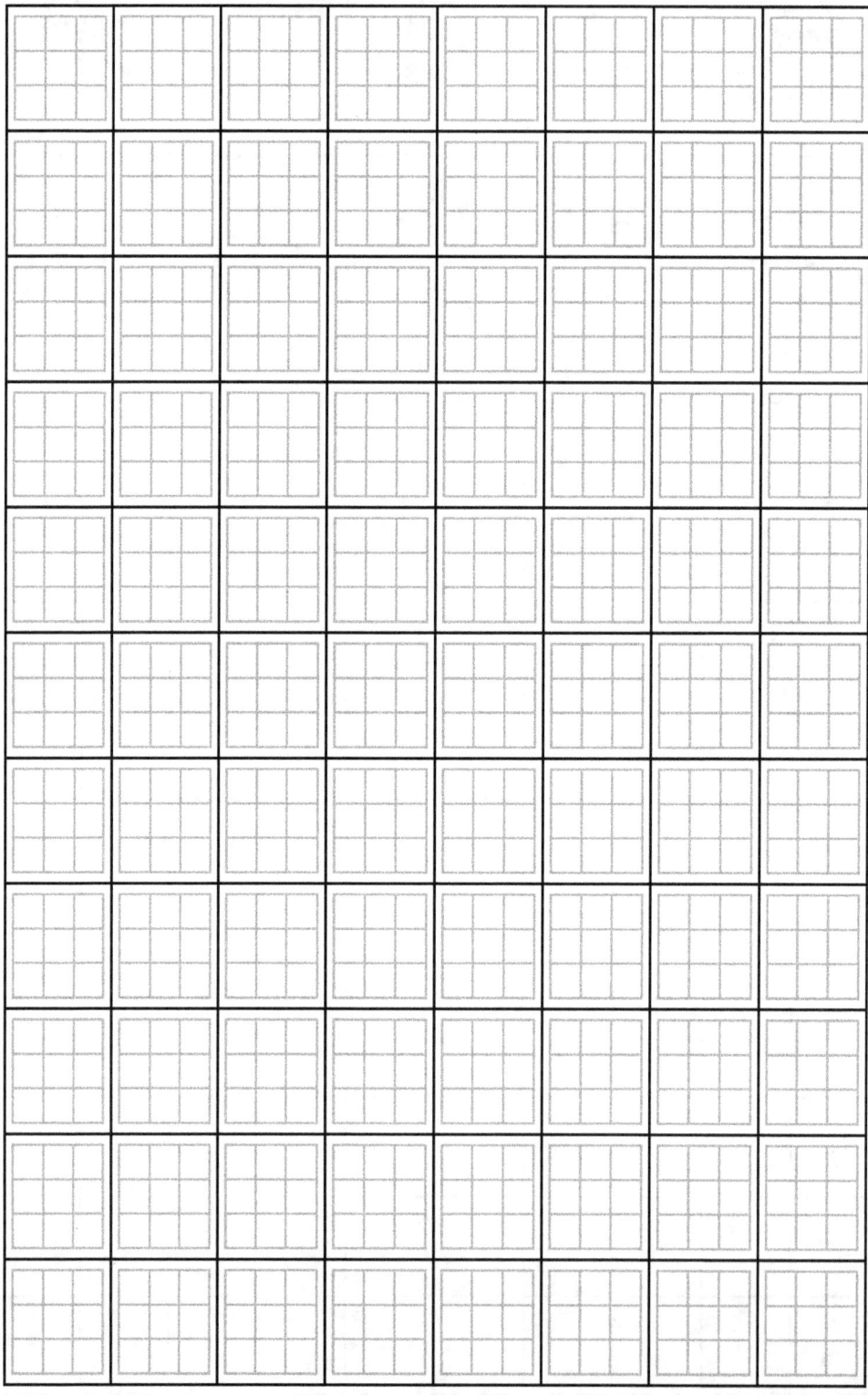

第三十一课　　　　Unit 31

这个 玩具 很 好玩, 我 要 它!
Zhè gè wán jù hěn hǎo wán, wǒ yào tā!
This toy is fun to play with. I want it!

不可以, 你 知道 为什么 吗?
Bù kě yǐ, nǐ zhī dào wèi shén me ma?
You cannot have it. Do you know why?

我 知道, 太贵了!
Wǒ zhī dào, tài guì le!
I know. It's too expensive!

好 孩子!
Hǎo hái zǐ!
Good boy!

This is a dialog between mother and child.
Mom is teaching the youngster a lesson about the value of money.

Dialog Vocabulary

玩具	wán jù	toy
可以	kě yǐ	can
知道	zhī dào	to know
玩	wán	fun/ to enjoy
孩子	hái zǐ	child
了	le	particle to urge

Useful Vocabulary

男孩子	nán hái zi	boy
女孩子	nǔ hái zi	girl
家具	jiā jù	furniture
工具	gōng jù	tool
美	měi	beautiful

Revision Vocabulary

这	zhè	this
它	tā	it
贵	guì	expensive
个	gè	general MW

Lesson Breakdown

> 不可以, 你 知道 为什么 吗?
> Bù kě yǐ, nǐ zhī dào wèi shén me ma?
> You cannot have it. Do you know why?

不可以　　bù kě yǐ　　cannot

可以 means *can* and therefore 不可以 means *cannot*.
It is common to put this phrase at the beginning of the sentence for **emphasis**, meaning that it is the main message of the sentence.
Following 不可以 is the *reason* why something is not allowed to be.

> 这个 玩具 很 好玩, 我要它!
> Zhè gè wán jù hěn hǎo wán, wǒ yào tā!
> This toy is fun to play with. I want it!

玩   wán   to play

This Verb can mean *to enjoy* or *to play* with something.
Let's look at two examples:
To enjoy:
这个玩具很好玩。
[Zhè gè wán jù hěn hǎo wán]
This toy is very enjoyable (fun to play with).

To play:
玩牌。
[wán pái]
To play cards.

> 我 知道, 太 贵 了!
> Wǒ zhī dào, tài guì le!
> I know. It's too expensive!

太   tài   too

We are already familiar with this word. It is an Adverb and it is used to indicate when something is *excessive*. It basically describes the **degree** of the Adjective.

It can be used with a negative (excessive) or positive (admiration) tone. In our example, it describes just "how expensive" it is.

In certain cases we can add a particle to put even **more emphasis** on the speaker's message. In the example sentence, 了 is added at the end of the sentence as a particle of emphasis. It reminds the listener that "I already know!". We use this structure:

太 + Adjective + 了

Example:
糖果太甜了。
[táng guǒ tài tián le]
The candy is too sweet.

Pay close attention to 了 because it is a very special particle with various meanings and applications.

Supplementary

Writing:
The word 具 means *tool or instrument*. It is thus quite logical to see it present in the following examples:

玩具 [wán jù] means: toy
家具 [jiā jù] means: furniture
工具 [gōng jù] means: work tool
文具 [wén jù] means: stationery
教具 [jiào jù] means: teaching aid
食具 [shí jù] means: utensil

Looking for these "clues" can simplify the recognition and memorizing of characters.

Download The Bonus Audio Files To Practice Your Pronunciation

My Progress

Words	QW's	MW's	TW's	Total
Count	7	6	4	180

Hint

One use of the particle 了 is for emphasis. It is often used with the Adverb 太.

Self-Practice

Connect and match:

玩具 •	• le •	• can
可以 •	• wán jù •	• toy
知道 •	• kě yǐ •	• fun
玩 •	• zhī dào •	• child
孩子 •	• hái zǐ •	• to know
了 •	• nǚ hái zǐ •	• to urge
男孩子 •	• nán hái zǐ •	• boy
女孩子 •	• wán •	• girl

Translate the following sentences into English:

1. Hǎo hái zǐ !
   _____

2. Wǒ zhī dào, tài guì le !
   _____

3. Bù kě yǐ, nǐ zhī dào wèi shén me ma?
   _____

4. Zhè gè wán jù hěn hǎo wán, wǒ yào tā !
   _____

Arrange the words into sentences:

1. 玩　　好　　玩具　　很　　个　　这。
   _____

2. 他　　孩子　　好　　是。
   _____

3. 知道　　为什么　　你　　吗？
   _____

4. 贵　　了　　太。
   _____

● Useful Words Stroke Order　　Character Stroke Order ●

工	教	可	以	孩
子	知	道	玩	具

Trace the following characters

工	工	工	工	工	工	工	工	工
教	教	教	教	教	教	教	教	教
可	可	可	可	可	可	可	可	可
以	以	以	以	以	以	以	以	以
孩	孩	孩	孩	孩	孩	孩	孩	孩
子	子	子	子	子	子	子	子	子
知	知	知	知	知	知	知	知	知
道	道	道	道	道	道	道	道	道
玩	玩	玩	玩	玩	玩	玩	玩	玩
具	具	具	具	具	具	具	具	具

Self-Practice

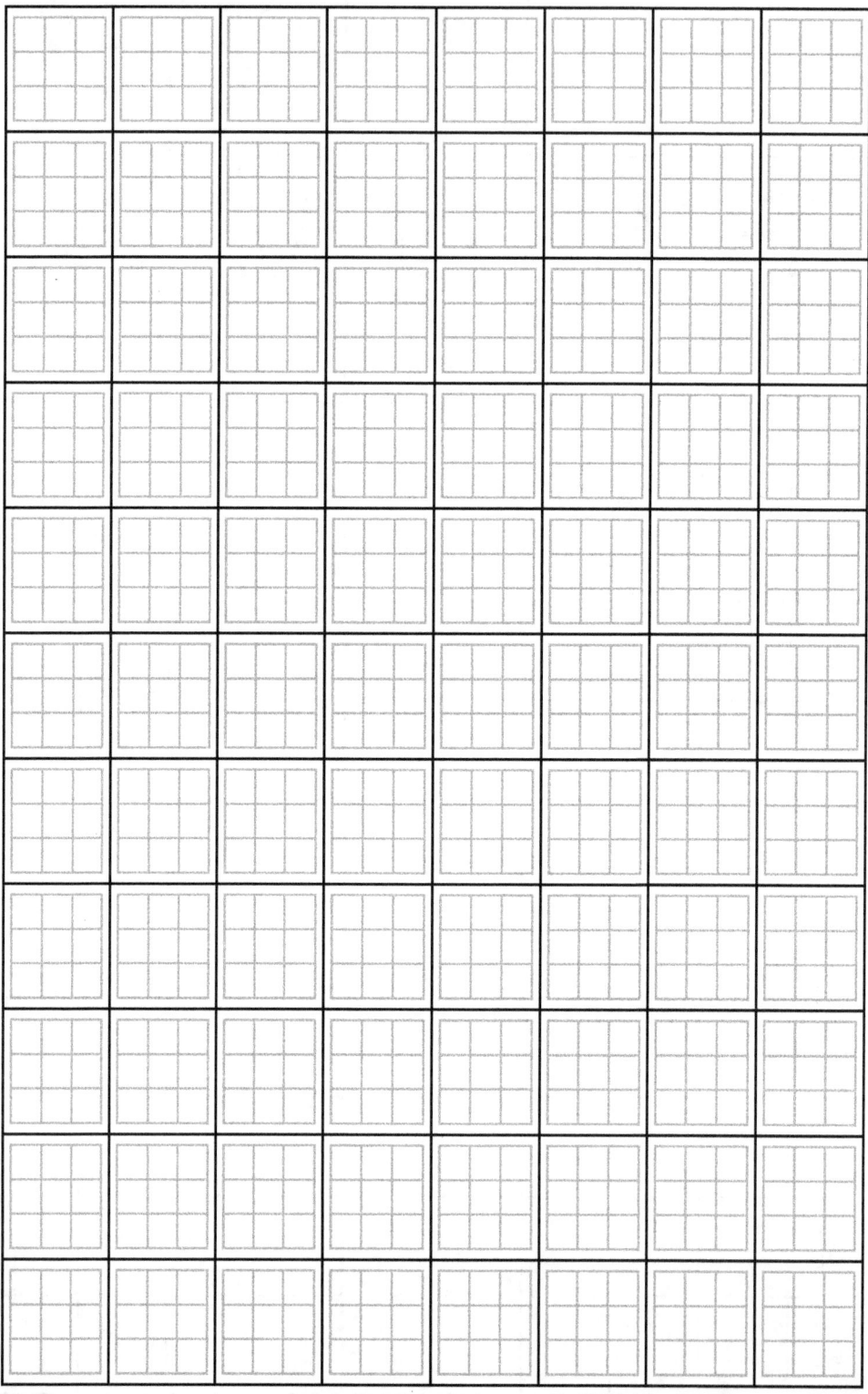

第三十二课   Unit 32

我 星期三 要 去 看 电影。
Wǒ xīng qī sān yào qù kàn diàn yǐng.
I want to go to the movies on Wednesday.

你 想 看 哪 一 部 电影?
Nǐ xiǎng kàn nǎ yí bù diàn yǐng ?
Which movie do you want to watch?

我 想 看 "猫 & 狗"。
Wǒ xiǎng kàn "māo & gǒu".
I would like to watch "Cats and Dogs".

但是 我 真的 想要 看 "动物园"!
Dàn shì wǒ zhēn de xiǎng yào kàn "dòng wù yuán"!
But, I really want to watch "The Zoo"!

This is a dialog between two friends who are in elementary school. Both want to go to the movies.

Dialog Vocabulary

星期三	xīng qī sān	Wednesday
动物园	dòng wù yuán	zoo
想	xiǎng	would like to
猫	māo	cat
狗	gǒu	dog

Useful Vocabulary

动物	dòng wù	animal
花园	huā yuán	garden
星期一	xīng qī yī	Monday
星期二	xīng qī èr	Tuesday
星期四	xīng qī sì	Thursday
星期五	xīng qī wǔ	Friday
星期六	xīng qī liù	Saturday
星期天	xīng qī tiān	Sunday

Revision Vocabulary

看	kàn	to watch
部	bù	MW for films
去	qù	go to
要	yào	to want
电影	diàn yǐng	film/ movie

Lesson Breakdown

我 星期三 要 去 看 电影。
Wǒ xīng qī sān yào qù kàn diàn yǐng.
I want to go to the movies on Wednesday.

星期三　　　xīng qī sān　　　Wednesday

This is a TW and if we break it down, we notice that 星期 [xīng qī] means *week* and 三 [sān] means *three*.
It literally means: "week three".
Therefore, we conclude that the *third day of the week* is **Wednesday**.

Unit 32

The days of the week are based on a simple numerical sequence. The Chinese week starts on a Monday and therefore it is the first day of the week.

Mon - Sat. follows this numeral trend as seen in the Useful Vocabulary list provided.

Sunday is the exception:

日 [rì] and 天 [tiān] both mean: day

星期日 [xīng qī rì] and 星期天 [xīng qī tiān] both mean: Sunday

Both are acceptable to use and literally mean: "week day".
Take note that 星期日 [xīng qī rì] is slightly more formal.

Another word used for week is: 礼拜 [lǐ bài]

This is a more informal expression:

礼拜一　　[lǐ bài yī]　　Monday
礼拜二　　[lǐ bài èr]　　Tuesday
礼拜三　　[lǐ bài sān]　　Wednesday
礼拜四　　[lǐ bài sì]　　Thursday
礼拜五　　[lǐ bài wǔ]　　Friday
礼拜六　　[lǐ bài liù]　　Saturday
礼拜天　　[lǐ bài tiān]　　Sunday

> 但是 我 真的 想要 看 "动物园"!
> Dàn shì wǒ zhēn de xiǎng yào kàn "dòng wù yuán"!
> But, I really want to watch "The Zoo"!

可是　VS　但是

Although both words mean "but", there is a minor difference in **mood** between the two words.

可是 is used when the speaker wants to put more emphasis on the statement that follows.

It is used **informally** and usually related to something negative.

我 喜欢 她, 可是 她 不喜欢 我。

[wǒ xǐ huan tā, kě shì tā bù xǐ huan wǒ]

I like her, but she does not like me.

但是 is used when the mood is a bit more **formal** and when the two statements (preceding and following) are incompatible. It is often present in written text and formal documents.

Supplementary

Writing:

> 动 物 园   dòng wù yuán   zoo

Look at the character 园 [yuán]. This character is used for various *open spaces*:

- 动物 园   [dòng wù yuán] meaning: zoo

Literally: "animal garden".

- 公 园   [gōng yuán] meaning: park

Literally: "public garden".

- 花 园   [huā yuán] meaning: garden

Literally: "flower garden".

- 乐 园 [lè yuán] meaning: amusement park

Literally: "happy garden".

Download The Bonus Audio Files To Practice Your Pronunciation

My Progress					Hint
Words	QW's	MW's	TW's	Total	The days of the week follow a simple numeral trend (1-6), with Sunday being the exception.
Count	7	6	5	185	

Self-Practice

Connect and match:

想	•	• māo •	• would like
狗	•	• gǒu •	• cat
猫	•	• xiǎng •	• animal
动物	•	• huā yuán •	• zoo
动物园	•	• dòng wù •	• dog
星期一	•	• dòng wù yuán •	• Monday
星期二	•	• xīng qī yī •	• Tuesday
花园	•	• xīng qī èr •	• garden

Rewrite the following sentences into Pinyin:

1. I want to go to the movies. _____
2. I want to go on Wednesday. _____
3. Which movie do you want to watch? _____
4. I want to go to the zoo. _____
5. The zoo has a garden. _____
6. I like animals. _____

Circle the correct character in every line:

1. 枸 , 佝 , 构 , 勾 , 狗
2. 湘 , 香 , 相 , 想 , 箱
3. 胜 , 生 , 腥 , 星 , 姓
4. 棋 , 琪 , 期 , 淇 , 其

● Useful Words Stroke Order   Character Stroke Order ●

礼	拜	花	动	物
园	星	期	狗	猫

Trace the following characters

礼	礼	礼	礼	礼	礼	礼	礼	礼	礼
拜	拜	拜	拜	拜	拜	拜	拜	拜	拜
花	花	花	花	花	花	花	花	花	花
动	动	动	动	动	动	动	动	动	动
物	物	物	物	物	物	物	物	物	物
园	园	园	园	园	园	园	园	园	园
星	星	星	星	星	星	星	星	星	星
期	期	期	期	期	期	期	期	期	期
狗	狗	狗	狗	狗	狗	狗	狗	狗	狗
猫	猫	猫	猫	猫	猫	猫	猫	猫	猫

Self-Practice

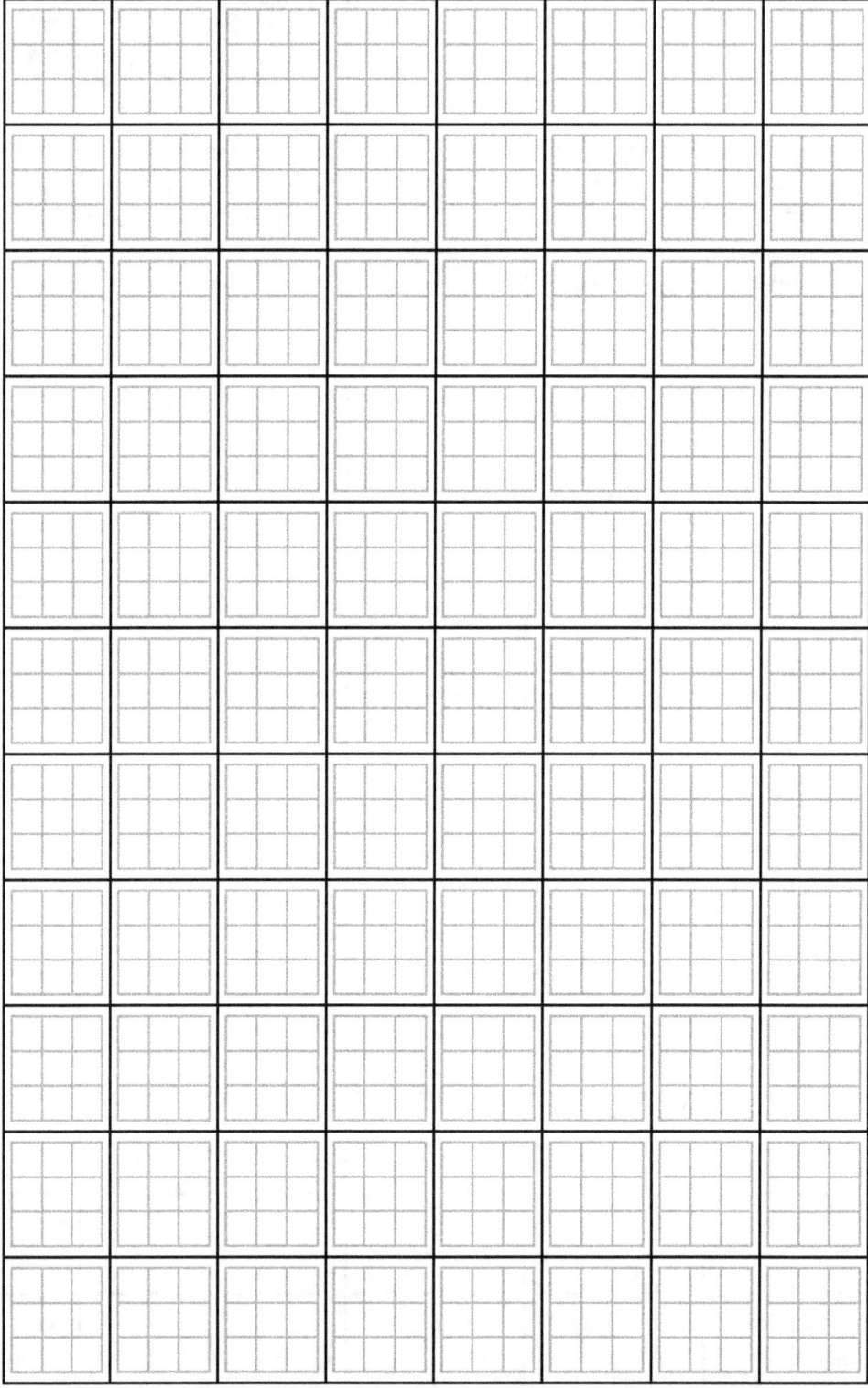

第三十三课 — Unit 33

这种 电脑 多少钱?
Zhè zhǒng diàn nǎo duō shǎo qián?
How much is this computer?

这种 电脑 很贵。
Zhè zhǒng diàn nǎo hěn guì.
This kind (of computer) is expensive.

好, 多少钱?
Hǎo, duō shǎo qián?
OK, how much is it?

这一个, 一百元。
Zhè yí gè, yì bǎi yuán.
This one is $100.

This is a dialog between sales clerk and customer.
The mood is casual and relaxed.

Dialog Vocabulary

多少	duō shǎo	how much/many
种	zhǒng	kind/ type
元	yuán	dollar (unit)
一百	yì bǎi	one hundred
钱	qián	money
电脑	diàn nǎo	computer

Useful Vocabulary

多	duō	many/ more
少	shǎo	few/ less
两百	liǎng bǎi	two hundred
三百	sān bǎi	three hundred
四百	sì bǎi	four hundred
五百	wǔ bǎi	five hundred
一千	yì qiān	one thousand

Revision Vocabulary

很	hěn	very
贵	guì	expensive
个	gè	general MW

Lesson Breakdown

> 这种 电脑 多少钱?
> Zhè zhǒng diàn nǎo duō shǎo qián ?
> How much is this computer?

种	zhǒng	kind/type MW

This is a Measure Word or classifier meaning *kinds of*.
It is normally followed by Nouns like: *things, books or people*.
Example:
苹果是一 种 水果。
[píng guǒ shì yī zhǒng shuǐ guǒ]
An apple is a kind of fruit.

> 多少   duō shǎo   How much?

This Question-word is mostly used with money matters, but not exclusively. It inquires after "how much?" or "how many?". In simpler terms, it has a similar feel to "much" as used in English.

Important to note that you do not need to put a MW at the back.

We use this structure:

多少 + Noun

It is normally used for amounts from ten upwards and especially for large numbers.

If we were to separate the two characters:

多 [duō]   means: more or many.

少 [shǎo] means: less or few.

> 这一个，一百元。
> Zhè yí ge, yì bǎi yuán.
> This one is $100.

> 元   yuán   Unit of money

The 元 [yuán] is a **unit for money** like the American Dollar, Japanese Yen, Chinese Yuan.

It is a more formal way to describe a "dollar" and it can be applied to any currency.

Example:

一百 元

[yī bǎi yuán]

$100

Supplementary

Large Numbers: Units of 10

零	líng	0
十	shí	10
二十	èr shí	20
三十	sān shí	30
四十	sì shí	40
五十	wǔ shí	50
六十	liù shí	60
七十	qī shí	70
八十	bā shí	80
九十	jiǔ shí	90
一百	yì bǎi	100

When counting in units of 100 we use the following structure. "Number add 100":

一百 = 1x100 = 100
两百 = 2x100 = 200
三百 = 3x100 = 300
四百 = 4x100 = 400

For the numbers in between, we simply add the numeral to the sequence used above:

一百二十五 = 100+25 = 125
三百四十六 = 300+46 = 346
六百二十一 = 600+21 = 621

Download The Bonus Audio Files To Practice Your Pronunciation

My Progress

Words	QW's	MW's	TW's	Total
Count	8	6	5	191

Hint

多少 is a QW that is mostly used with money matters. It has a similar feel to "much" in English.

Self-Practice

Connect and match:

多少 •	• yì bǎi •	• how much
种 •	• diàn nǎo •	• computer
元 •	• yuán •	• few/ less
钱 •	• qián •	• many/ more
一百 •	• duō shǎo •	• one hundred
电脑 •	• zhǒng •	• kind/ type
多 •	• duō •	• money
少 •	• shǎo •	• dollar

Translate the following sentences into English:

1. Zhè yí gè, yì bǎi yuán.
   _____

2. Hǎo, duō shǎo qián ?
   _____

3. Zhè zhǒng diàn nǎo duō shǎo qián ?
   _____

4. Zhè zhǒng diàn nǎo hěn guì.
   _____

Arrange the words into sentences:

1. 钱　　多少　　电脑　　种　　这？
   _____

2. 多少　　电视　　这　　种　　钱？
   _____

3. 个　　一　　元　　这　　一百。
   _____

4. 种　　这　　很　　电脑　　贵。
   _____

● Useful Words Stroke Order　　Character Stroke Order ●

千	零	电	脑	百
多	少	元	种	钱

Trace the following characters

千	千	千	千	千	千	千	千	千	千
零	零	零	零	零	零	零	零	零	零
电	电	电	电	电	电	电	电	电	电
脑	脑	脑	脑	脑	脑	脑	脑	脑	脑
百	百	百	百	百	百	百	百	百	百
多	多	多	多	多	多	多	多	多	多
少	少	少	少	少	少	少	少	少	少
元	元	元	元	元	元	元	元	元	元
种	种	种	种	种	种	种	种	种	种
钱	钱	钱	钱	钱	钱	钱	钱	钱	钱

Self-Practice

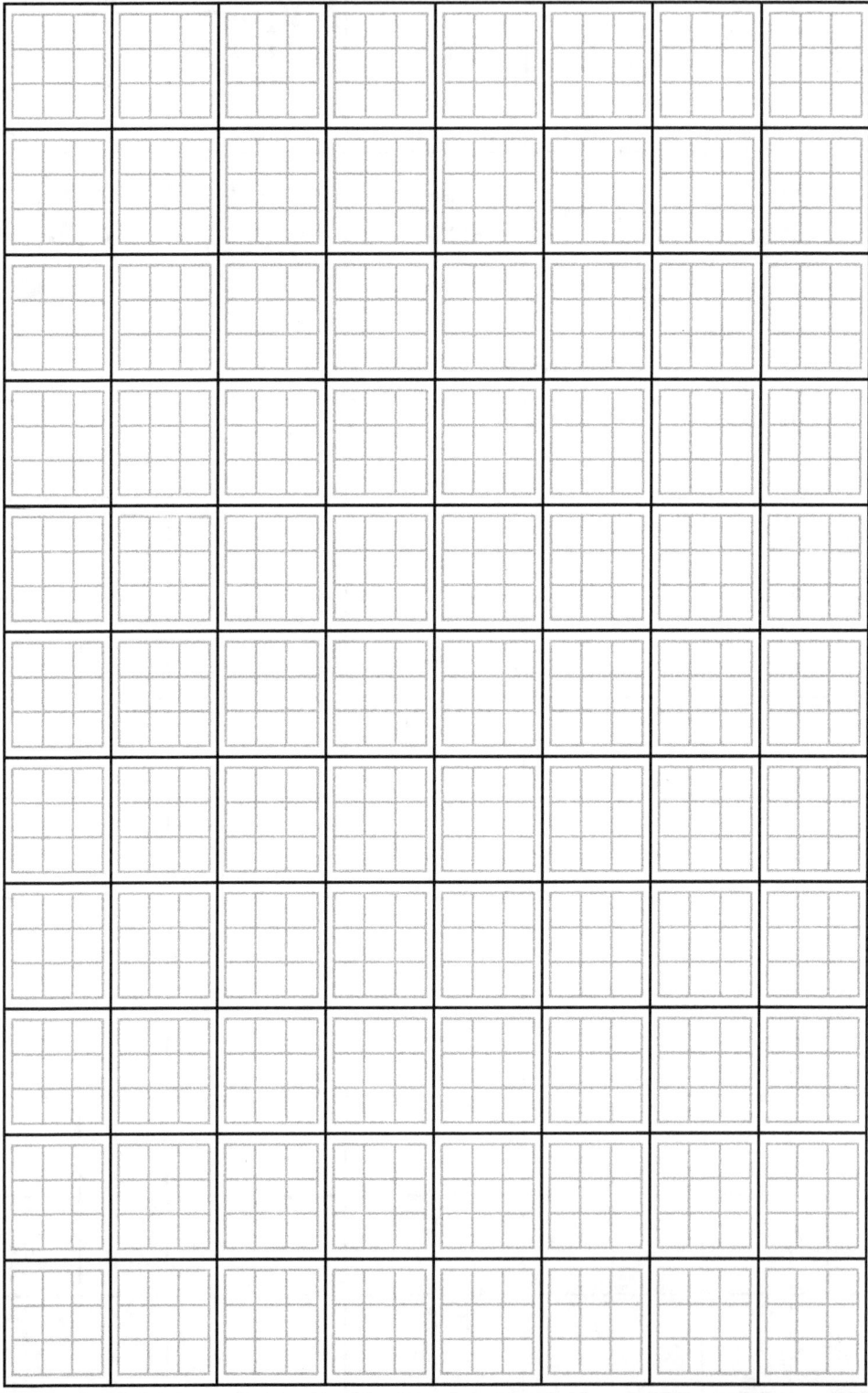

第三十四课　　Unit 34

这是一支好的笔。
Zhè shì yì zhī hǎo de bǐ.
This is a good pen.

我喜欢。
Wǒ xǐ huan.
I do like it.

你需要几支笔?
Nǐ xū yào jǐ zhī bǐ?
How many pens do you need?

我要两支笔,一支给我一支给我太太。
Wǒ yào liǎng zhī bǐ, yì zhī gěi wǒ yì zhī gěi wǒ tài tai.
I want two. One for me and one for my wife.

This is a dialog between customer and sales clerk.
The purchase is a simple one and the mood is relaxed.

Dialog Vocabulary

笔	bǐ	pen
几	jǐ	how many
给	gěi	to give
需要	xū yào	to need
支 / 枝	zhī	MW for long, thin, objects

Useful Vocabulary

胶带	jiāo dài	tape
胶水	jiāo shuǐ	glue
纸	zhǐ	paper
铅笔	qiān bǐ	pencil
尺	chǐ	ruler

Revision Vocabulary

要	yào	to want
喜欢	xǐ huan	to like
太太	tài tai	wife
两	liǎng	two, before MW

Lesson Breakdown

> 这是 一支 好的 笔。
> Zhè shì yì zhī hǎo de bǐ.
> This is a good pen.

支／枝　　zhī　　Specific MW

This is a Specific MW that is used for **twig-like objects**.

These objects must be long, thin and hard, like a pen, marker or pencil. Both characters provided can be used. The difference is that the 2nd character has been re-clarified with the radical for "tree" (木), which implies *made of wood*.

> 你 需要 几 支 笔?
> Nǐ xū yào jǐ zhī bǐ ?
> How many pens do you need?

> 几   jǐ   how many?

This Question-word is generally used for **amounts smaller than ten** and it means "how many". It has a similar feel to "many" as used in English, which is used for countable objects. It is very important to note that it must be **used together with a MW,** to follow. We use the following structure:

几 + MW + Noun

Example:

你有几支笔?

[Nǐ yǒu jǐ zhī bǐ ?]

How many pens do you have?

In this case the MW is 支 and the expected amount is obviously smaller than ten. Generally speaking we do not use this QW for matters revolving around money (see 多少).

We can also use it for inquiries about the **date or the time**:

今天 几 号?

[jīn tiān jǐ hào]

What's the date today?

现在 几 点?

[xiàn zài jǐ diǎn]

What time is it?

> 我要 两 支 笔, 一支 给 我 一支 给 我太太。
> Wǒ yào liǎng zhī bǐ, yì zhī gěi wǒ yì zhī gěi wǒ tài tai.
> I want two. One for me and one for my wife.

This is quite a mouthful. Let's look at the action of "handing" *something* to *somebody*.

给   gěi   to give

This Verb is used to indicate that something is being given to *somebody*. Therefore, it is always followed by a Pronoun, "somebody".

Example:
他 给 我 钱。
[tā gěi wǒ qián]
He gives me money.
我要给他这支笔。
[wǒ yaò gěi tā zhè zhī bǐ]
I want to give this pen to him.

Supplementary

Writing: Radicals
- The "bamboo radical" (⺮) is present in characters, where traditionally the object was made out of *bamboo*.

笔 This character consists of two compounds:

⺮ + 毛 = the bamboo radical + brush = a writing instrument.

- Similarly, look for the "grass radical" (⺿) which is present in characters, that represent plants or *products made out of plants*.

⺿ This is a picture of two shoots of grass.

It is present in words like: tea 茶 [chá] and medicine 药 [yào].

Download The Bonus Audio Files To Practice Your Pronunciation

My Progress

Words	QW's	MW's	TW's	Total
Count	9	7	5	196

Hint

几 is mostly used for amounts smaller than ten. It must be used together with a MW that follows it.

Self-Practice

Connect and match:

笔 •	• jiāo dài •	• MW thin objects
给 •	• bǐ •	• paper
几 •	• jǐ •	• pen
需要 •	• gěi •	• to give
支 •	• xū yào •	• to need
纸 •	• jiāo shuǐ •	• how many
胶带 •	• zhī •	• tape
胶水 •	• zhǐ •	• glue

Write questions for the following answers:

1. _____?
我 需要 一支 笔。

2. _____?
对,我 喜欢 这支 笔。

3. _____?
这 种 电脑 一百 元。

4. _____?
我 不需要 胶水。

Circle the correct character in every line:

1. 乙 , 几 , 叫 , 片 , 九
2. 守 , 拿 , 手 , 毛 , 笔
3. 红 , 盒 , 合 , 给 , 給
4. 两 , 雪 , 需 , 雨 , 而

○ Useful Words Stroke Order　　Character Stroke Order ●

铅	带	胶	纸	尺
笔	几	给	需	支

Trace the following characters

铅	铅	铅	铅	铅	铅	铅	铅	铅
带	带	带	带	带	带	带	带	带
胶	胶	胶	胶	胶	胶	胶	胶	胶
纸	纸	纸	纸	纸	纸	纸	纸	纸
尺	尺	尺	尺	尺	尺	尺	尺	尺
笔	笔	笔	笔	笔	笔	笔	笔	笔
几	几	几	几	几	几	几	几	几
给	给	给	给	给	给	给	给	给
需	需	需	需	需	需	需	需	需
支	支	支	支	支	支	支	支	支

Unit 34

Self-Practice

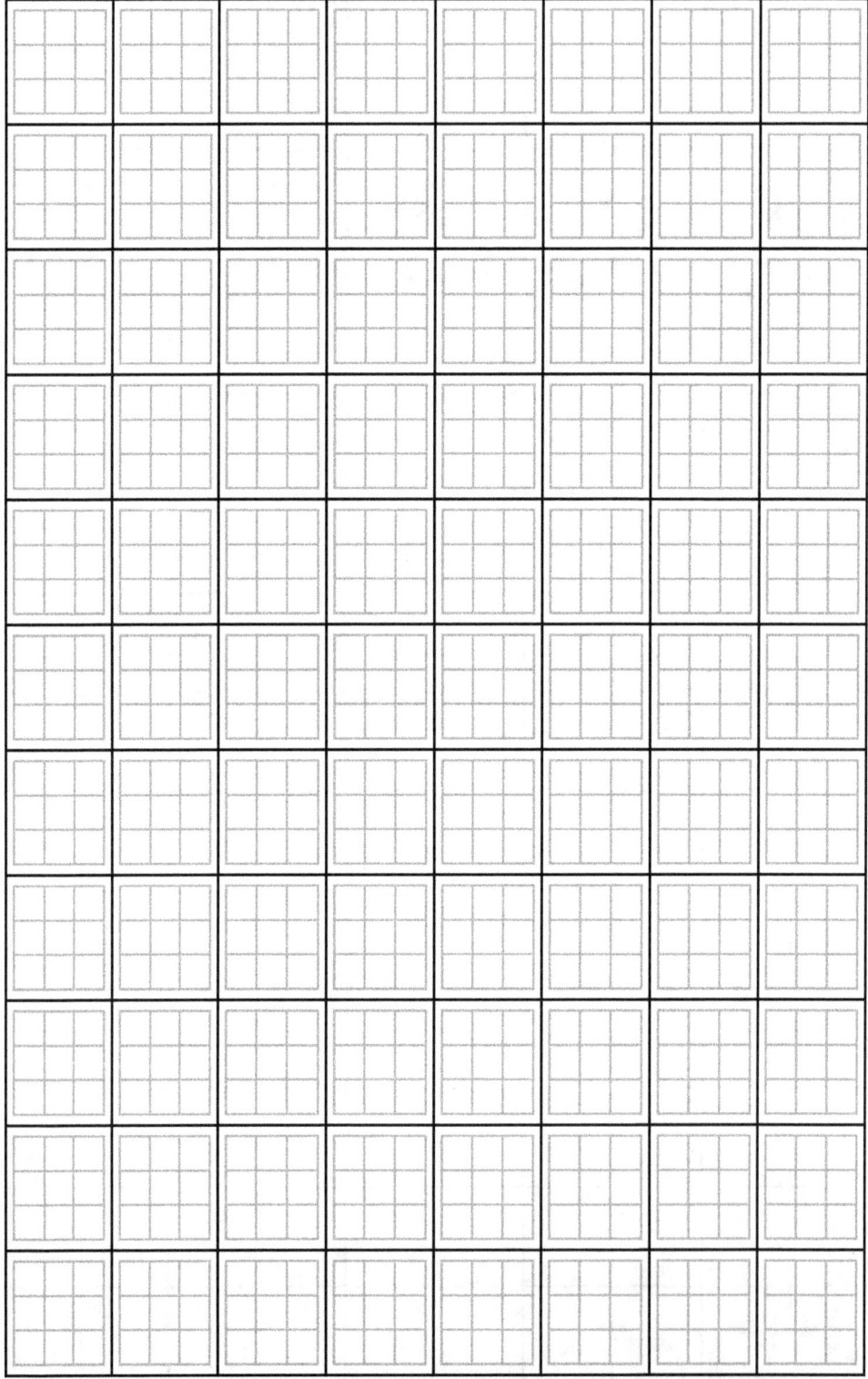

第三十五课　Unit 35

早，我要买一杯咖啡。
Zǎo, wǒ yào mǎi yì bēi kā fēi.
Morning! I want to buy a cup of coffee.

好，我们的咖啡很不错！
Hǎo, wǒ men de kā fēi hěn bú cuò!
Good! Our coffee is excellent!

一杯多少钱?
Yì bēi duō shǎo qián?
How much is it?

一杯五块钱。
Yì bēi wǔ kuài qián.
Five dollars a cup.

This is a dialog at a coffee shop between customer and shop assistant. The mood is relaxed and polite.

Dialog Vocabulary

买	mǎi	to buy
杯	bēi	a cup of
咖啡	kā fēi	coffee
不错	bú cuò	pretty good
五	wǔ	five
块	kuài	MW for dollars

Useful Vocabulary

茶	chá	tea
果汁	guǒ zhī	fruit juice
牛奶	niú nǎi	milk
水	shuǐ	water
好喝	hǎo hē	tastes good (drink)
好吃	hǎo chī	tastes good (food)

Revision Vocabulary

多少	duō shǎo	how much?
钱	qián	money
要	yào	to want

Lesson Breakdown

好, 我们的 咖啡 很 不错!
Hǎo, wǒ men de kā fēi hěn bú cuò!
Good! Our coffee is excellent!

不错   bú cuò   pretty good

This word is an Adjective.

It tells us (describes) just *how good* the coffee is.

New students should not get confused with the 不 present in 不错 [búcuò].

It is not a negative and the word means "pretty good".

> 早，我 要 买 一 杯 咖啡。
> Zǎo, wǒ yào mǎi yì bēi kā fēi.
> Morning! I want to buy a cup of coffee.

要　　　yào　　　to want to

This Verb means "to want" and it is used to express the need of the Subject *to do* something.

The example given is an interesting sentence in that we have the two Verbs (要 and 买) right next to each other. We see that 要 [yào] acts as an Auxiliary Verb, to assist 买 [mǎi] the main Verb.

What makes this Verb special is that it can act as the main Verb in one sentence, and also as the Auxiliary Verb in another.

As the main Verb, it can be used in a typical SVO sentence:

I **want** candy.

As the Auxiliary Verb it can be used as:

I **want** *to eat* candy.

We employ the following structure:

Subject + 要 + Verb

Example:
我 要 去 美国。
[wǒ yào qù měi guó]
I **want** *to go to* America.

This is a very handy Verb and it can be used for all kinds of desires like: to eat, to sleep, to cook, to do, to study, to go, etc.

> 一 杯 五 块 钱。
> Yì bēi wǔ kuài qián.
> Five dollars a cup.

| 块 | kuài | MW (dollars) |

This is an informal MW that is used **colloquially** for gold, silver or normal dollars:

一块钱　　[yì kuài qián]　　$ 1.00
两块钱　　[liǎng kuài qián]　$ 2.00
三块钱　　[sān kuài qián]　　$ 3.00

It is also acceptable to omit the last monetary unit 钱 [qián] when discussing money matters.

一百块
[yī bǎi kuài]
$100

Besides money, it can also be used as a MW for a piece of cake or soap. Basically it represents a *chunk of something*.

Supplementary

List of common drinks:

红茶	hóng chá	black tea	啤酒	pí jiǔ	beer
绿茶	lǜ chá	green tea	牛奶	nǎi	milk
果汁	guǒ zhī	juice	水	shuǐ	water
咖啡	kā fēi	coffee	可乐	kě lè	Coke

Download The Bonus Audio Files To Practice Your Pronunciation

My Progress

Words	QW's	MW's	TW's	Total
Count	9	8	5	202

Hint

Remember that the Verb 要 can be used as the main Verb and also as an Auxiliary Verb.

Self-Practice

Connect and match:

买 •	• chá •	• juice
杯 •	• guǒ zhī •	• tea
五 •	• kuài •	• coffee
块 •	• wǔ •	• to buy
咖啡 •	• bú cuò •	• pretty good
不错 •	• mǎi •	• cup
茶 •	• bēi •	• MW dollars
果汁 •	• kā fēi •	• five

Translate the following sentences into English:

1. Hǎo wǒ men de kā fēi hěn bú cuò !
   _____

2. Zǎo, wǒ yào mǎi yì bēi kā fēi.
   _____

3. Yì bēi wǔ kuài qián.
   _____

4. Yì bēi duō shǎo qián ?
   _____

Arrange the words into sentences:

1. 多少 钱 杯 一？
   _____

2. 杯 这 咖啡 不错。
   _____

3. 咖啡 杯 要 一 我 买。
   _____

4. 要 茶 杯 一 我。
   _____

● Useful Words Stroke Order   Character Stroke Order ●

| 吃 | 茶 | 牛 | 奶 | 买 |
| 杯 | 咖 | 啡 | 错 | 块 |

Trace the following characters

吃									
茶									
牛									
奶									
买									
杯									
咖									
啡									
错									
块									

Unit 35

Self-Practice

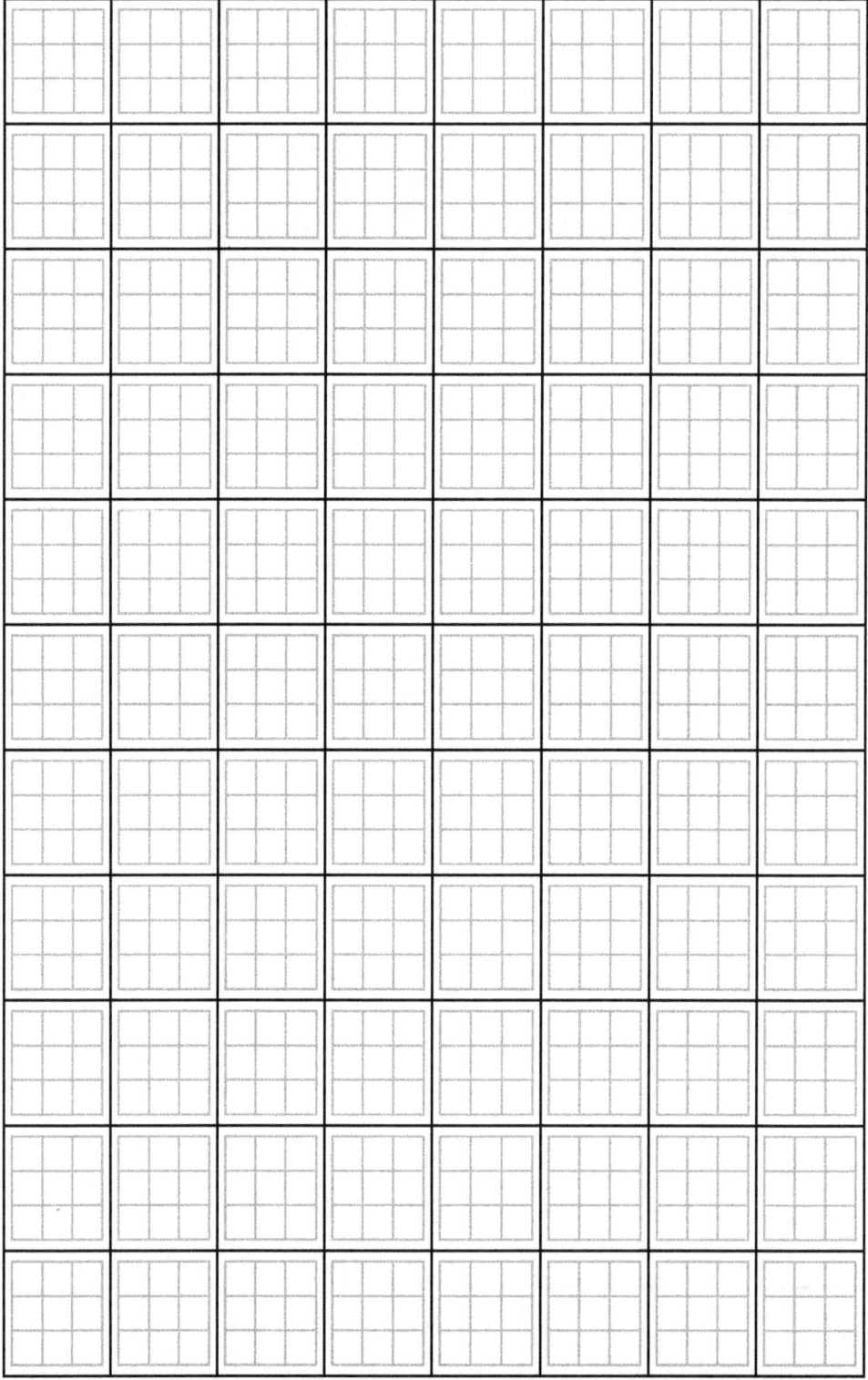

第三十六课　Unit 36

我 喜欢 这间 店的 糖果。
Wǒ xǐ huan zhè jiān diàn de táng guǒ.
I like this store's candy.

我们 去 买 吧!他们 也有 卖 冰淇淋!
Wǒ men qù mǎi bā! Tā men yě yǒu mài bīng qí lín !
Let's go buy some! They also sell ice-cream!

我有 五 块 钱。
Wǒ yǒu wǔ kuài qián.
I have five dollars.

我也 有 五 块 钱, 我们 总共 有 十 块 钱!
Wǒ yě yǒu wǔ kuài qián, wǒ men zǒng gòng yǒu shí kuài qián !
I also have five dollars. Together we have ten dollars!

This is a dialog between two young children.
Both are eager to visit the candy store.

Dialog Vocabulary

总共	zǒng gòng	together
店	diàn	store
十	shí	ten
冰淇淋	bīng qí lín	ice-cream
糖果	táng guǒ	candy
卖	mài	to sell
吧	bā	particle(to suggest)
间	jiān	MW (rooms)

Useful Vocabulary

六	liù	six
七	qī	seven
八	bā	eight
九	jiǔ	nine
糖	táng	sugar
一起	yī qǐ	together

Revision Vocabulary

买	mǎi	to buy
有	yǒu	to have
也	yě	also
钱	qián	money

Lesson Breakdown

> 我 喜欢 这间 店的 糖果。
> Wǒ xǐ huan zhè jiān diàn de táng guǒ.
> I like this store's candy.

| 间 | jiān | MW for rooms |

This MW is used for small spaces like rooms.

In our example it is used for a shop, because it is basically just a small room. This is very common in China, where we find that the first floor of the house can be used for the family business and upstairs as living space for the family members.

For bigger establishments (restaurants, stores, companies) we use the Measure Word 家 [jiā].

> 我们 去 买 吧!
> Wǒ men qù mǎi bā!
> Let's go buy some!

吧　　bā　　particle

This is simply a particle that we place at the end of a sentence when we want to make a **suggestion** or a **proposal**.
It basically implies "... OK?"　or　"... Right?"

We use the following structure:
Suggestion + 吧

Example:
我们 走 吧。
[wǒ men zǒu ba]
Let's go.

The speaker is making a suggestion for them *to leave*.
The use is similar to asking a question and the tone is friendly and polite.

We have now been introduced to **three question particles** used in Mandarin:

吗 [ma] used for questions where a Yes/ No answer is expected.
呢 [ne] used where the speaker redirects the question back.
吧 [ba] used for suggestions or proposals.

Besides these three particles, we can also use QWs to ask questions of a more complex nature.

Supplementary

卖 VS 买

These two words are used very often, for obvious reasons. Although their respective pronunciations seem very similar, their tones do set them apart.

- 买

[mǎi]

to buy (V)

Notice the 3rd tone and also the character shape.

- 卖

[mài]

to sell (V)

Notice the 4th tone and the addition of a new radical on top of the original character used above.

Note the tones for pronunciation of these characters. It is essential to understand the importance of tones from the start!

冰淇淋   bīng qí lín   ice-cream

Two radicals present in this word.

In 冰 the 冫-radical means ice and is used to describe anything related to ice.

In 淇 the 氵-radical means water and is used to describe anything related to water.

Download The Bonus Audio Files To Practice Your Pronunciation

My Progress

Words	QW's	MW's	TW's	Total
Count	9	9	5	210

Hint

We place question particle 吧 at the end of a sentence when we want to make a suggestion.

Self-Practice

Connect and match:

总共 •	• zǒng gòng •	• store
店 •	• jiān •	• together
十 •	• bā •	• ice cream
糖果 •	• mài •	• MW (room)
卖 •	• shí •	• to sell
吧 •	• diàn •	• ten
间 •	• táng guǒ •	• to suggest
冰淇淋 •	• bīng qí lín •	• candy

Rewrite the following sentences into Pinyin:

1. I like candy. _____
2. I like ice cream. _____
3. I like this store's candy. _____
4. This store's candy is pretty good. _____
5. I have ten dollars. _____
6. Together we have one hundred dollars. _____

Circle the correct character in every line:

1. 猓 ， 涷 ， 東 ， 课 ， 果
2. 芭 ， 吧 ， 爸 ， 把 ， 巴
3. 扪 ， 问 ， 间 ， 门 ， 们
4. 踮 ， 掂 ， 点 ， 店 ， 站

Useful Words Stroke Order — Character Stroke Order

总	共	钱	店	间
吧	糖	果	卖	十

Trace the following characters

总									
共									
钱									
店									
间									
吧									
糖									
果									
卖									
十									

Self-Practice

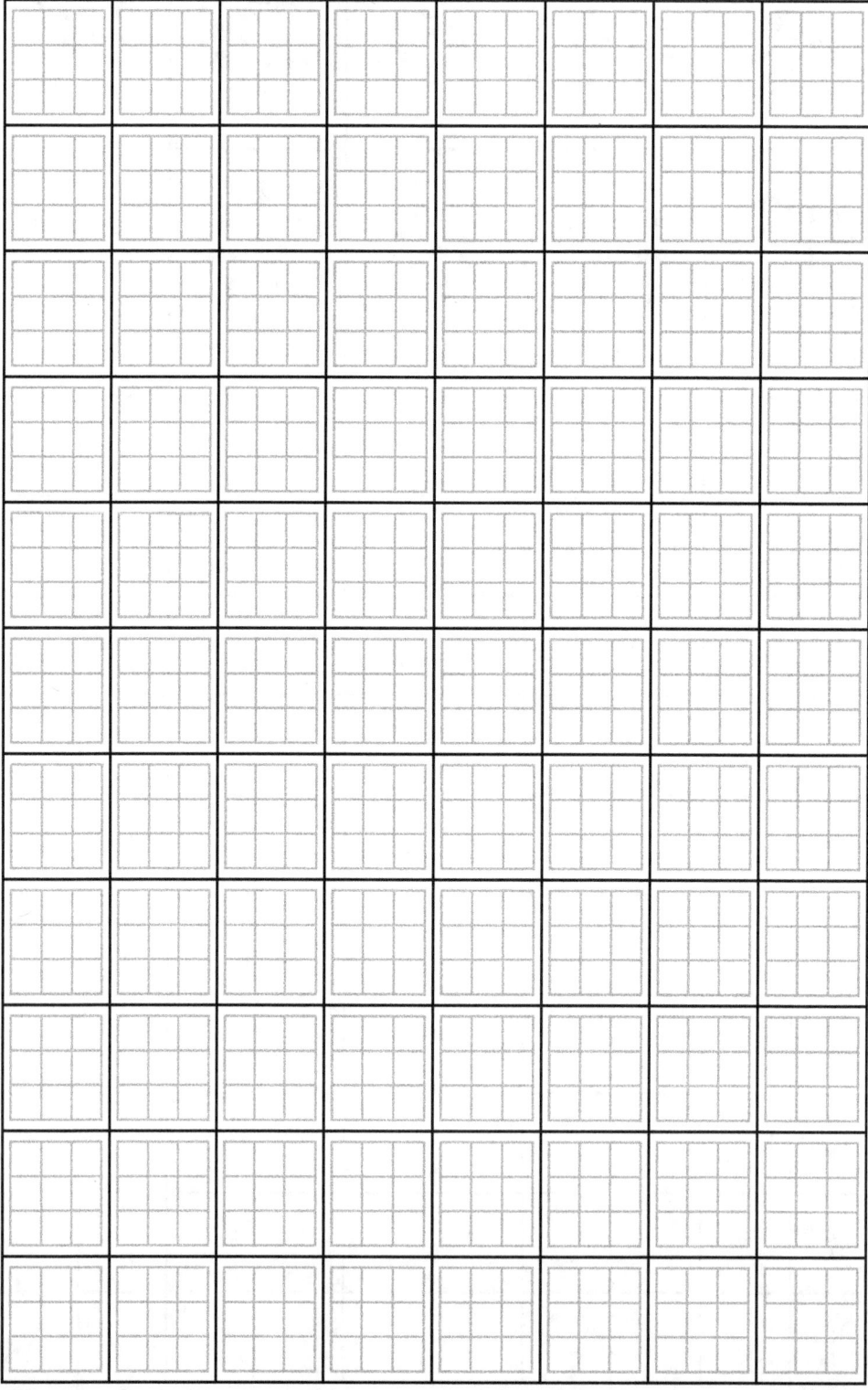

Unit 37

这件 衣服 一百元。
Zhè jiàn yīfu yì bǎi yuán.
This piece of clothing is one hundred dollars, please.

好, 可以 便宜 一点 吗?
Hǎo, kě yǐ pián yi yì diǎn ma ?
Ok, can you lower the price a bit?

不好意思, 我们 没有 折扣。
Bù hǎo yì sī, wǒ men méi yǒu zhé kòu.
Sorry, no discount.

谢谢。
Xiè xie.
Thank you.

This is a dialog between customer and clerk at a clothing store. The customer asks for discount, but the clerk refuses with a polite tone.

Dialog Vocabulary

折扣	**zhé kòu**	discount
衣服	**yī fu**	clothing
便宜	**pián yi**	cheap
一点	**yì diǎn**	a bit/ a little
件	**jiàn**	MW (clothing)

Useful Vocabulary

长裤	**cháng kù**	trousers
内裤	**nèi kù**	underwear
袜子	**wà zi**	socks
帽子	**mào zi**	hat/ cap
穿	**chuān**	to put on clothes

Revision Vocabulary

没有	méi yǒu	not to have
我们	wǒmen	we/ us
可以	kě yǐ	can/ may
元	yuán	dollar (unit)
不好意思	bù hǎo yì sī	excuse me

Lesson Breakdown

> 这件 衣服 一百元。
> Zhè jiàn yīfu yì bǎi yuán.
> This piece of clothing is one hundred dollars, please.

件　　　jiàn　　　MW (clothes)

This is a Specific Measure Word.

It is used specifically for **clothing** (especially the top part of clothes). When used in a sentence, immediately following 件, is the article of clothing.

(Take note that it can also be used for *matters or affairs* that need your attention.)

> 不好意思，我们 没有 折扣。
> Bù hǎo yì sī, wǒ men méi yǒu zhé kòu.
> Sorry, no discount.

折扣　　zhé kòu　　discount

- This Noun means "discount" and asking for discount is quite straight forward. Let's look at the individual characters:

折 [zhé] means: discount

扣 [kòu] means: to deduct

The tricky part is understanding how discount is measured in China.

Example:

A product costs $100.

English interpretation: A sign with 10% discount, means 10% off the asking price. The percentage value indicates the money saved. Thus you pay $90.

Chinese interpretation: A sign that equates to 10%, indicates the **final price after the discount has been applied**. That would mean 90% off and a price of $10!

The structure for discounts is:

Number + 折

8 折 means: 20% off

6 折 means: 40% off

2.5 折 means: 75% off

It is clear that discounts in Mandarin are expressed as the opposite of the English expression.

> 好, 可以 便宜 一点 吗?
> Hǎo, kě yǐ pián yi yì diǎn ma ?
> Ok, can you lower the price a bit?

一点   yì diǎn   a little bit

This phrase is used with an Adjective to express *degree*.
It can also be written as 一点儿 [yì diǎnr].
便宜
[pián yi]
means: cheap
It is an Adjective that is used to describe the quality of the Noun (price).
We use this structure:
Adjective + 一点

Some **examples** of 一点 used with Adjectives to indicate degree:

快 一 点 [kuài yì diǎn]   faster
慢 一 点 [màn yì diǎn]   slower
好 一 点 [hǎo yì diǎn]   better
累 一 点 [lèi yì diǎn]   more tired

The opposite of cheap, is expensive 贵 [guì].
(An Adjective is also called a Stative Verb.)

Download The Bonus Audio Files To Practice Your Pronunciation

My Progress

Words	QW's	MW's	TW's	Total
Count	9	10	5	215

Hint

In Chinese, discounts are expressed as the opposite of the standard English expression.

Self-Practice

Connect and match:

折扣 •	• jiàn •	• to put on
衣服 •	• zhé kòu •	• socks
便宜 •	• pián yi •	• hat
件 •	• yì diǎn •	• MW clothes
一点 •	• chuān •	• discount
穿 •	• yī fu •	• cheap
帽子 •	• wà zi •	• clothes
袜子 •	• mào zi •	• a bit

Translate the following sentences into English:

1. Hǎo, kě yǐ pián yi yì diǎn ma ?
   _____

2. Zhè jiàn yī fu yì bǎi yuán.
   _____

3. Bù hǎo yì sī, wǒ men méi yǒu zhé kòu.
   _____

4. Bù hǎo yì sī.
   _____

Arrange the words into sentences:

1. 便宜   吗   一点   可以？
   _____

2. 没有   折扣   我们。
   _____

3. 一百   元   衣服   这   件。
   _____

4. 要   我   衣服   穿。
   _____

● Useful Words Stroke Order   Character Stroke Order ●

| 帽 | 穿 | 便 | 宜 | 件 |
| 点 | 衣 | 服 | 折 | 扣 |

Trace the following characters

帽									
穿									
便									
宜									
件									
点									
衣									
服									
折									
扣									

Self-Practice

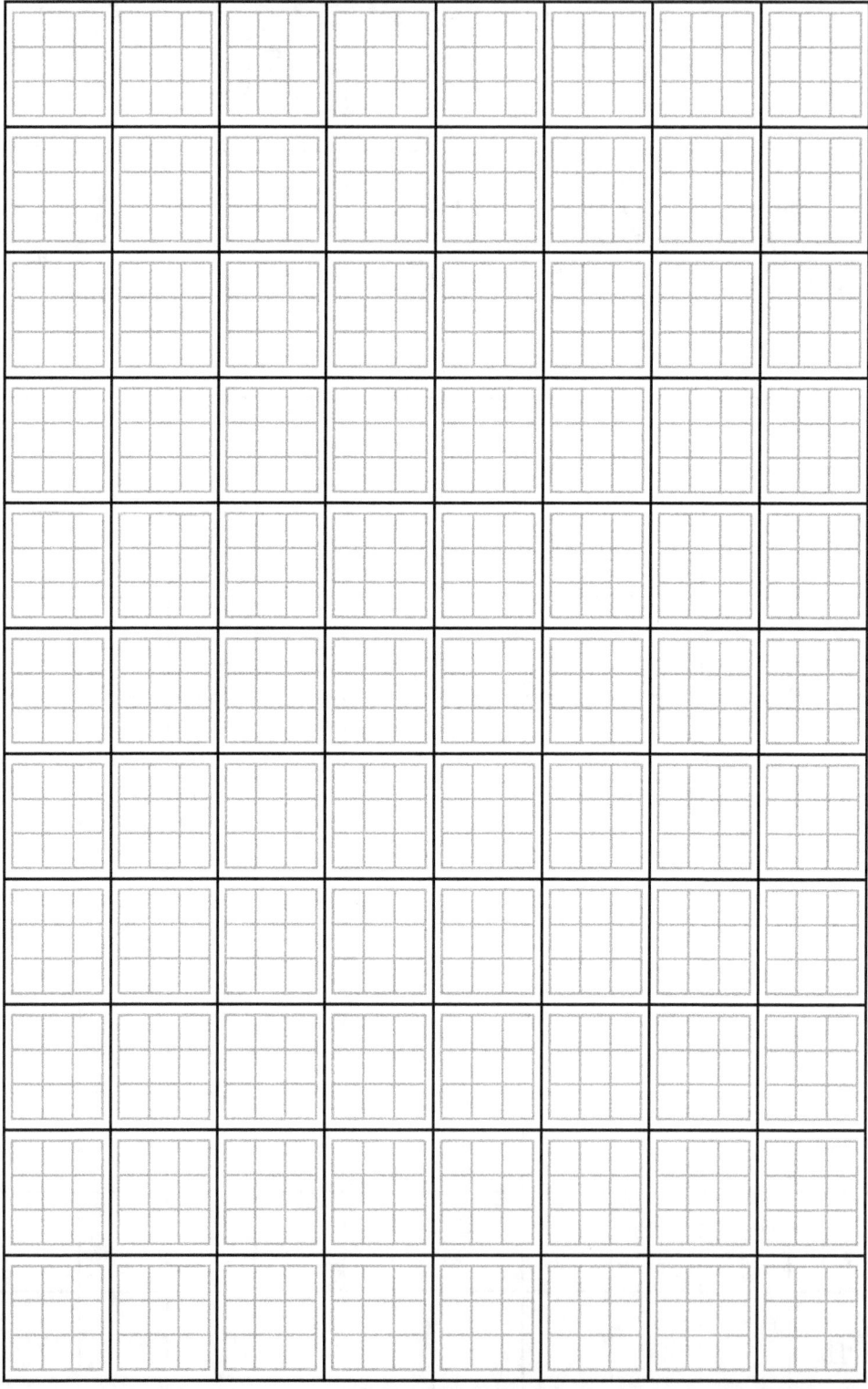

第三十八课 Unit 38

我要 这顶 红色的 帽子。
Wǒ yào zhè dǐng hóng sè de mào zi.
I want that red hat, please.

这顶 帽子 很不错。
Zhè dǐng mào zi hěn bú cuò.
This hat is pretty nice.

我也要 这顶 黄色的 帽子。
Wǒ yě yào zhè dǐng huáng sè de mào zi.
I also want that yellow one.

总共 八 块 钱。
Zǒng gòng bā kuài qián.
Together it's eight dollars.

This is a dialog between customer and clerk.
The mood is polite and relaxed.

Dialog Vocabulary

红色	hóng sè	red
黄色	huáng sè	yellow
帽子	mào zi	hat/ cap
八	bā	eight
顶	dǐng	MW for hat

Useful Vocabulary

颜色	yán sè	color
蓝色	lán sè	blue
白色	bái sè	white
金色	jīn sè	golden
绿色	lǜ sè	green

Revision Vocabulary

也要	yě yào	also want
总共	zǒng gòng	together
不错	bú cuò	pretty good

Lesson Breakdown

这顶 帽子 很不错。
Zhè dǐng mào zi hěn bú cuò.
This hat is pretty nice.

顶　　　dǐng　　MW (hats)

顶 [dǐng] is a specific MW used for things we *wear on our heads*. It can be used for most head-wear like hats, helmets, caps, etc.
It is also interesting to note that it can be used for umbrellas and tents, both of which are used to protect our heads from the elements.

> 我要 这顶 红色的 帽子。
> Wǒ yào zhè dǐng hóng sè de mào zi.
> I want that red hat, please.

红色　　　hóng sè　　　red

In Mandarin colors end with 色. We can therefore safely say that all colors have two or three syllables. (A syllable represents one character present in a word.)

When we use colors to describe a Noun, we employ the following structure:

Color + 的 + Noun

Example:
红色 的 帽子。
[hóng sè de mào zi]
The red helmet.

If you just want to name a color there is no need to add the possessive particle 的 [de].

Example:
我 喜欢 蓝色。
[wǒ xǐ huan lán sè]
I like blue.

Colors function as Adjectives.

This begs the question, what is the rule that determines whether you should put particle 的 behind the Adjective or not?

The general rule is:

Place 的 after words with two or more syllables and don't put it after single syllable Adjectives.

Supplementary

Writing: Radicals

钱   qián   money

Notice when writing the character for money, that there is a special radical at the front of the character.

This is the radical 钅 [jīn] which is used for gold and precious **metals**.

We find this radical in all things of a metallic nature:

铁　[tiě]　　iron (metal)
铜　[tóng]　copper/ brass (metal)
锁　[suǒ]　　lock (metal)
钥匙　[yào shi]　key (metal)

This is one way in which to learn the characters.

In Chinese elementary schools, every character is dissected and radicals are isolated for better comprehension.

All students of Mandarin should be aware of these subtle hints of *where* a character comes from and *how* it is implemented.

Download The Bonus Audio Files To Practice Your Pronunciation

My Progress

Words	QW's	MW's	TW's	Total
Count	9	11	5	220

Hint

When dealing with colors, particle 的 is placed after words with two or more syllables.

Self-Practice

Connect and match:

八 •	• bái sè •	• red
红色 •	• yán sè •	• white
顶 •	• mào zi •	• blue
黄色 •	• lán sè •	• yellow
蓝色 •	• bā •	• MW hats
帽子 •	• huáng sè •	• eight
颜色 •	• dǐng •	• color
白色 •	• hóng sè •	• hat/ cap

Write questions for the following answers:

1. _____?
对, 我 要 红色 的 帽子。

2. _____?
这 顶 帽子 一百 元。

3. _____?
对, 我 喜欢 黄色。

4. _____?
不好 意思, 我们 没有 折扣。

Circle the correct character in every line:

1. 且 , 日 , 目 , 白 , 自
2. 芭 , 爸 , 巴 , 吧 , 色
3. 叮 , 町 , 顶 , 叮 , 订
4. 江 , 虹 , 给 , 給 , 红

Useful Words Stroke Order — Character Stroke Order

颜	蓝	金	白	绿
红	黄	色	帽	顶

Trace the following characters

颜	颜	颜	颜	颜	颜	颜	颜	颜	颜
蓝	蓝	蓝	蓝	蓝	蓝	蓝	蓝	蓝	蓝
金	金	金	金	金	金	金	金	金	金
白	白	白	白	白	白	白	白	白	白
绿	绿	绿	绿	绿	绿	绿	绿	绿	绿
红	红	红	红	红	红	红	红	红	红
黄	黄	黄	黄	黄	黄	黄	黄	黄	黄
色	色	色	色	色	色	色	色	色	色
帽	帽	帽	帽	帽	帽	帽	帽	帽	帽
顶	顶	顶	顶	顶	顶	顶	顶	顶	顶

Self-Practice

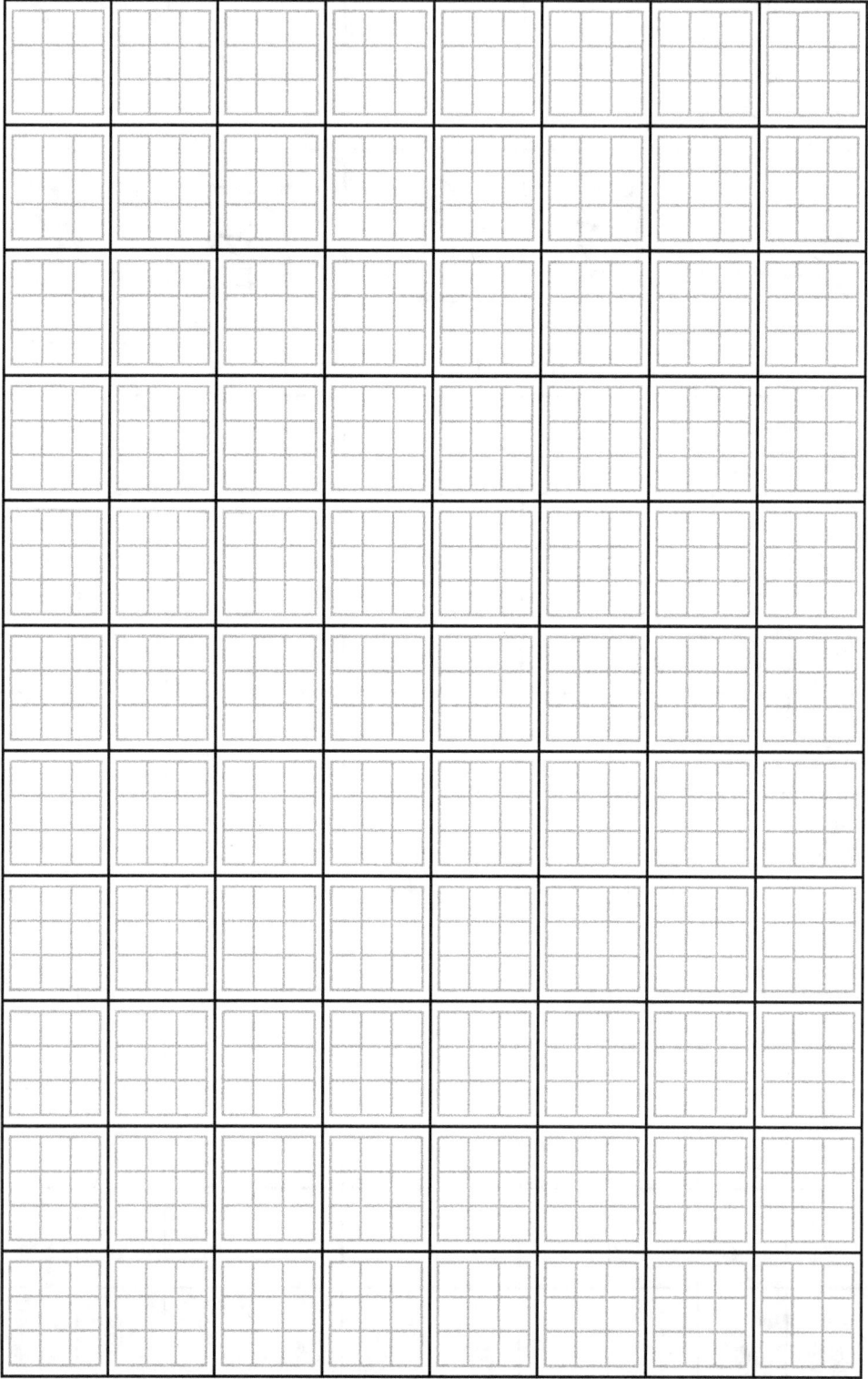

第三十九课 Unit 39

我 喜欢 这 些 蓝色的 贴纸。
Wǒ xǐ huan zhè xiē lán sè de tiē zhǐ.
I like these blue stickers.

你 有 多少 张 贴纸?
Nǐ yǒu duō shǎo zhāng tiē zhǐ?
How many do you have?

我 有 二十张, 你 有 怎么 多吗?
Wǒ yǒu èr shí zhāng, nǐ yǒu zěn me duō ma?
I have twenty. Do you have that many?

我 没有, 你 应该 跟我 分享。
Wǒ méi yǒu, nǐ yīng gāi gēn wǒ fēn xiǎng.
No, I don't. You should share them with me.

This is a dialog between two classmates.
The mood is friendly and they are good friends.

Dialog Vocabulary

贴纸	tiē zhǐ	stickers
跟	gēn	with
应该	yīng gāi	should/ ought to
分享	fēn xiǎng	to share
蓝色	lán sè	blue
二十	èr shí	twenty
张	zhāng	MW for paper
些	xiē	MW meaning some/few

Useful Vocabulary

三十	sān shí	thirty
四十	sì shí	forty
五十	wǔ shí	fifty
绿色	lǜ sè	green
黑色	hēi sè	black
白色	bái sè	white

Revision Vocabulary

有	yǒu	to have
怎么	zěn me	how?
多少	duō shǎo	how many
多	duō	many
喜欢	xǐ huan	to like

Lesson Breakdown

> 我 喜欢 这 些 蓝色的 贴纸。
> Wǒ xǐ huan zhè xiē lán sè de tiē zhǐ.
> I like these blue stickers.

些	xiē	some (MW)

This is a Specific Measure Word and it means *some* or a *few*. In the dialog, it literally means: "I like these *few* blue stickers." It indicates a *small amount or number*.

Example:
这些
[zhè xiē]
these few

> 你 有 多少 张 贴纸?
> Nǐ yǒu duō shǎo zhāng tiē zhǐ?
> How many stickers do you have?

| 张 | zhāng | MW (paper) |

This is a Specific Measure word and it is used for objects *made of paper* and take note that it is also used for objects with *flat segments* like tables and beds.

(Anything that you can visualize with a nice flat and open surface area.)

Note the use of 贴 [tiē], which means *to stick,* in the word for sticker:

贴纸 [tiē zhǐ]

It literally means: "sticky paper".

> 我 没有, 你 应该 跟我 分享。
> Wǒ méi yǒu, nǐ yīng gāi gēn wǒ fēn xiǎng.
> No, I don't. You should share them with me.

| 应该 | yīng gāi | should |

This word functions as an Auxiliary verb and is used to express *should*. It is a very important word that is used daily in conversations all over China.

We use the following structure:

Subject + 应该 + Verb + Object

Example:

你 应该 回家。

[nǐ yīng gāi huí jiā]

You should go home.

Supplementary

Colors:

Colors play an important role in Chinese culture.

A good example is *red* which is a very popular color and visible throughout the nation. It is considered the color of "good luck".

白色	**bái sè**	White
蓝色	**lán sè**	Blue
黄色	**huáng sè**	Yellow
绿色	**lǜ sè**	Green
红色	**hóng sè**	Red
橘色	**jú sè**	Orange
咖啡色	**kā fēi sè**	Brown
黑色	**hēi sè**	Black
紫色	**zǐ sè**	Purple
灰色	**huī sè**	Grey

Download The Bonus Audio Files To Practice Your Pronunciation

My Progress

Words	QW's	MW's	TW's	Total
Count	9	13	5	228

Hint

应该 is used pretty much in the same way that we use it in English. It's followed by a Verb "to do".

Self-Practice

Connect and match:

贴纸 •	• sān shí •	• twenty
跟 •	• tiē zhǐ •	• with
应该 •	• èr shí •	• thirty
分享 •	• gēn •	• to share
二十 •	• yīng gāi •	• stickers
张 •	• fēn xiǎng •	• MW paper
些 •	• zhāng •	• MW some/few
三十 •	• xiē •	• should

Translate the following sentences into English:

1. Nǐ yǒu duō shǎo zhāng tiē zhǐ?
   _____

2. Wǒ yǒu èr shí zhāng.
   _____

3. Wǒ xǐ huan zhè xiē lán sè de tiē zhǐ.
   _____

4. Nǐ yīng gāi gēn wǒ fēn xiǎng.
   _____

Arrange the words into sentences:

1. 贴纸   张   多少   你   有？
   _____

2. 张   我   二十   有。
   _____

3. 分享   跟   我   你   应该。
   _____

4. 你的   我   喜欢   贴纸。
   _____

Useful Words Stroke Order — Character Stroke Order

贴	纸	跟	应	该
分	享	蓝	张	些

Trace the following characters

贴	贴	贴	贴	贴	贴	贴	贴	贴	贴
纸	纸	纸	纸	纸	纸	纸	纸	纸	纸
跟	跟	跟	跟	跟	跟	跟	跟	跟	跟
应	应	应	应	应	应	应	应	应	应
该	该	该	该	该	该	该	该	该	该
分	分	分	分	分	分	分	分	分	分
享	享	享	享	享	享	享	享	享	享
蓝	蓝	蓝	蓝	蓝	蓝	蓝	蓝	蓝	蓝
张	张	张	张	张	张	张	张	张	张
些	些	些	些	些	些	些	些	些	些

Self-Practice

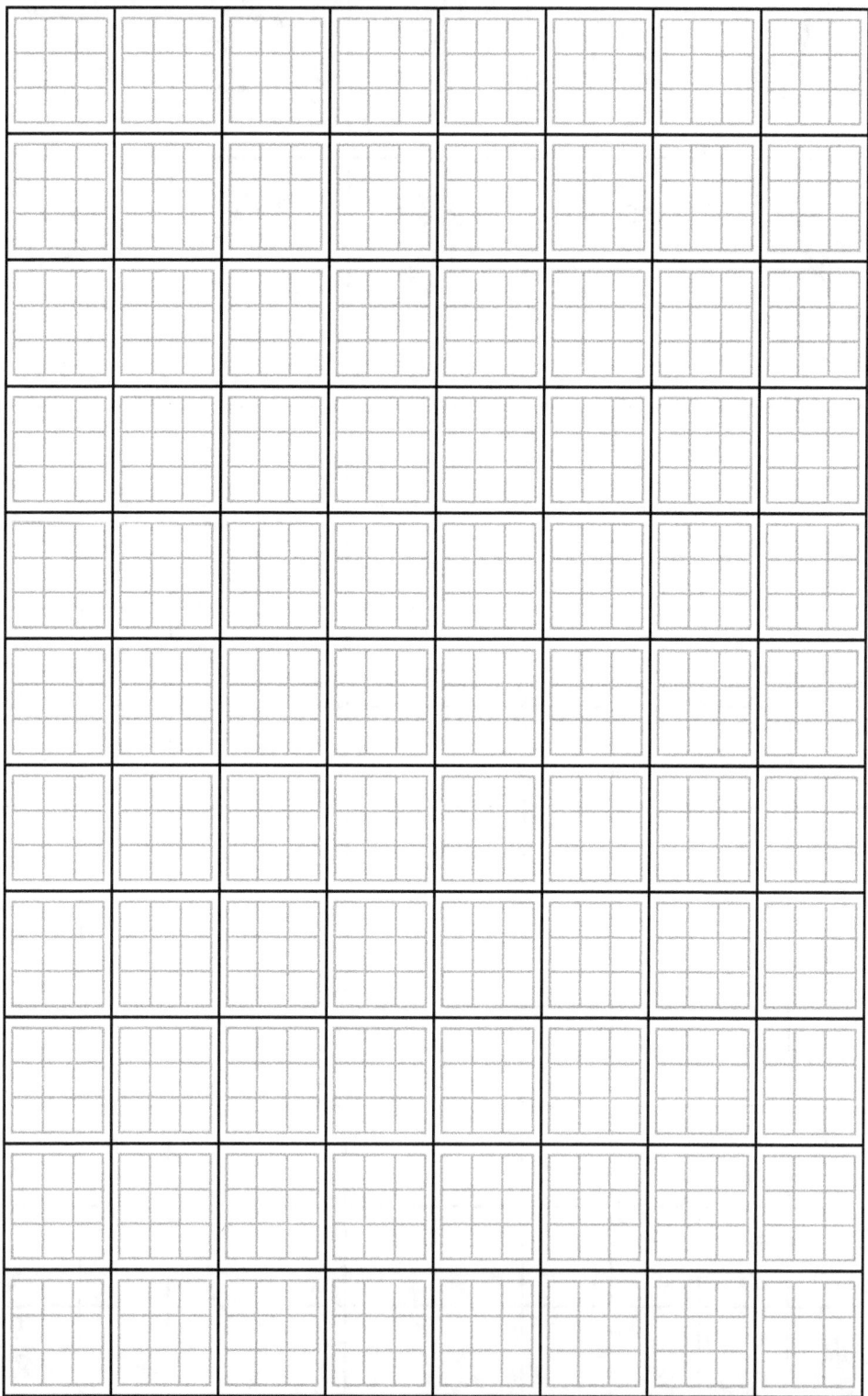

第四十课　　　　Unit 40

一瓶 可乐 五毛钱。
Yì píng kě lè wǔ máo qián.
A bottle of coke is fifty cents.

请 帮 我 买 一瓶?
Qǐng bāng wǒ mǎi yì píng ?
Please help me buy one?

好,这 真的 很 便宜。
Hǎo, zhè zhēn de hěn pián yi.
OK, it's really very cheap.

谢谢!
Xièxie !
Thank you!

This is a dialog between two friends.
They are good friends and the one is glad to help the other.

Dialog Vocabulary

瓶	píng	bottle
毛	máo	ten cents
可乐	kě lè	Coke
帮	bāng	to help
请	qǐng	please/ would you

Useful Vocabulary

茶	chá	tea
啤酒	pí jiǔ	beer
果汁	guǒ zhī	fruit juice
杯	bēi	cup
请问	qǐng wèn	Excuse me (polite)

Revision Vocabulary

谢谢	xiè xie	thank you
买	mǎi	to buy
便宜	pián yi	cheap

Lesson Breakdown

请 帮 我 买 一瓶?
Qǐng bāng wǒ mǎi yì píng ?
Please help me buy a bottle?

| 请 | qǐng | please |

This word functions as a Verb and it is used as a polite way of expressing the need for assistance or to *request something*.

It basically means: Will you please?

(It can also mean *to invite*.)

The word order is important.

When requesting assistance, we always place this word before Verbs and at the beginning of the sentence to convey a feeling of warmth or hospitality.

> 瓶　　píng　　bottle

This is a Noun and it means *bottle* which is used for measurements (a bottle of something).

It is interesting to note that it can also act as a **Measure Word**.

The good news is that this MW behaves in a similar way as we would use it in the English language.

Example:
三 瓶 水。
[sān píng shuǐ]
Three bottles of water.

Only certain MWs behave like their English counterparts.
Here is a list of the most common ones:

杯	**bēi**	cups of…
块	**kuài**	chunks of…
双	**shuāng**	pairs of…
碗	**wǎn**	bowls of…
种	**zhǒng**	kinds of…
包	**bāo**	packets of…
盒	**hé**	small boxes of…

> 一瓶 可乐 五毛钱。
> Yìpíng kělè wǔmáo qián.
> A bottle of coke is fifty cents.

毛　　máo　　10 cents

To understand money matters, you need to understand numbers and currency.

The official currency of China is the 人民币 [rén mín bì].

Concerning the Chinese language, there are two ways to use currency: formally and informally (colloquially).

- **Formal** use of money:

A $1.00 unit equals 1.00 元 [yuán].

Ten 角 [jiǎo] is one 元 [yuán].

(One 角 [jiǎo] is ten cents or a dime.)

- **Informal** use of money:

A $1.00 unit equals 1.00 块 [kuài].

Ten 毛 [máo] is one 块 [kuài].

(One 毛 [máo] is ten cents or a dime.)

Examples of the informal use of currency:

五毛 [wǔ máo] $ 0.50

二十二块 [èr shí èr kuài] $ 22.00

二十二块两毛五 [èr shí èr kuài liǎng máo wǔ] $ 22.25

Download The Bonus Audio Files To Practice Your Pronunciation

My Progress

Words	QW's	MW's	TW's	Total
Count	9	14	5	233

Hint

Make sure you know which words are used for currency, whether formal or informal.

Self-Practice

Connect and match:

瓶	•	• kě lè •	• Coke
可乐	•	• píng •	• beer
毛	•	• bāng •	• juice
帮	•	• máo •	• ten cents
请	•	• qǐng •	• please
杯	•	• bēi •	• cup
果汁	•	• pí jiǔ •	• to help
啤酒	•	• guǒ zhī •	• bottle

Rewrite the following sentences into Pinyin:

1. A bottle of Coke is fifty cents. _____
2. Thank you. _____
3. It's really very cheap. _____
4. Please help me buy one? _____
5. How much is one cup of Coke? _____
6. I do not like beer. _____

Circle the correct character in every line:

1. 瓶 , 开 , 蚜 , 邢 , 頻
2. 冋 , 句 , 司 , 同 , 可
3. 清 , 请 , 情 , 晴 , 凊
4. 梛 , 绑 , 帮 , 邦 , 棒

● Useful Words Stroke Order   Character Stroke Order ●

啤	酒	汁	茶	问
毛	请	瓶	乐	帮

Trace the following characters

啤	啤	啤	啤	啤	啤	啤	啤	啤	啤
酒	酒	酒	酒	酒	酒	酒	酒	酒	酒
汁	汁	汁	汁	汁	汁	汁	汁	汁	汁
茶	茶	茶	茶	茶	茶	茶	茶	茶	茶
问	问	问	问	问	问	问	问	问	问
毛	毛	毛	毛	毛	毛	毛	毛	毛	毛
请	请	请	请	请	请	请	请	请	请
瓶	瓶	瓶	瓶	瓶	瓶	瓶	瓶	瓶	瓶
乐	乐	乐	乐	乐	乐	乐	乐	乐	乐
帮	帮	帮	帮	帮	帮	帮	帮	帮	帮

Self-Practice

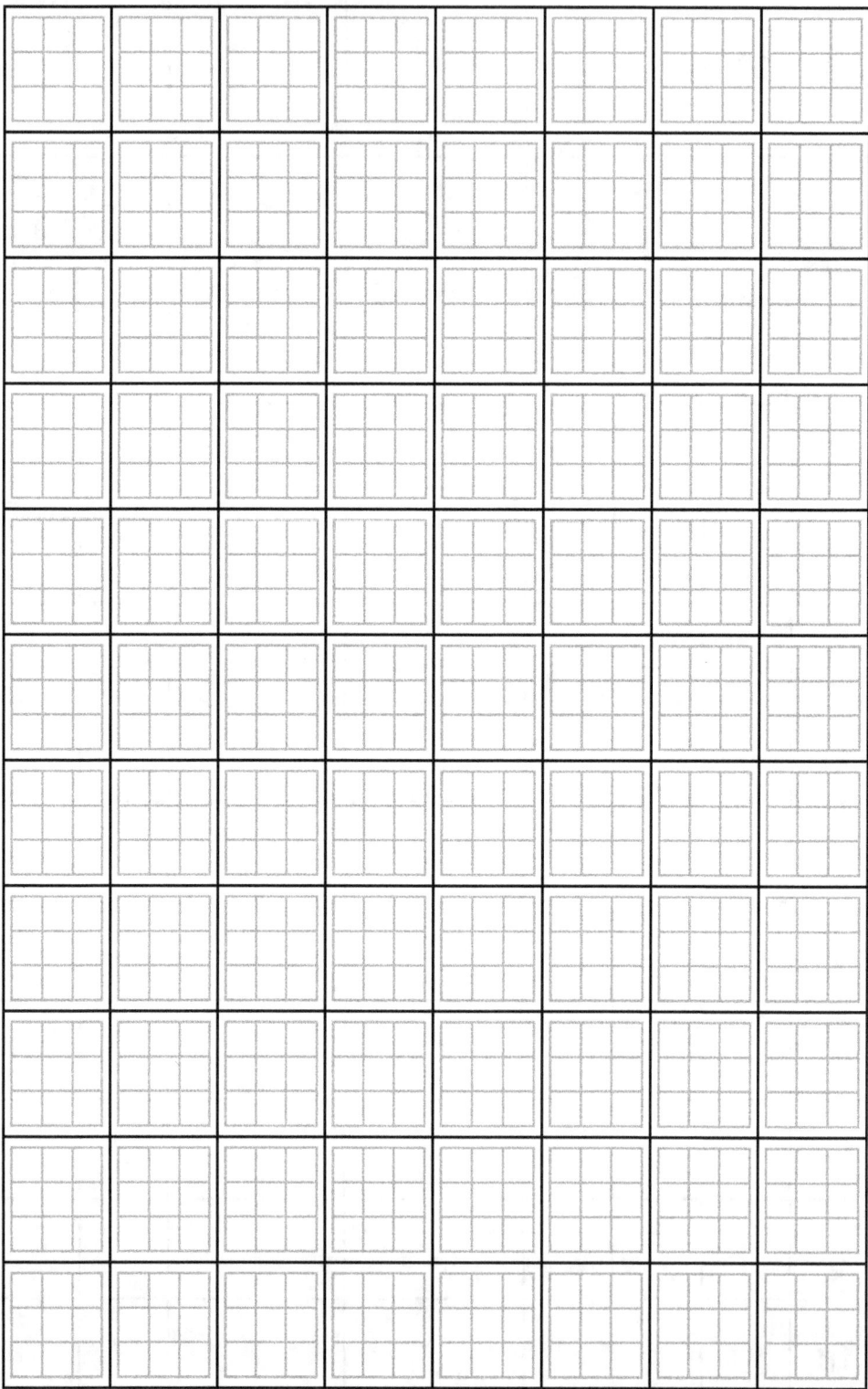

第四十一课　　　Unit 41

今天 有卖 蛋糕 吗?
Jīn tiān yǒu mài dàn gāo ma?
Do you have cake (for sale), today?

有的, 今天 有 巧克力 蛋糕。
Yǒu de, jīn tiān yǒu qiǎo kè lì dàn gāo.
We have some. We have chocolate cake.

我要 两片 蛋糕。
Wǒ yào liǎng piàn dàn gāo.
I want two slices.

好的, 今天的 蛋糕 很好吃!
Hǎo de, jīn tiān de dàn gāo hěn hǎo chī!
OK, the cake is very delicious today.

This is a dialog between customer and shop assistant.
The mood is friendly and polite.

Dialog Vocabulary

蛋糕	dàn gāo	cake
片	piàn	slice (MW)
好吃	hǎo chī	delicious
巧克力	qiǎo kè lì	chocolate
有的	yǒu de	some

Useful Vocabulary

面包	miàn bāo	bread
蛋	dàn	egg
三明治	sān míng zhì	sandwich
杯子蛋糕	bēi zi dàn gāo	cup cake
香草	xiāng cǎo	vanilla
草莓	cǎo méi	strawberry

Revision Vocabulary

有	yǒu	to have
今天	jīn tiān	today
卖	mài	to sell
两	liǎng	two (with MW)

Lesson Breakdown

我要 两片 蛋糕。
Wǒ yào liǎng piàn dàn gāo.
I want two slices of cake.

片   piàn   slice MW

This is a Specific MW for flat, thin-looking objects like slices, tablets, lakes, CDs, etc.

You can also use 块 [kuài] for a piece of cake, when it is not necessarily in the shape of a slice.

Unit 41

> 有的, 今天 有 巧克力 蛋糕。
> Yǒu de, jīn tiān yǒu qiǎo kè lì dàn gāo.
> We have some. We have chocolate cake.

有的   yǒu de   some

This word can be used in a number of expressions.
The theme is centered around "having some" of *a specific something*.

Examples:

有的 人 [yǒu de rén] meaning: *some people*
Literally: "to have some people"

有的 卖 [yǒu de mài] meaning: *to have for sale*
Literally: "to have some for sale"

有的 时候 [yǒu de shí hòu] meaning: *sometimes*
Literally: "to have at sometime"

> 好的, 今天的 蛋糕 很 好吃!
> Hǎo de, jīn tiān de dàn gāo hěn hǎo chī!
> OK, the cake is very delicious today.

好吃   hǎo chī   delicious

We already know that 好 [hǎo] means *good*, but it can also be used as an Adverb to describe when something is **good to do** or **easy to do**.
To achieve this, it must be used with a Verb to indicate the action.

We use this structure:

Subject + 好 + Verb

Take note that this Adverb is placed directly in front of the Verb.

Examples of "easy to do":

好写　[hǎo xiě]　　easy to write

好做　[hǎo zuò]　　easy to make

好用　[hǎo yòng]　easy to use

It can also be combined with Verbs that we use for our senses, like smell, look, taste, etc. It indicates that something is **good to do**:

Examples of "good to do":

好吃　[hǎo chī]　good to eat (delicious)

好喝　[hǎo hē]　 good to drink

好看　[hǎo kàn] good-looking

好听　[hǎo tīng] good-sounding

好玩　[hǎo wán] fun

Supplementary

Writing: Radicals

蛋糕　　　dàn gāo　　cake

Note the left radical 米 in the character 糕.

The radical is often used in nouns to describe anything to do with seeds, rice, powders or flour (here used in a cake).

米粉　[mǐ fěn]　rice flour

粉笔　[fěn bǐ]　chalk (blackboard)

Download The Bonus Audio Files To Practice Your Pronunciation

My Progress

Words	QW's	MW's	TW's	Total
Count	9	15	5	238

Hint

Both 难 and 好 can be used as an Adverb, to describe when something is *hard* or *easy* to do.

Self-Practice

Connect and match:

蛋糕 •	• yǒu de •	• cake
好吃 •	• piàn •	• some
片 •	• hǎo chī •	• bread
有的 •	• miàn bāo •	• slice
面包 •	• dàn •	• delicious
蛋 •	• sān míng zhì •	• sandwich
三明治 •	• cǎo méi •	• strawberry
草莓 •	• dàn gāo •	• egg

Translate the following sentences into English:

1. Hǎo de, jīn tiān de dàn gāo hěn hǎo chī !
   _____

2. Wǒ yào liǎng piàn dàn gāo.
   _____

3. Yǒu de, jīn tiān yǒu qiǎo kè lì dàn gāo.
   _____

4. Jīn tiān yǒu mài dàn gāo ma ?
   _____

Arrange the words into sentences:

1. 要 我 片 两 蛋糕。
   _____

2. 的 蛋糕 今天 很 吃 好。
   _____

3. 今天 卖 有 吗 蛋糕？
   _____

4. 有 草莓 蛋糕 今天。
   _____

● Useful Words Stroke Order   Character Stroke Order ●

面	包	草	莓	香
蛋	糕	片	有	吃

Trace the following characters

面	面	面	面	面	面	面	面	面
包	包	包	包	包	包	包	包	包
草	草	草	草	草	草	草	草	草
莓	莓	莓	莓	莓	莓	莓	莓	莓
吃	吃	吃	吃	吃	吃	吃	吃	吃
蛋	蛋	蛋	蛋	蛋	蛋	蛋	蛋	蛋
糕	糕	糕	糕	糕	糕	糕	糕	糕
片	片	片	片	片	片	片	片	片
有	有	有	有	有	有	有	有	有
吃	吃	吃	吃	吃	吃	吃	吃	吃

Self-Practice

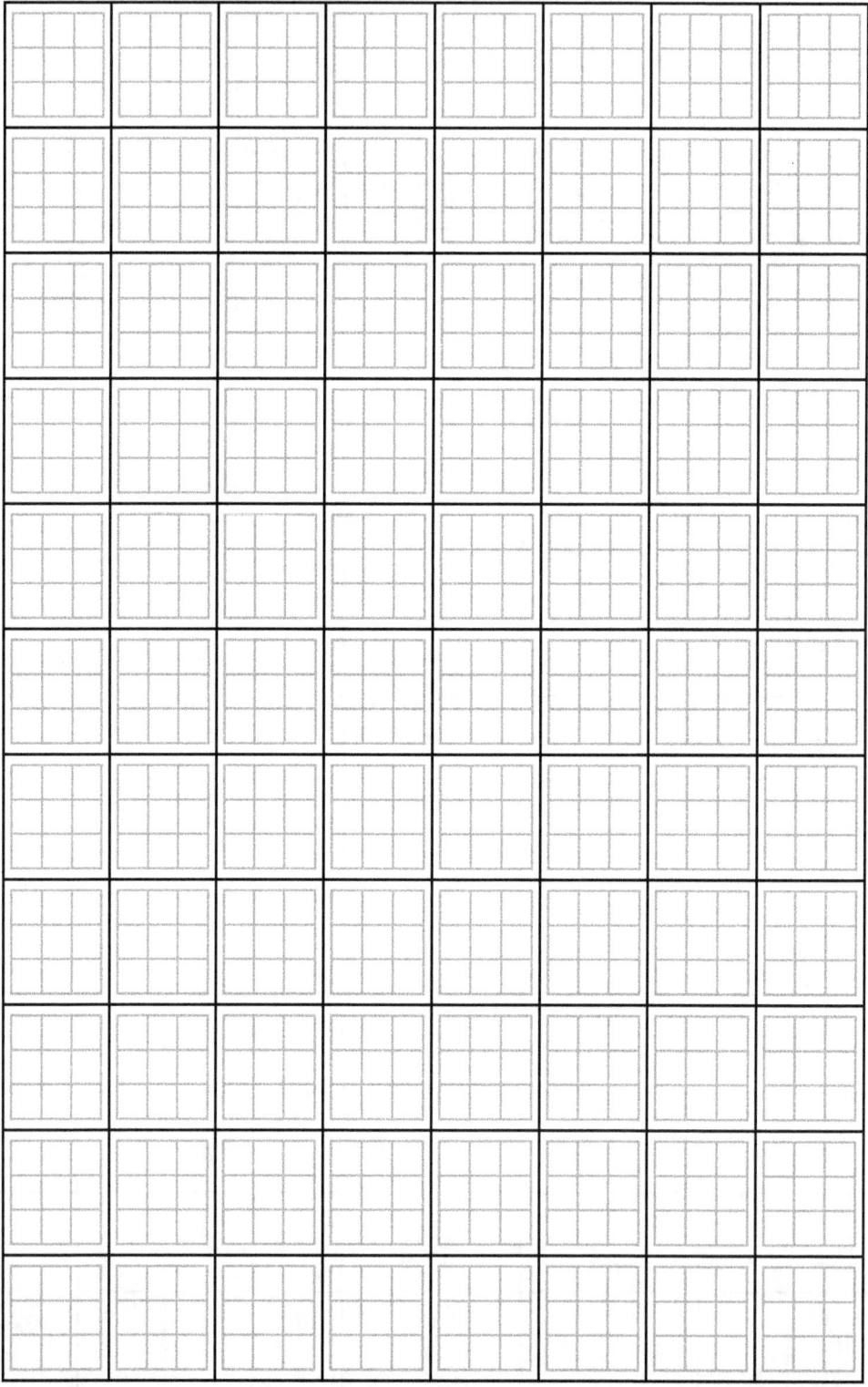

第四十二课 Unit 42

我要买 两个 绿色的 苹果。
Wǒ yào mǎi liǎng gè lǜ sè de píng guǒ.
I want two green apples.

在 这里!
Zài zhè li!
Here you go.

你 找 我 多少 钱?
Nǐ zhǎo wǒ duō shǎo qián?
How much is the change?

我 找 你 六 块 钱。
Wǒ zhǎo nǐ liù kuài qián.
I'll give you six dollars.

This is a dialog between customer and fruitmonger.
The mood is casual.

Dialog Vocabulary

绿色	lǜ sè	green
苹果	píng guǒ	apple
六	liù	six
这里	zhè li	here
找	zhǎo	to return change

Useful Vocabulary

水果	shuǐ guǒ	fruit
蔬菜	shū cài	vegetables
市场	shì chǎng	market
给	gěi	to give objects
农场	nóng chǎng	farm

Revision Vocabulary

钱	qián	money
在	zài	to be at/ in/ on
两	liǎng	two (with MW)
块	kuài	MW for dollars

Lesson Breakdown

我要买 两个 绿色的 苹果。
Wǒ yào mǎi liǎng gè lǜ sè de píng guǒ.
I want to buy two green apples.

This sentence is filled with elements that should be familiar to us by now. It is actually a classic SVO sentence and although it may seem quite long and complicated, the elements present are all quite easy to recognize.

We can break it down as follow:

Subject + Auxiliary Verb + Verb + MW + Adjective + Object

- 我 [wǒ]

This is the Subject of the sentence and the **doer** of the action.

- 要买 [yào mǎi]

Following the Subject is the Auxiliary Verb (要) and the normal Verb (买) (Remember: Subject + 要 + Verb)

- 两个 [liǎng gè]

Quantity expressed with a general MW.

- 绿色的 [lǜ sè de]

This is the Adjective that **describes the quality of the Noun** and Object of the sentence.

- 苹果 [píng guǒ]

This is the Object of the sentence and the **receiver** of the action.

Take note of the roles of all parts of speech and what their functions are in the sentence.

你 找 我 多少钱?

Nǐ zhǎo wǒ duō shǎo qián ?

How much is the change?

找   zhǎo   to return change

找 is a Verb and is used when returning change after a purchase.
It is often used with money:
我 找 钱。
[wǒ zhǎo qián]
I return your change

It is not used for returning or giving objects. There is a specific word for this purpose:

给

[gěi]

to give

It is used specifically for giving stuff/ objects.

(Keep in mind that 找 is one of those words that also have a second meaning which is "to look for".)

Supplementary

List of common fruits:

李子	**lǐ zǐ**	plum
柚子	**yòu zi**	pomelo
椰子	**yē zi**	coconut
桃子	**táo zi**	peach
西瓜	**xī guā**	watermelon
木瓜	**mù guā**	papaya
草莓	**cǎo méi**	strawberry
香蕉	**xiāng jiāo**	banana
芒果	**máng guǒ**	mango
菠萝	**bō luó**	pineapple
葡萄	**pú tao**	grape

Download The Bonus Audio Files To Practice Your Pronunciation

My Progress

Words	QW's	MW's	TW's	Total
Count	9	15	5	243

Hint

With complex sentences, determine the *parts of speech* and what their functions are.

Self-Practice

Connect and match:

六 •   • liù •   • apple
苹果 •   • zhǎo •   • green
这里 •   • píng guǒ •   • return change
找 •   • nóng chǎng •   • six
市场 •   • gěi •   • here
农场 •   • shì chǎng •   • market
给 •   • lǜ sè •   • farm
绿色 •   • zhè li •   • to give

Write questions for the following answers:

1._____?
我找你六块钱。

2._____?
有的,今天有巧克力蛋糕。

3._____?
对,我喜欢吃苹果。

4._____?
我要一瓶可乐。

Circle the correct character in every line:

1. 硪 , 及 , 代 , 找 , 我
2. 坪 , 萍 , 评 , 苹 , 平
3. 帀 , 巾 , 什 , 市 , 师
4. 炀 , 场 , 杨 , 扬 , 疡

● Useful Words Stroke Order   Character Stroke Order ●

| 给 | 市 | 场 | 水 | 菜 |
| 绿 | 找 | 苹 | 果 | 里 |

Trace the following characters

给	给	给	给	给	给	给	给	给
市	市	市	市	市	市	市	市	市
场	场	场	场	场	场	场	场	场
水	水	水	水	水	水	水	水	水
菜	菜	菜	菜	菜	菜	菜	菜	菜
绿	绿	绿	绿	绿	绿	绿	绿	绿
找	找	找	找	找	找	找	找	找
苹	苹	苹	苹	苹	苹	苹	苹	苹
果	果	果	果	果	果	果	果	果
里	里	里	里	里	里	里	里	里

Self-Practice

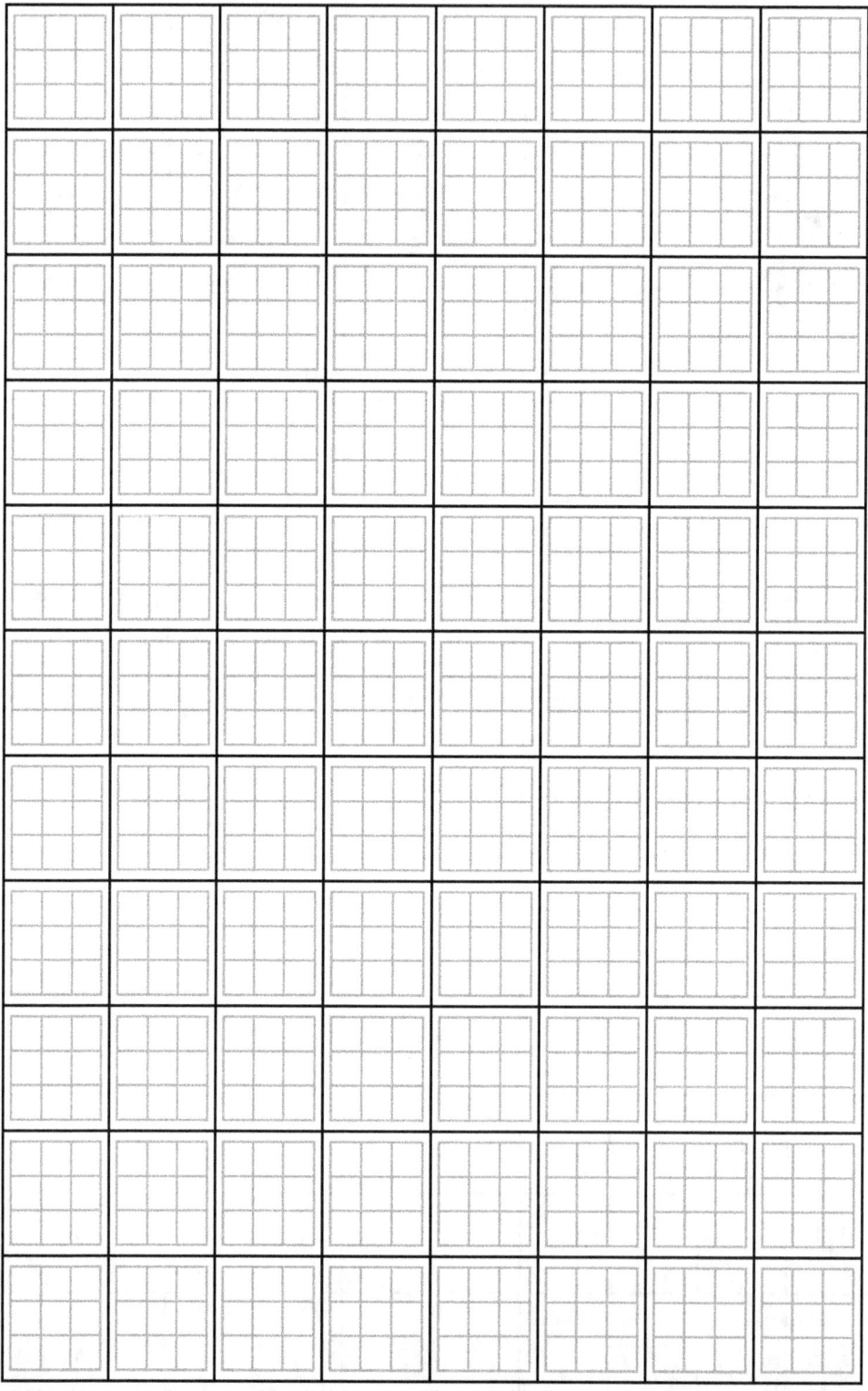

第四十三课　Unit 43

我要十个小鸡块,谢谢!
Wǒ yào shí gè xiǎo jī kuài, xiè xie!
I want ten chicken nuggets. Thanks!

现在我没有那么多。
Xiàn zài wǒ méi yǒu nà me duō.
I do not have that many at the moment.

那你现在有几块?
Nà nǐ xiàn zài yǒu jǐ kuài?
Then, how many do you have?

现在我只有八块。
Xiàn zài wǒ zhǐ yǒu bā kuài.
At this moment I only have eight pieces.

This is a dialog between customer and store owner.
The mood is casual.

Dialog Vocabulary

鸡块	jī kuài	chicken nuggets
块	kuài	piece (MW)
现在	xiàn zài	now/at present
那么	nà me	like that/ so
多	duō	many/ much
只	zhǐ	only/ just/ merely

Useful Vocabulary

最多	zuì duō	most
冰块	bīng kuài	ice
鸡	jī	chicken
鸡肉	jī ròu	chicken meat
炸	zhá	to deep fry

Revision Vocabulary

十	shí	ten
八	bā	eight
小	xiǎo	small
几	jǐ	how many
那	nà	then/ in that case

Lesson Breakdown

现在 我没有 那么多。
Xiàn zài wǒ méi yǒu nà me duō.
I don't have that many at the moment.

那么   nà me   like that/so

This word is placed in front of the Adjective to exaggerate the extend of the Adjective.

Example:

"You are **so** smart. / She is **so** tall."

You can use 这么 [zhè me] for *close objects*.

We use 那么 [nà me] for things that are *far away* or "unreachable".

> 那 你 现在 有 几 块?
> Nà nǐ xiàn zài yǒu jǐ kuài ?
> Then, how many do you have?

| 那 | nà | then/in that case |

This is a Conjunction.

Conjunctions are used in Chinese (and in English) to connect things or ideas.

They show the relationship between these ideas.

This specific Conjunction must be used in context of a preceding statement.

Immediately following 那 is a statement or a question **that is related to the original and preceding statement**.

Let's use an example to clarify.

- Original statement:

I don't have that many!

- Question:

Then, how many do you have?

Following the Conjunction (then), is a question that is related to the original statement.

It is very similar to the use of "*in that case*" in English.

It is obvious that he relationship between the two ideas is very clear.

Example:
他 不在 家。
[tā bú zài jiā]
He is not at home.

那 他一定 在 学校。
[nà, tā yí dìng zài xué xiào]
In that case, he must be at school then.

> 现在 我 只有 八块。
> Xiàn zài wǒ zhǐ yǒu bā kuài.
> At this moment I only have eight pieces.

现在   xiàn zài   now/at this moment

It literally means: "at the present moment".
We usually place this Time Word at the front of a sentence since it presents us with the time when an action is taking place.
(Other TWs include: the days of the week, today, yesterday, last year, now, in the future, etc.)

只   zhǐ   only

This Adverb is used to describe the *Verb that will follow*.
We use this structure:

只 + Verb

In our example it is used with the Verb 有 [yǒu] meaning "to have".
我 只有
[wǒ zhǐ yǒu]
I only have...

This is a very common structure and it is usually used with :
我 只有 一个。   [wǒ zhǐ **yǒu** yī gè] I only have one.
他 只给 我 三个。 [tā zhǐ **geǐ** wǒ sān gè] He only gave me three.
我 只想 看 电视。 [wǒ zhǐ **xiǎng** kàn diàn shì] I only want to watch television.

Download The Bonus Audio Files To Practice Your Pronunciation

My Progress

Words	QW's	MW's	TW's	Total
Count	9	15	6	249

Hint

The Conjunction 那 is used when replying to an original statement or question.

Unit 43

Self-Practice

Connect and match:

鸡块 •   • zhǐ •   • like that
只 •   • duō •   • piece
多 •   • jǐ kuài •   • now
那么 •   • xiàn zài •   • many/ much
现在 •   • kuài •   • chicken nugget
块 •   • jī •   • chicken
鸡 •   • jī ròu •   • only/ just
鸡肉 •   • nà me •   • chicken meat

Translate the following sentences into English:

1. Xiàn zài wǒ zhǐ yǒu bā kuài.
   _____

2. Nà nǐ xiàn zài yǒu jǐ kuài ?
   _____

3. Xiàn zài wǒ méi yǒu nà me duō.
   _____

4. Wǒ yào shí gè xiǎo jī kuài, xiè xie !
   _____

Arrange the words into sentences:

1. 你　　有　　几　　块　　现在？
   _____

2. 只有　　八　　我　　块。
   _____

3. 鸡块　　小　　个　　要　　十　　我。
   _____

4. 多　　我　　没有　　那么。
   _____

● Useful Words Stroke Order   Character Stroke Order ●

多	肉	炸	最	鸡
现	在	只	那	么

Trace the following characters

多	多	多	多	多	多	多	多	多
肉	肉	肉	肉	肉	肉	肉	肉	肉
炸	炸	炸	炸	炸	炸	炸	炸	炸
最	最	最	最	最	最	最	最	最
鸡	鸡	鸡	鸡	鸡	鸡	鸡	鸡	鸡
现	现	现	现	现	现	现	现	现
在	在	在	在	在	在	在	在	在
只	只	只	只	只	只	只	只	只
那	那	那	那	那	那	那	那	那
么	么	么	么	么	么	么	么	么

Self-Practice

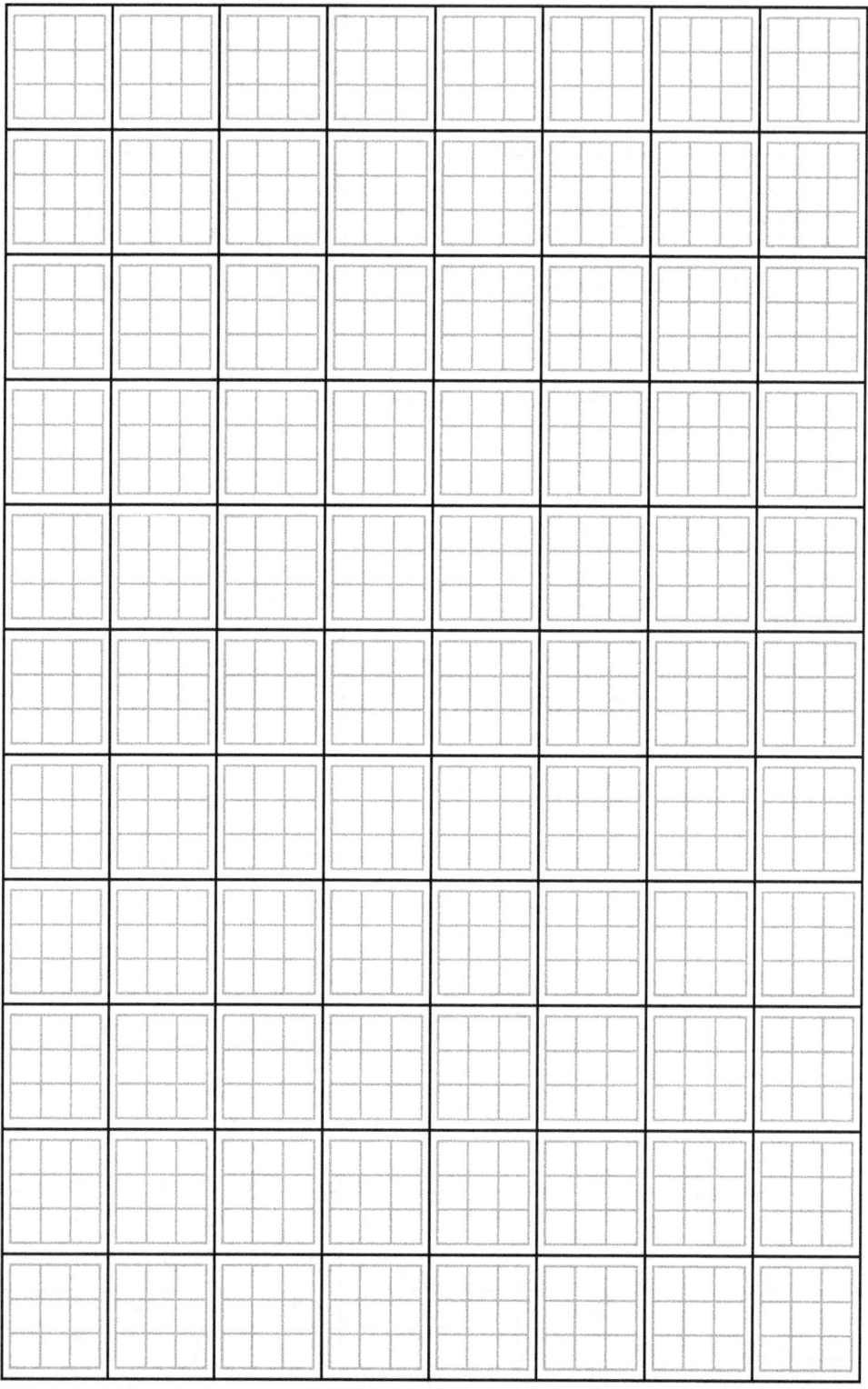

第四十四课   Unit 44

你妹妹几岁? 我喜欢她。

Nǐ mèi mei jǐ suì ? Wǒ xǐ huan tā.

How old is your sister? I like her.

什么? 你是 认真的 吗?

Shén me ? Nǐ shì rèn zhēn de ma ?

What? Are you serious?

对, 她 什么时候 有 时间 跟我 一起 出去玩?

Duì, tā shén me shí hòu yǒu shí jiān gēn wǒ yī qǐ chū qù wán ?

Yes, when does she have time to go out with me?

不要 问 我!

Bú yào wèn wǒ !

Don't ask me!

This is a dialog between two friends.
The mood is tense and the topic is sensitive.

Dialog Vocabulary

妹妹	mèi mei	younger sister
认真	rèn zhēn	to be serious
一起	yī qǐ	together
出去	chū qù	to go out
什么时候	shén me shí hòu	when?
时间	shí jiān	time
问	wèn	to ask
岁	suì	MW (age)

Useful Vocabulary

姐姐	jiě jie	older sister
哥哥	gē ge	older brother
弟弟	dì di	younger brother
爸爸	bà ba	father
妈妈	mā ma	mother

Revision Vocabulary

什么	shén me	what?
有	yǒu	to have
几	jǐ	how many?
玩	wán	to play
跟	gēn	with

Lesson Breakdown

你 妹妹 几 岁？我 喜欢 她。

Nǐ mèi mei jǐ suì ? Wǒ xǐ huan tā.

How old is your sister? I like her.

岁	suì	MW for age

This word is a MW and it always **used with age**.

It is the official classifier for age and we have to follow a specific sentence structure:

Subject + Age + 岁

Let's look at some **example** sentences:

你几岁？[nǐ jǐ suì]
How old are you?

我十岁。[wǒ shí suì]
I am ten years old.

Take note that it is not necessary to add another MW. It is also unnecessary to add 是 meaning "to be". In English we use "am, is, are" to indicate a person's age, but it is not necessary in Chinese.

> 对, 她 什么时候 有 时间 跟我 一起 出去玩？
> Duì, tā shén me shí hòu yǒu shí jiān gēn wǒ yī qǐ chū qù wán ?
> Yes, when does she have time to go out with me?

什么时候   shén me shí hòu   when?

This is another QW that is quite easy to use. When using this word, we have to follow a specific structure:

Subject + 什么 时候 + Predicate

(The Predicate is the part of the sentence that expresses what is said about the Subject.)

Example:
他 什么时候 要 回去？
[tā shén me shí hòu yào húi qù]
When does he want to go home?

出去   chū qù   to go out

This word is a compliment of direction. It means "to go out" or "to leave". Let's look at the individual characters.

The Verb 出 [chū] means: to go or come **out**.

The Verb 去 [qù] means: to **go**.

Directional complements follow a specific structure:
Verb + 去／来 (The direction can be *away* or *towards* speaker.)
Example:
- 出去 [chū qù] means "go out".

The movement is out and **away from** the speaker.
"The picnic is under the tree. Let's **go outside**." (**Speaker is inside.**)

- 出来 [chū lái] means "come out".

The movement is out and **towards** the speaker.
"The house has a gas leak. **Come outside**!" (**Speaker is outside.**)

> 不要问我! 你 太老了!
> Bú yào wèn wǒ ! Nǐ tài lǎo le !
> Don't ask me. You are too old!

| 不要 | bú yào | Don't! |

This is a command that is used to tell somebody **not to do something**. This command follows a specific structure:
(Subject) + 不要 + Verb
Note that normally the Subject is omitted.
Example:
不要 推 我!
[bú yào tuī wǒ]
Don't push me!
The mood is stern and urgent; typical of a command.

Download The Bonus Audio Files To Practice Your Pronunciation

My Progress

Words	QW's	MW's	TW's	Total
Count	10	16	6	257

Hint

A command does not need a Subject. They are usually short reprimands.

Self-Practice

Connect and match:

妹妹 •	• shénme shí hòu •	• MW age
认真 •	• mèi mei •	• to ask
一起 •	• rèn zhēn •	• time
出去 •	• suì •	• when
时间 •	• wèn •	• to go out
问 •	• shí jiān •	• together
岁 •	• chū qù •	• to be serious
什么时候 •	• yī qǐ •	• younger sister

Rewrite the following sentences into Pinyin:

1. How old is you sister? _____
2. How old are you? _____
3. Are you serious? _____
4. Don't ask me! _____
5. I like your sister. _____
6. Do you have time at the moment? _____

Circle the correct character in every line:

1. 赿 ， 走 ， 越 ， 起 ， 超
2. 崼 ， 世 ， 比 ， 山 ， 出
3. 发 ， 岁 ， 学 ， 歹 ， 岑
4. 籵 ， 忊 ， 旿 ， 寸 ， 时

Useful Words Stroke Order — Character Stroke Order

妹	问	认	真	起
出	候	时	间	岁

Trace the following characters

妹	妹	妹	妹	妹	妹	妹	妹	妹	妹
问	问	问	问	问	问	问	问	问	问
认	认	认	认	认	认	认	认	认	认
真	真	真	真	真	真	真	真	真	真
起	起	起	起	起	起	起	起	起	起
出	出	出	出	出	出	出	出	出	出
候	候	候	候	候	候	候	候	候	候
时	时	时	时	时	时	时	时	时	时
间	间	间	间	间	间	间	间	间	间
岁	岁	岁	岁	岁	岁	岁	岁	岁	岁

Self-Practice

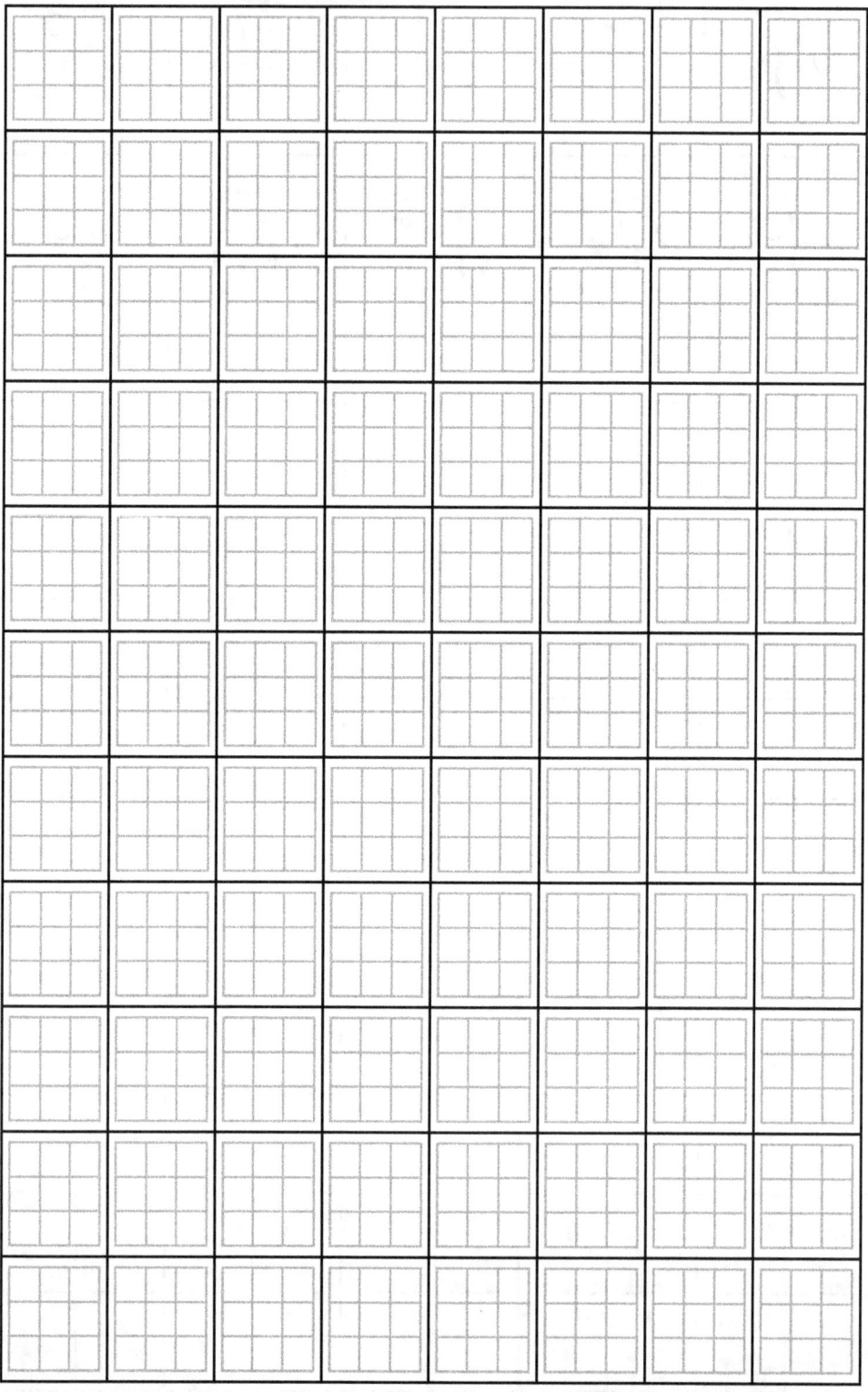

第四十五课　　Unit 45

你有 弟弟 可以 一起 玩 吗?
Nǐ yǒu dì di kě yǐ yì qǐ wán ma ?
Do you have a (younger) brother to play with?

对, 我们 两个 常常 一起玩。
Duì, wǒ men liǎng gè cháng cháng yì qǐ wán.
Yes, the two of us often play together.

我有 两个 姐姐。
Wǒ yǒu liǎng gè jiě jie.
I have two (older) sisters.

我没有姐姐, 没有人 可以 照顾 我。
Wǒ méi yǒu jiě jie, méi yǒu rén kě yǐ zhào gù wǒ.
I don't have a sister or anyone who can take care of me.

This is a dialog between two children.
Both are young and innocent.

Dialog Vocabulary

弟弟	dì di	younger brother
姐姐	jiě jie	older sister
照顾	zhào gù	to take care of
可以	kě yǐ	can/ may
常常	cháng cháng	often

Useful Vocabulary

抱	bào	to hug
好玩	hǎo wán	fun/ amusing
年轻	nián qīng	young
介绍	jié sháo	to introduce
兄弟	xiōng di	brothers
姐妹	jiě mèi	sisters

Revision Vocabulary

有	yǒu	to have
没有	méi yǒu	not to have
两	liǎng	two (MW)
玩	wán	to play
一起	yì qǐ	together

Lesson Breakdown

> 没有人 可以 照顾 我。
> Méi yǒu rén kě yǐ zhào gù wǒ.
> I don't have anyone who can take care of me.

没有人   méi yǒu rén   nobody

This phrase literally means: "do not have a person".
Correctly translated it means *nobody*.
These days it's common for people to omit the 有 and to say:
没人 [méi rén]

As mentioned earlier (Unit 25) this Verb is used not only for objects, but also for people.

When using the Verb "to have" and also "not to have", note that both 有 [yǒu] and 没有 [méi yǒu] are followed by Nouns.

These Nouns can represent people, animals, things, time, manners, etc.

> 你跟弟弟 可以 一起 玩 吗?
> Nǐ gēn dì di kě yǐ yì qǐ wán ma ?
> Do you have a (younger)brother to play with?

弟弟　　　dì di　　　younger brother

This is the word for younger brother.

Important to note the importance of distinguishing between *siblings*. This is related to the position and responsibilities of each family member.

Besides younger brother, we can also look at the word for older brother.

哥哥 [gēge] means: older brother

When we want to speak about brothers in general, we use a more informal description:

兄弟

[xiōng dì]

brothers

This is a Noun and it is used colloquially when we are not sure who the elder sibling of the two is.

Example:
他们 两个 是 兄弟。
[tāmen liǎng gè shì xiōng dì]
Those two are brothers.

> 我有 两个 姐姐。
> Wǒ yǒu liǎng gè jiě jie.
> I have two (older) sisters.

姐姐　　　**jiě jie**　　　older sister

This is the word for older sister. We distinguish between the younger and older female siblings, just as we did with the brothers.

妹妹

[meìmei]

younger sister (N)

When we want to speak about sisters in general, we use a more informal description:

姐妹

[jiě meì]

sisters

This is a Noun and it is also used colloquially when we are not sure who the elder sibling of the two is.

Example:

她们 两个 是 姐妹。

[tāmen liǎng gè shì jiě meì]

Those two are sisters.

Writing: Radicals

Look at the following two characters:

妹妹 and 姐姐

When writing these characters, note that the female radical 女 is present in both of these words.

(See Unit 47 for the Chinese family member list.)

Download The Bonus Audio Files To Practice Your Pronunciation

My Progress

Words	QW's	MW's	TW's	Total
Count	10	16	6	262

Hint

The Chinese family tree is quite complex. Make sure you are familiar with immediate family.

Self-Practice

Connect and match:

弟弟 •	• cháng cháng •	• younger brother
姐姐 •	• jiě mèi •	• brothers
照顾 •	• xiōng di •	• sisters
可以 •	• bào •	• often
常常 •	• jiě jie •	• can
抱 •	• dì di •	• to hug
兄弟 •	• kě yǐ •	• to take care of
姐妹 •	• zhào gù •	• older sister

Translate the following sentences into English:

1. Wǒ méi yǒu jiě jie, méi yǒu rén kě yǐ zhào gù wǒ.
   _____

2. Wǒ yǒu liǎng gè jiě jie.
   _____

3. Duì, wǒ men liǎng gè cháng cháng yì qǐ wán.
   _____

4. Nǐ yǒu dì di kě yǐ yì qǐ wán ma?
   _____

Arrange the words into sentences:

1. 玩　　一起　　可以　　吗　　我们？
   _____

2. 一起　　我们　　常常　　玩。
   _____

3. 弟弟　　我　　没有。
   _____

4. 姐姐　　个　　我　　两　　有。
   _____

Useful Words Stroke Order — Character Stroke Order

姐	年	轻	介	绍
弟	照	顾	以	常

Trace the following characters

姐	姐	姐	姐	姐	姐	姐	姐	姐	姐
年	年	年	年	年	年	年	年	年	年
轻	轻	轻	轻	轻	轻	轻	轻	轻	轻
介	介	介	介	介	介	介	介	介	介
绍	绍	绍	绍	绍	绍	绍	绍	绍	绍
弟	弟	弟	弟	弟	弟	弟	弟	弟	弟
照	照	照	照	照	照	照	照	照	照
顾	顾	顾	顾	顾	顾	顾	顾	顾	顾
以	以	以	以	以	以	以	以	以	以
常	常	常	常	常	常	常	常	常	常

Self-Practice

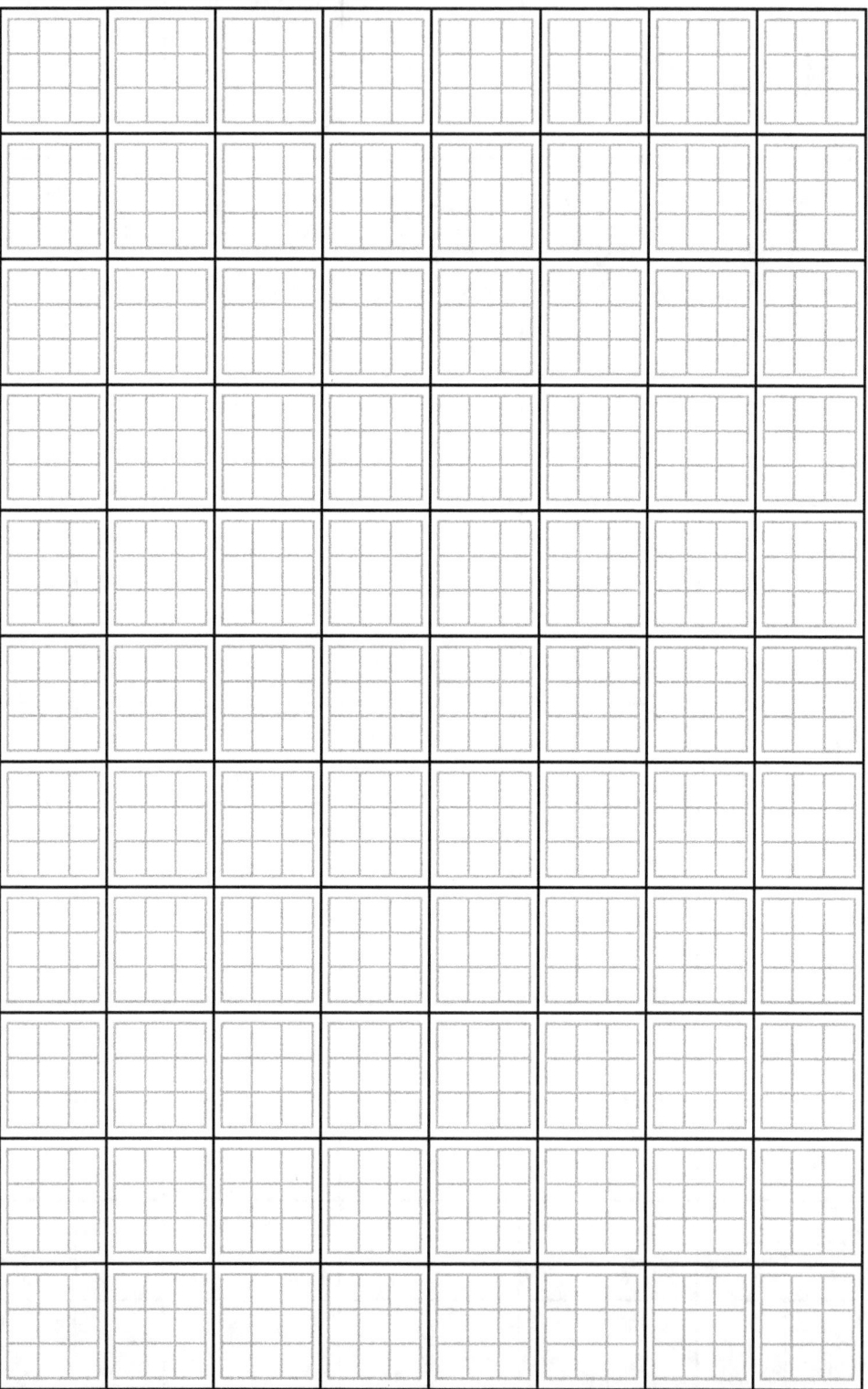

第四十六课　　　Unit 46

我爸爸是日本人，他住在日本。
Wǒ bà ba shì rì běn rén, tā zhù zài rì běn.
My father is Japanese. He lives in Japan.

那你妈妈呢?
Nà nǐ mā ma ne?
And your mother?

她是美国人，她也住在日本。
Tā shì měi guó rén, tā yě zhù zài rì běn.
She is American. She also lives in Japan.

哇～你们家好特别!
Wā, nǐ men jiā hǎo tè bié!
Wow! Your family is quite special.

This is a dialog between two classmates.
Both are curious about the other.

Dialog Vocabulary

爸爸	bà ba	father
妈妈	mā ma	mother
住	zhù	to live
特别	tè bié	special
哇	wā	Wow! (surprise)

Useful Vocabulary

父母	fù mǔ	parents
母	mǔ	mother
父	fù	father
外国人	wài guó rén	foreigner
家庭	jiā tíng	family/household

Revision Vocabulary

日本人	rì běn rén	Japanese
美国人	měi guó rén	American
呢	ne	what about...?
家	jiā	home/ family
那	nà	then/ in that case

Lesson Breakdown

哇～你们家 好 特别!
Wā, nǐ men jiā hǎo tè bié!
Wow! Your family is quite special.

哇	wā	Wow!

This is an Exclamative particle of *wonder*.
It is used to indicate *surprise and approval*.
When used for this specific purpose, we place the particle at the beginning of the sentence.

> 我爸爸是日本人,他住在日本。
> Wǒ bà ba shì rì běn rén , tā zhù zài rì běn .
> My father is Japanese. He lives in Japan.

住　　　zhù　　　to live/stay

This Verb can mean *to live* at a place like a country, town or a house. It can also mean *to stay* at a hotel, dormitory, hospital, etc. It usually (but not exclusively) follows a specific structure:

Subject + 住 + 在 + Place

Note that 住 is followed by 在 [zài] which indicates *at, on, in*.

Example:
他住在哪里?
[tā zhù zài nǎ li]
Where does he live?

> 你们家好特别!
> Nǐ men jiā hǎo tè bié !
> Your family is quite special.

特别　　　tè bié　　　special

This word functions as an Adjective in our example. When used as an Adjective or SV it means *to be special*.

It can also function as an Adverb. As an Adverb it will be used in a sentence to describe the Verb/ Adjective and it means *especially*.

Example:
他做的菜特别好吃。
[tā zuò de cài tè bié hǎo chī]
His food is **especially** delicious.
她特别漂亮。
[tā tè bié piào liang]
She is **especially** beautiful.

Supplementary

Writing: Radicals

妈妈　　mā ma　　mother

We continue to look for ways to recognize and understand the individual characters. Let's take a closer look at the word for "mother".

The first radical present is the *female radical*:

女 [nǔ] woman

This clearly adds the female element (mother) and sets it apart from similar characters like:

马 and 吗

Thus, when we combine the radical with the word the result is:

女 + 马 = 妈

爸爸　　bà ba　　father

Similarly, let's look at the word for "father". The first radical on top is the *father radical*:

父 [fù] father

This adds the *male* element. It is different from similar characters like:

巴 , 吧 , 把

Thus, when we combine the radical with the word the result is:

父 + 巴 = 爸

Download The Bonus Audio Files To Practice Your Pronunciation

My Progress

Words	QW's	MW's	TW's	Total
Count	10	16	6	267

Hint

The Verb 住 is followed by 在 which acts as a Preposition to tell us *where the place is*.

Self-Practice

Connect and match:

爸爸 •   • tè bié •   • mother
妈妈 •   • zhù •   • father
住 •   • wā •   • Wow!
哇 •   • mā ma •   • to live
特别 •   • bà ba •   • special
父母 •   • mǔ •   • parents
父 •   • fù mǔ •   • mother
母 •   • fù •   • father

Write questions for the following answers:

1._____?
我 妈妈 是 日本人。
2._____?
我 爸爸 住 在 日本。
3._____?
我 没有 姐姐。
4._____?
我 妹妹 十八 岁。

Circle the correct character in every line:

1. 每 , 丹 , 莓 , 每 , 母
2. 柱 , 注 , 住 , 往 , 主
3. 兄 , 男 , 别 , 另 , 另
4. 得 , 夺 , 时 , 待 , 特

Useful Words Stroke Order   Character Stroke Order

Trace the following characters

父									
母									
外									
国									
庭									
爸									
妈									
住									
特									
别									

Self-Practice

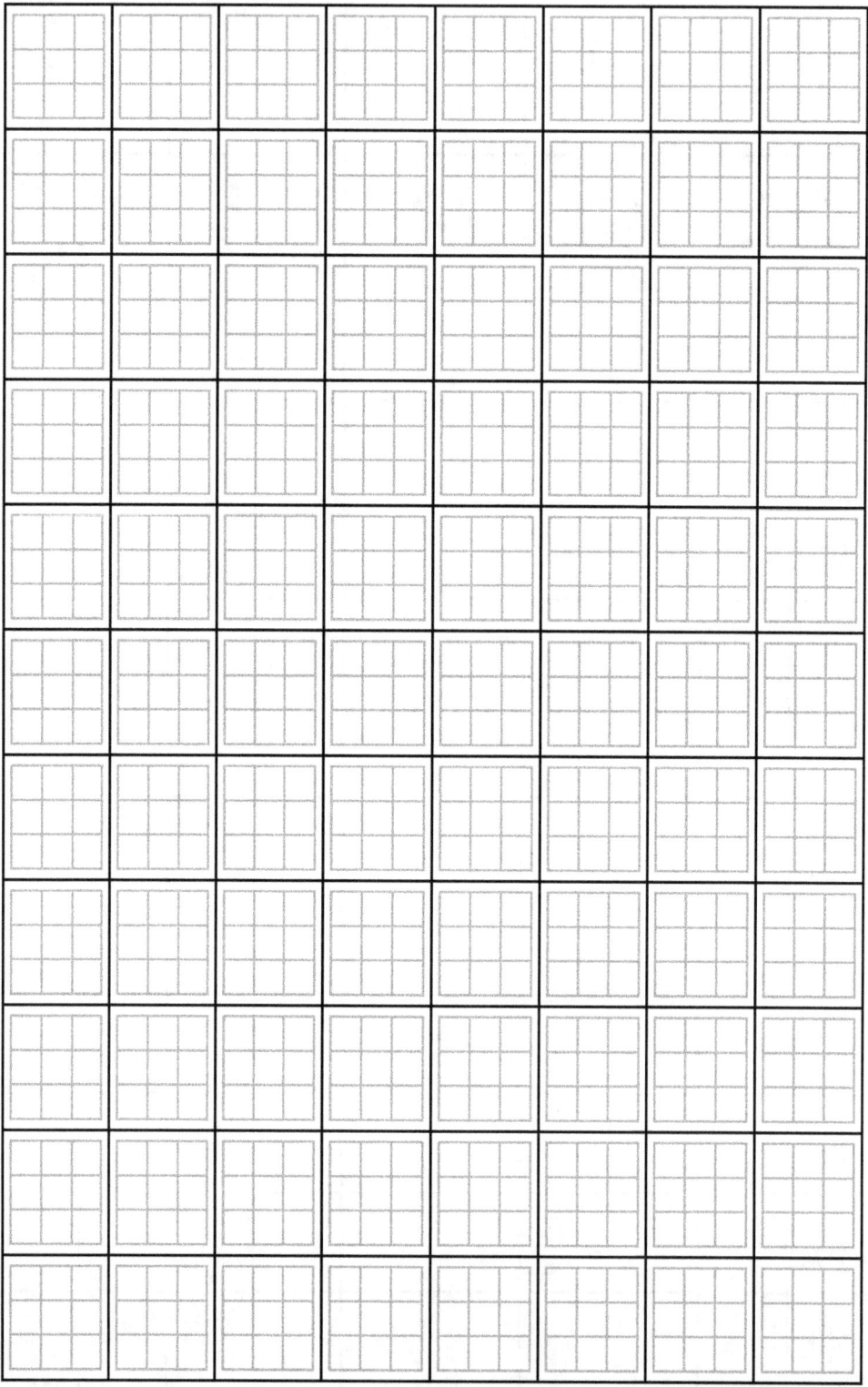

第四十七课　　Unit 47

你看这张照片，这是我的家人。
Nǐ kàn zhè zhāng zhào piàn, zhè shì wǒ de jiā rén.
Look at this photo. It's my family.

这是谁?
Zhè shì shéi?
Who is this?

这是我哥哥。
Zhè shì wǒ gē ge.
This is my older brother.

他很高，很瘦又很帅。
Tā hěn gāo, hěn shòu yòu hěn shuài.
He is tall, skinny and handsome.

This is a dialog between two friends who are browsing through a family album. They are old friends and the mood is casual.

Dialog Vocabulary

高	gāo	to be tall
哥哥	gē ge	older brother
照片	zhào piàn	photo
帅	shuài	to be handsome
张	zhāng	MW photo, paper

Useful Vocabulary

聪明	cōng míng	to be smart
强壮	qiáng zhuàng	strong/ capable
害羞	hài xiū	to be shy
胖	pàng	to be fat
矮	ǎi	to be short
像	xiàng	to resemble
再说	zài shuō	besides

Revision Vocabulary

家人	jiā rén	family
谁	shéi	who
也	yě	also
又	yòu	furthermore/also

Lesson Breakdown

> 他很高。
> Tā hěn gāo.
> He is tall.

In English, **Adjectives** are used to describe Nouns.

Example: The car is **blue**.

(Blue describes the car.)

Throughout this guide, we have been using the word "Adjectives", to avoid confusion. Take note that, **in Chinese, Adjectives are called Stative Verbs** and, not only do they describe the Noun, they also describe the **quality** of the Subject or the Noun.

We use words like 很 , 好 , 真 , 非常 to connect the Stative verb to the subject or Noun.

We can call them joining words:

他 很 高。　　[Tā hěn gāo]　　　He is (**quite**) tall.
他 好 高。　　[Tā hǎo gāo]　　　He is **very** tall.
他 真 高。　　[Tā zhēn gāo]　　　He is **really** tall.
他 非常 高。　[Tā fēi cháng gāo]　He is **extremely** tall.

Notice the *degree of tallness*.

So the function of 很 is to connect the Subject/ Noun and the Stative Verb by indicating the degree of quality. That's why we call 很 a "joining word". This is an extremely important concept and one that we have stressed continuously throughout this guide.

Summary: 很 normally means quite or very. However, when 很 is used to connect a subject and a Stative verb, its function is to indicate degree or quality.

Don't get confused: An Adjective = a Stative Verb.

> 你 看 这 张 照片，这 是 我的 家人。
> Nǐ kàn zhè zhāng zhào piàn, zhè shì wǒ de jiā rén.
> Look at this photo. It's my family.

这　　　　zhè　　　　this

This word is a Demonstrative Pronoun. If you use it before a Noun, you need to **include a Measure Word**. In our example the Measure Word is 张 [zhāng], as mentioned in Unit 39. (This MW is used for objects made out of paper. This includes photographs and pictures.)

We use the following structure:

这 + MW + Noun

Example:
这 瓶 水。
[zhè píng shuǐ]
This bottle of water.

Supplementary

General list of family members:

(A complete list would take up to 3 pages of space!)

爸爸	bà ba	your dad
妈妈	mā ma	your mom
爷爷	yé ye	dad's dad
奶奶	nǎi nai	dad's mom
外公	wài gōng	mom's dad
姥姥	lǎo lao	mom's mom
哥哥	gē ge	older brother
弟弟	dì di	younger brother
姐姐	jiě jie	older sister
妹妹	mèi mei	younger sister
伯伯	bó bo	dad's older brother
叔叔	shū shu	dad's younger brother
姑姑	gū gu	dad's sister
舅舅	jiù jiu	mom's brother
阿姨	ā yí	mom's sister

Download The Bonus Audio Files To Practice Your Pronunciation

My Progress

Words	QW's	MW's	TW's	Total
Count	10	17	6	272

Hint

To memorize family members, **associate** a name of an actual family member with the word.

Self-Practice

Connect and match:

哥哥 •	• qiáng zhuàng •	• MW photo
照片 •	• cōng míng •	• older brother
帅 •	• hài xiū •	• photo
张 •	• xiàng •	• to be smart
聪明 •	• gē ge •	• strong
害羞 •	• zhào piàn •	• to be shy
像 •	• shuài •	• to resemble
强壮 •	• zhāng •	• to be handsome

Translate the following sentences into English:

1. Tā hěn gāo, hěn shòu yòu hěn shuài.
   _____

2. Zhè shì wǒ gē ge.
   _____

3. Zhè shì shéi ?
   _____

4. Nǐ kàn zhè zhāng zhào piàn, zhè shì wǒ de jiā rén.
   _____

Arrange the words into sentences:

1. 看　你　照片　张　这。
   _____

2. 是　这　谁？
   _____

3. 我　这　是　家人。
   _____

4. 是　我　哥哥　他。
   _____

● Useful Words Stroke Order   Character Stroke Order ●

| 聪 | 明 | 害 | 胖 | 像 |
| 照 | 片 | 张 | 哥 | 帅 |

Trace the following characters

聪	聪	聪	聪	聪	聪	聪	聪	聪	聪
明	明	明	明	明	明	明	明	明	明
害	害	害	害	害	害	害	害	害	害
胖	胖	胖	胖	胖	胖	胖	胖	胖	胖
像	像	像	像	像	像	像	像	像	像
照	照	照	照	照	照	照	照	照	照
片	片	片	片	片	片	片	片	片	片
张	张	张	张	张	张	张	张	张	张
哥	哥	哥	哥	哥	哥	哥	哥	哥	哥
帅	帅	帅	帅	帅	帅	帅	帅	帅	帅

Self-Practice

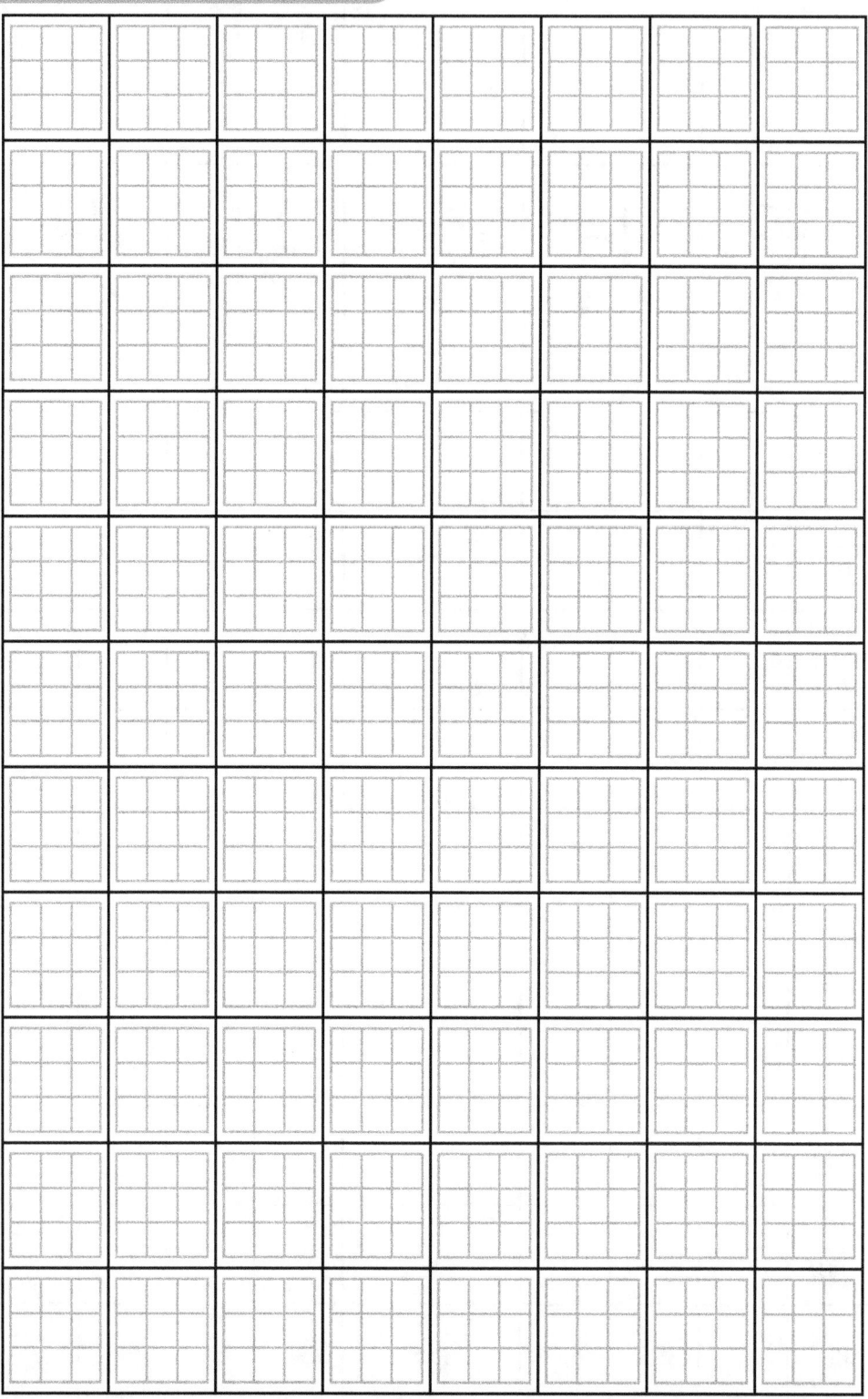

第四十八课　Unit 48

你弟弟是做什么的?
Nǐ dì di shì zuò shén me de?
What does your younger brother do?

我弟弟是医生,在成功医院。
Wǒ dì di shì yī shēng, zài Chéng Gōng yī yuàn.
My younger brother is a doctor at Cheng Gong hospital.

那很不错,他应该很有钱。
Nà hěn bú cuò, tā yīng gāi hěn yǒu qián.
Very nice. He must be rich.

我哥哥是老师。
Wǒ gē ge shì lǎo shī.
My older brother is a teacher.

This is a dialog between two friends.
The mood is pleasant and relaxed.

Dialog Vocabulary

医生	yī shēng	doctor
老师	lǎo shī	teacher
有钱	yǒu qián	to be rich
做	zuò	to do
医院	yī yuàn	hospital
成功	Chéng Gōng	success

Useful Vocabulary

律师	lǜ shī	lawyer
护士	hù shì	nurse
厨师	chú shī	chef
薪水	xīn shuǐ	salary/ wage
工作	gōng zuò	to work/ operate

Revision Vocabulary

弟弟	dì di	younger brother
哥哥	gē ge	older brother
应该	yīng gāi	should/ ought to
不错	bú cuò	excellent
那	nà	then/ in that case

Lesson Breakdown

你弟弟 是 做什么的?

Nǐ dì di shì zuò shén me de?

What does your younger brother do?

The use of 是....的 simply **puts emphasis on a specific part of the sentence**.

The part of the sentence to be emphasized can represent Time, Place or Means of an action.

We notice that 是 is immediately followed by a Verb (indicating the action, to do) and then followed by particle 的.

We use the following structure:
Subject + 是 + Part to emphasize + Verb + 的

Example:
他 是 昨天来 的。
[tā shì zuó tiān lái de]
He came yesterday.

This structure is often present when describing actions that took place in the past or that have been taking place for a while.

When using this pattern, keep in mind what exactly needs to be emphasized and simply place it in between 是 and 的.

You can **emphasize** the **Time, the Place, the Means or Specific detail** concerning the action.

> 做   zuò   to do

This is a Verb that means *to do, or to engage in* and it can describe quite a few activities. Let's look at our example sentence:

你弟弟 是 做 什么 的?
[nǐ dì di shì zuò shén me de?]
What does he do?

We can change the meaning of the Verb by adding an Object or an Adverb.

• **Adding an Adverb (在) :**
他 在 做 什么?
[tā zài zuò shén me?]
What is he **doing now**?

We added the Adverb 在 [zài] to indicate that the action is **ongoing and happening now**. This is similar to the Continuous tense in English (Verb + ing).

We can use this Adverb with various activities:
What is he doing, writing, cooking, saying, making, etc.

• **Adding an Object and creating a VO compound:**

做 饭

[zuò fàn]

to cook (VO)

We added the Object 饭 [fàn] meaning *food*.

他 在 做 饭。

[tā zài zuò fàn]

He is cooking.

(Compare this with Unit 23 where we discussed the VO compounds.)

> 那 很 不错, 他 应该 很 有钱。
> Nà hěn bú cuò, tā yīng gāi hěn yǒu qián.
> Very nice. He must be rich.

有钱   yǒu qián   to be rich

This is an Adjective.

To "have" money in Chinese, generally means: to be rich.

Interesting to note, that "face" is very important in Chinese culture. You are supposed to present yourself as a successful individual and the belief is, that this attitude will inspire good fortune and wealth.

This, combined with the Chinese mantra:

"努力 工作 会 成功 了!"

[nǔ lì gōng zuò huì chéng gōng le]

Work hard and you'll succeed!

...makes the Chinese a very industrious nation.

Download The Bonus Audio Files To Practice Your Pronunciation

My Progress

Words	QW's	MW's	TW's	Total
Count	10	17	6	278

Hint

When visiting China, don't feel offended when asked about your salary or bank balance. Normal.

Self-Practice

Connect and match:

医生 •	• yī yuàn •	• doctor
老师 •	• zuò •	• to work
有钱 •	• hù shì •	• to be rich
医院 •	• chéng gōng •	• hospital
做 •	• yǒu qián •	• teacher
成功 •	• lǎo shī •	• to do
护士 •	• gōng zuò •	• success
工作 •	• yī shēng •	• nurse

Rewrite the following sentences into Pinyin:

1. He much be rich. _____
2. My brother is a doctor. _____
3. My sister is a nurse. _____
4. What does your younger brother do. _____
5. My mother is a teacher. _____
6. I am not a teacher. _____

Circle the correct character in every line:

1. 区, 匝, 匡, 医, 叵
2. 谅, 亮, 挽, 园, 院
3. 老, 教, 者, 尧, 先
4. 柿, 币, 市, 师, 帅

• Useful Words Stroke Order   Character Stroke Order •

作	护	士	老	师
做	医	院	成	功

Trace the following characters

作	作	作	作	作	作	作	作	作
护	护	护	护	护	护	护	护	护
士	士	士	士	士	士	士	士	士
老	老	老	老	老	老	老	老	老
师	师	师	师	师	师	师	师	师
做	做	做	做	做	做	做	做	做
医	医	医	医	医	医	医	医	医
院	院	院	院	院	院	院	院	院
成	成	成	成	成	成	成	成	成
功	功	功	功	功	功	功	功	功

Self-Practice

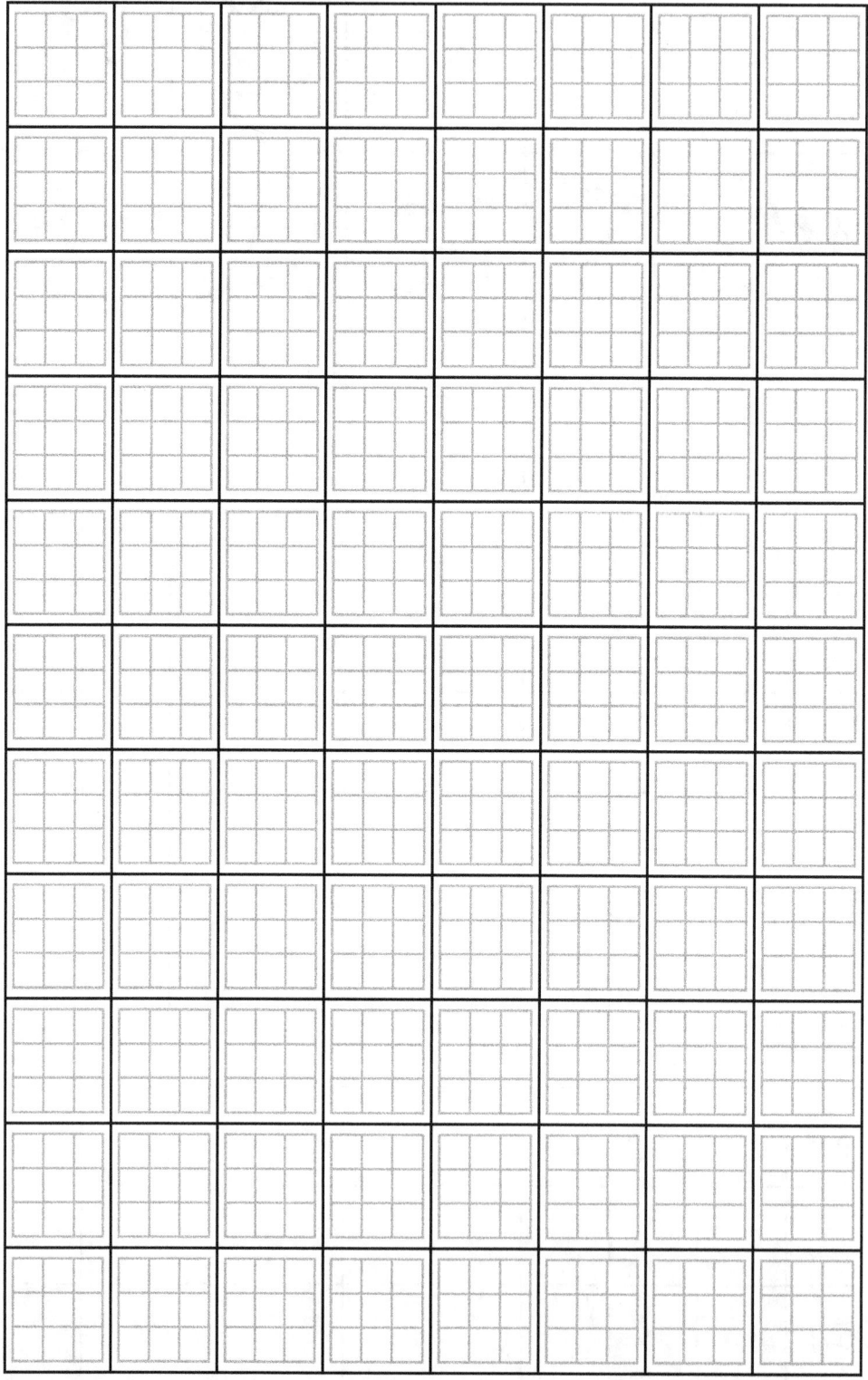

第四十九课　　Unit 49

我们家 是个 大 家庭。
Wǒ men jiā shì gè dà jiā tíng.
We have a large household.

你的 家庭 有 几个 小孩?
Nǐ de jiā tíng yǒu jǐ gè xiǎo hái?
How many children in your household?

十一个 小孩, 我们 都 很 用功。
Shí yī gè xiǎo hái, wǒ men dōu hěn yòng gōng.
Eleven children. We are all very diligent.

我知道, 你们 都 很 用功 又很 有礼貌。
Wǒ zhī dào, nǐ men dōu hěn yòng gōng yòu hěn yǒu lǐ mào.
I know. You are all very diligent and very courteous.

This is a dialog between two friends in high school.
Both are top students and the mood is polite.

Dialog Vocabulary

大	dà	large
小孩	xiǎo hái	child(ren)
十一	shí yī	eleven
用功	yòng gōng	diligent
有礼貌	yǒu lǐ mào	to be polite
家庭	jiā tíng	family/household

Useful Vocabulary

十二	shí èr	twelve
十三	shí sān	thirteen
十四	shí sì	fourteen
十五	shí wǔ	fifteen
房子	fáng zi	house

Revision Vocabulary

家	jiā	home
几	jǐ	how many
都	dōu	all/ both
知道	zhī dào	to know
又	yòu	furthermore/ also

Lesson Breakdown

> 我们家 是个 大 家庭。
> Wǒ men jiā shì gè dà jiā tíng.
> We have a large household.

家庭	jiā tíng	household

This Noun implies the general household as made up by the members living in the house.

To avoid confusion, let's make a comprehensive comparison of the words related to *house, household and family*.

家庭 vs. 家 vs. 房子

- 房子 [fángzi] house

This word is a Noun and it implies the actual **physical house** as made from brick and mortar:

我的 房子 很大。
[wǒ de fáng zi hěn dà]
My house is large.

- 家庭 [jiā tíng] household

This Noun implies the **general household** as made up by the members living in the house:

每个 家庭 都有电视。
[měi ge jiā tíng dōu yǒu diàn shì]
Every household has a TV.

- 家 [jiā] home

This Noun implies the **place** where a person lives. It can be any type of building:

我 回 家。
[wǒ huí jiā]
I go home.

| 个 | gè | general MW |

In our example sentence this general MW is used with 是 as:

... 是 个 大家庭 [...shè gè dà jiā tíng]

Usually this MW is used with the standard structure as:

Number + 个 + Noun

However, if the number used is **one** (1), then we can **omit** it. It allows us to use a simpler structure:

Verb + 个 + Noun

Example:

他 是 个 好人。
[tā shì gè hǎo rén]
He is a good person.

> 你们 都 很 用功 又很 有礼貌。
> Nǐ men dōu hěn yòng gōng yòu hěn yǒu lǐ mào.
> You are all very diligent and very courteous.

有礼貌   yǒu lǐ mào   to be well-mannered

This word means: to be polite/ courteous

礼 貌

[lǐ mào]

manners (N)

Note that this word functions as a Noun. To use it as an Adjective to describe a person, we need to add the Verb "to have".

有 礼貌

[yǒu lǐ mào]

to be polite (Adj)

It literally means: "*to have* manners".

没 礼貌

[meí lǐ mào]

to be rude (Adj)

This expression literally means: "*not to have* manners".

Take note of the use of (没)有 when changing the meaning of an Adjective (SV).

Download The Bonus Audio Files To Practice Your Pronunciation

My Progress

Words	QW's	MW's	TW's	Total
Count	10	17	6	284

Hint

Always be on best behavior when meeting new Chinese friends. Rudeness is truly frowned upon.

Self-Practice

Connect and match:

小孩 •	• shí yī •	• thirteen
十一 •	• shí èr •	• child
用功 •	• shí sān •	• eleven
家庭 •	• fáng zi •	• household
礼貌 •	• lǐ mào •	• twelve
房子 •	• yòng gōng •	• house
十二 •	• jiā tíng •	• polite
十三 •	• xiǎo hái •	• diligent

Translate the following sentences into English:

1. Wǒ men jiā shì gè dà jiā tíng.
   _____

2. Nǐ de jiā tíng yǒu jǐ gè xiǎo hái?
   _____

3. Shí yī gè xiǎo hái.
   _____

4. Nǐ men dōu hěn yòng gōng.
   _____

Arrange the words into sentences:

1. 小孩　个　几　家庭　有　你的？
   _____

2. 你们　都　用功　很。
   _____

3. 有　很　礼貌　他。
   _____

4. 家　是　大　家庭　我们　一。
   _____

● Useful Words Stroke Order   Character Stroke Order ●

都	知	道	几	房
用	小	孩	礼	貌

Trace the following characters

都	都	都	都	都	都	都	都	都
知	知	知	知	知	知	知	知	知
道	道	道	道	道	道	道	道	道
几	几	几	几	几	几	几	几	几
房	房	房	房	房	房	房	房	房
用	用	用	用	用	用	用	用	用
小	小	小	小	小	小	小	小	小
孩	孩	孩	孩	孩	孩	孩	孩	孩
礼	礼	礼	礼	礼	礼	礼	礼	礼
貌	貌	貌	貌	貌	貌	貌	貌	貌

Self-Practice

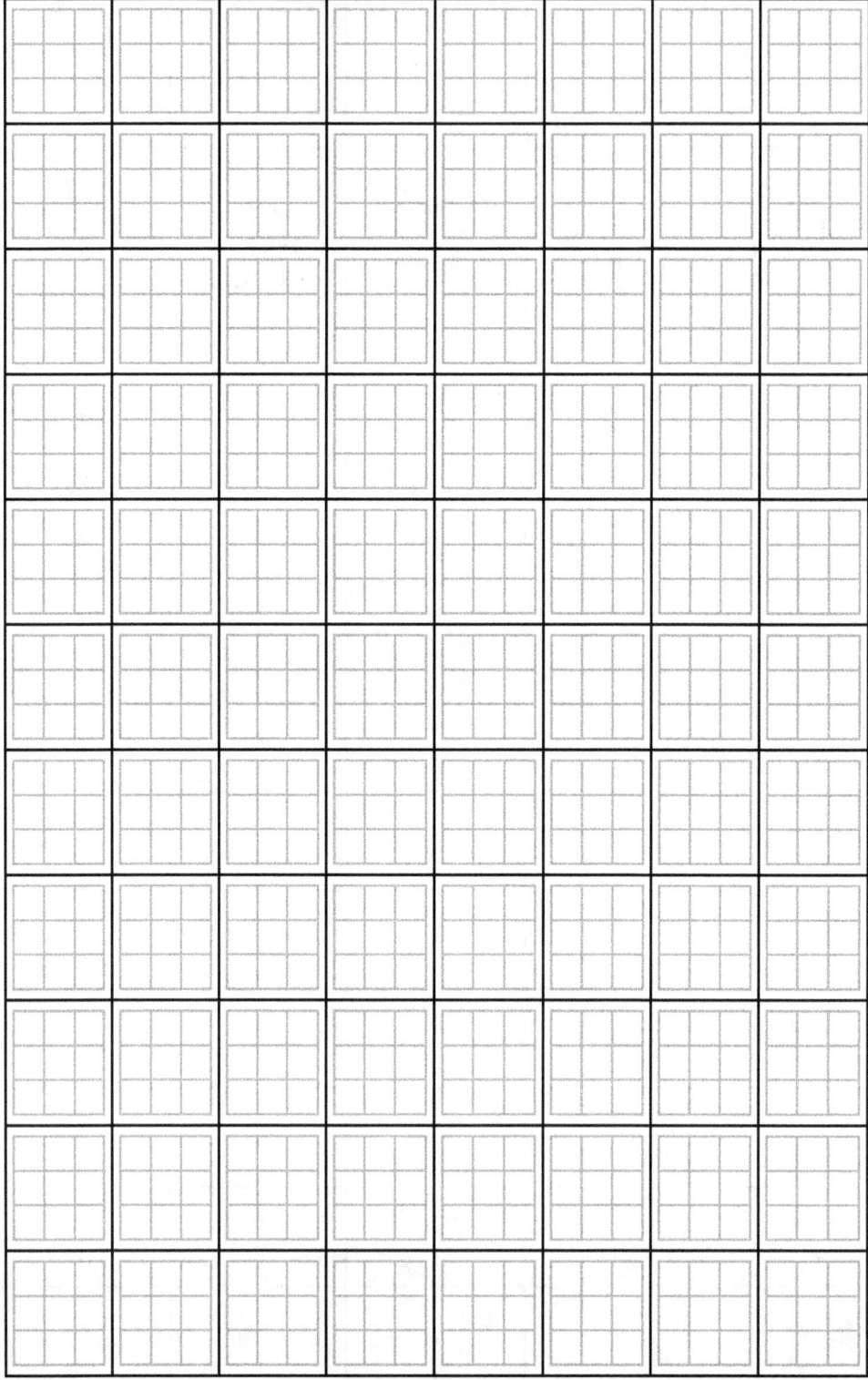

第五十课　　　　　Unit 50

This unit is dedicated to the writing of characters.

Throughout the book, at the end of every unit, we provide a list of characters with small numbers scattered in between the strokes.

These numbers are stroke numbers and they represent one completed stroke, as drawn with a calligraphy pen.

We call them the **Stroke Order** of the character.

The concept of a numbered "stroke order" is to help the student to write the character by following the correct and fixed order.

These stroke orders help you to acquire correct habits early on.

Keep characters uniform in size and position and use the guide (grid) to assist you.

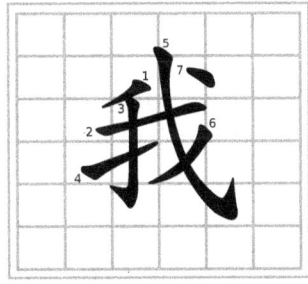

How to Write

At first glance, the grouping of strokes within a character might seem just plain random and disorganized; this is a normal reaction that every new student of Mandarin will experience. If we look a bit deeper, we see that there is definitely a natural order present, which allows the brush to move and flow in a natural, effortless motion.

Let's look at the following diagram provided.
It presents us with the layout of the stroke order of a character.

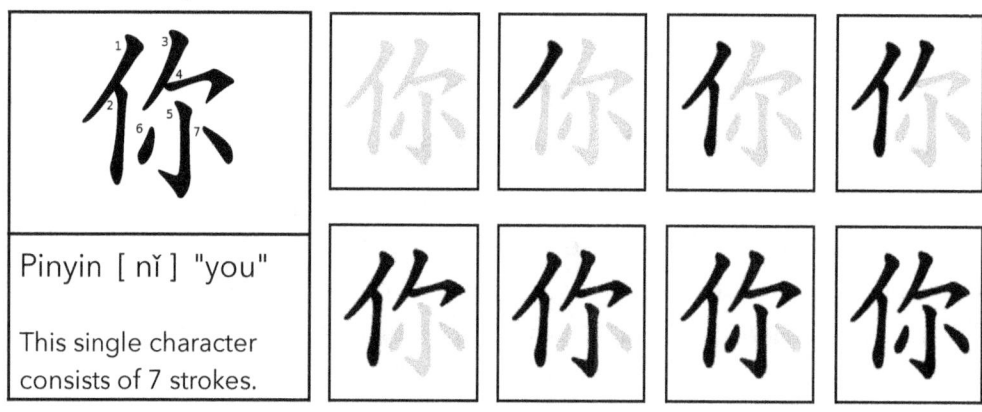

Pinyin [nǐ] "you"

This single character consists of 7 strokes.

Chinese characters consist of pictures or symbols.
When we *write* characters, we are actually *drawing*.
Traditionally, a brush is used for calligraphy, but of course every stroke can also be drawn with a pen or a pencil.

An individual character represents a single *syllable*.
A word can consist of one, two or more syllables.

Many characters consist of a graphical component called a *radical*. This radical helps to identify the *meaning* of the character. In the example provided, we notice that the character for "you" can be divided into the following components: 亻 + 尔 = 你

The radical 亻 means "man", as in a *person*. It helps us to identify the word and to comprehend its meaning. Always keep an eye out for radicals when introduced to new characters. Knowing the radical, helps us to *identify* and to *memorize* the character.

Look at the character diagram provided on the left.

To write characters, we follow a simple yet specific order:

1. **Top to bottom.**
Stroke 1, before Stroke 2.

2. **Left to right.**
Stroke 1+2 completed the "person" radical. It is completed before the rest of the character on the right.

3. **Upper left corner to lower right corner.**
Stroke 3 - Stroke 7

4. **Outside to inside.**
This is normally for characters with "boxes". The box is drawn first.

5. **When two strokes cross, the horizontal stroke is drawn first.** The vertical last.

6. **With slanted strokes, the slanting stroke to the left is drawn before the one slanting to the right.**
Stroke 1 before Stroke 2.

7. **When a character component looks symmetrical, we draw the center stroke first, followed by the symmetrical wings.**
Stroke 5 first, followed by 6 and 7.

These are the rules to be followed. Take note that these seven rules are in place to help you become more efficient at writing.

The secret to writing characters is practice.

Look at the character, dissect it by looking at the recognizable radicals and components present. Then, write it down as many times as possible on Chinese writing paper. Remember to stay within the margins of the boxes provided and to keep characters uniform in size.

We provide you with a list of more than 200 radicals that you should practice before you start this book. These radicals are extremely helpful and will provide a strong foundation for mastering the art of character writing.

Practice Radicals

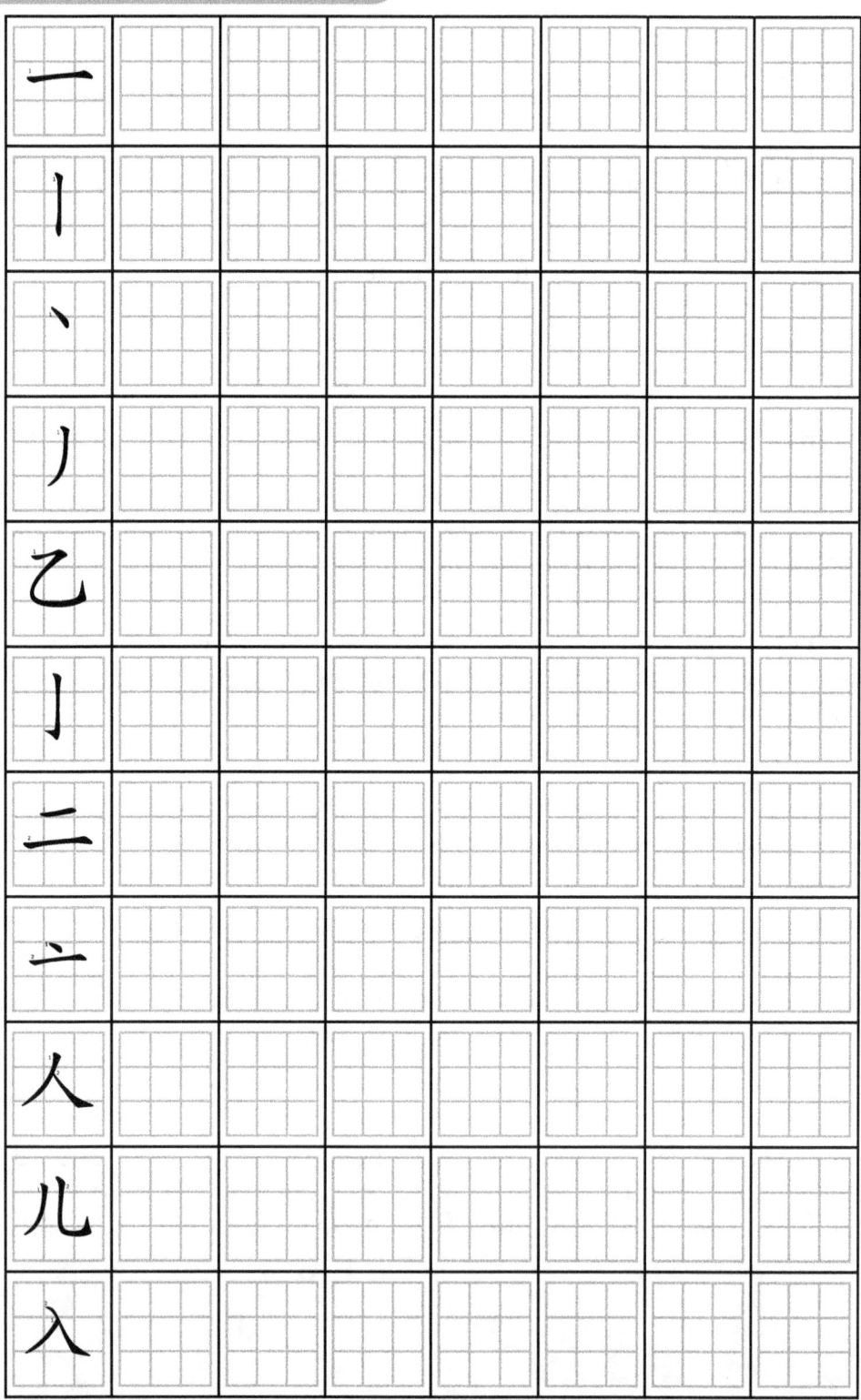

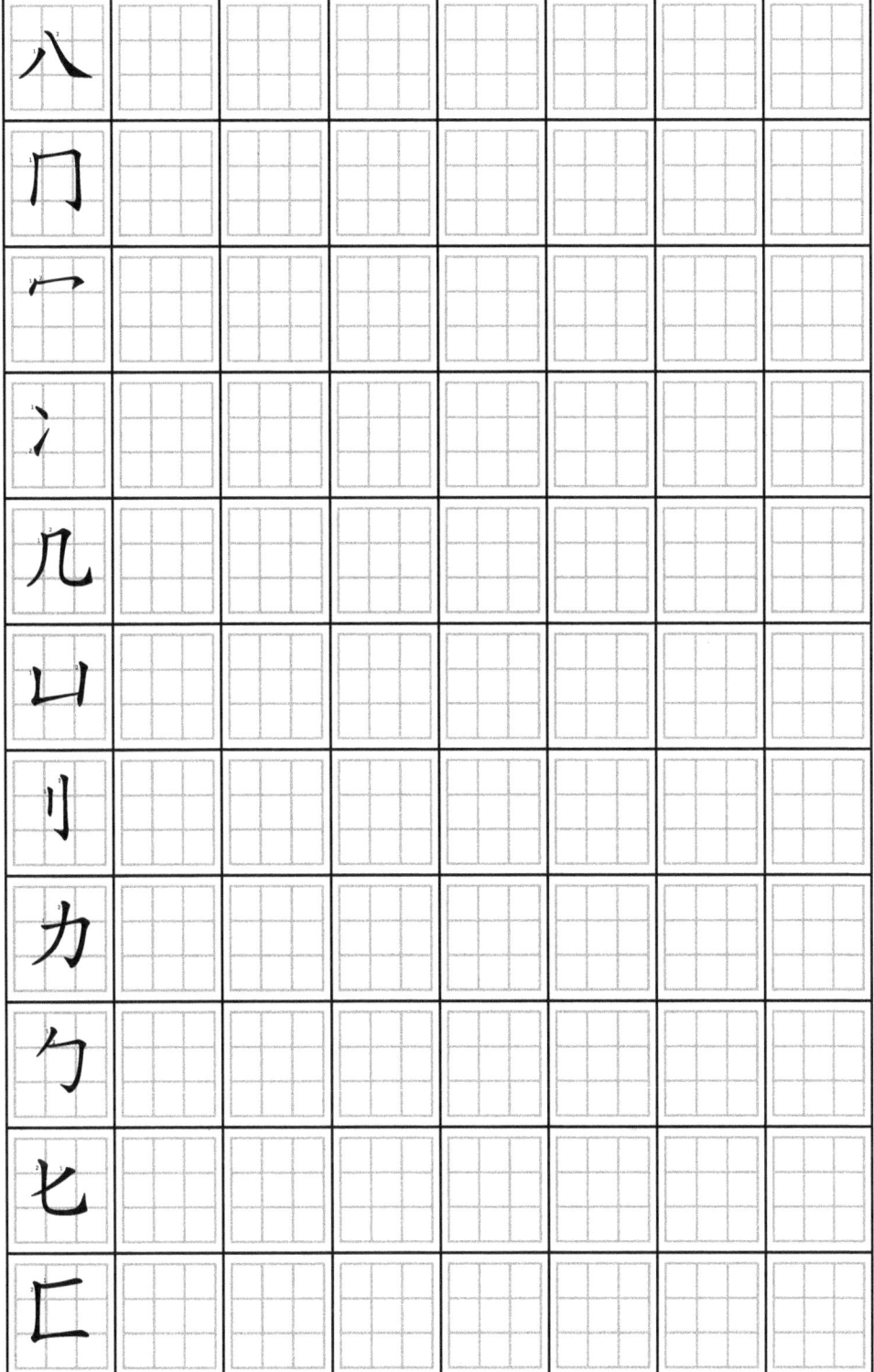

Practice Radicals

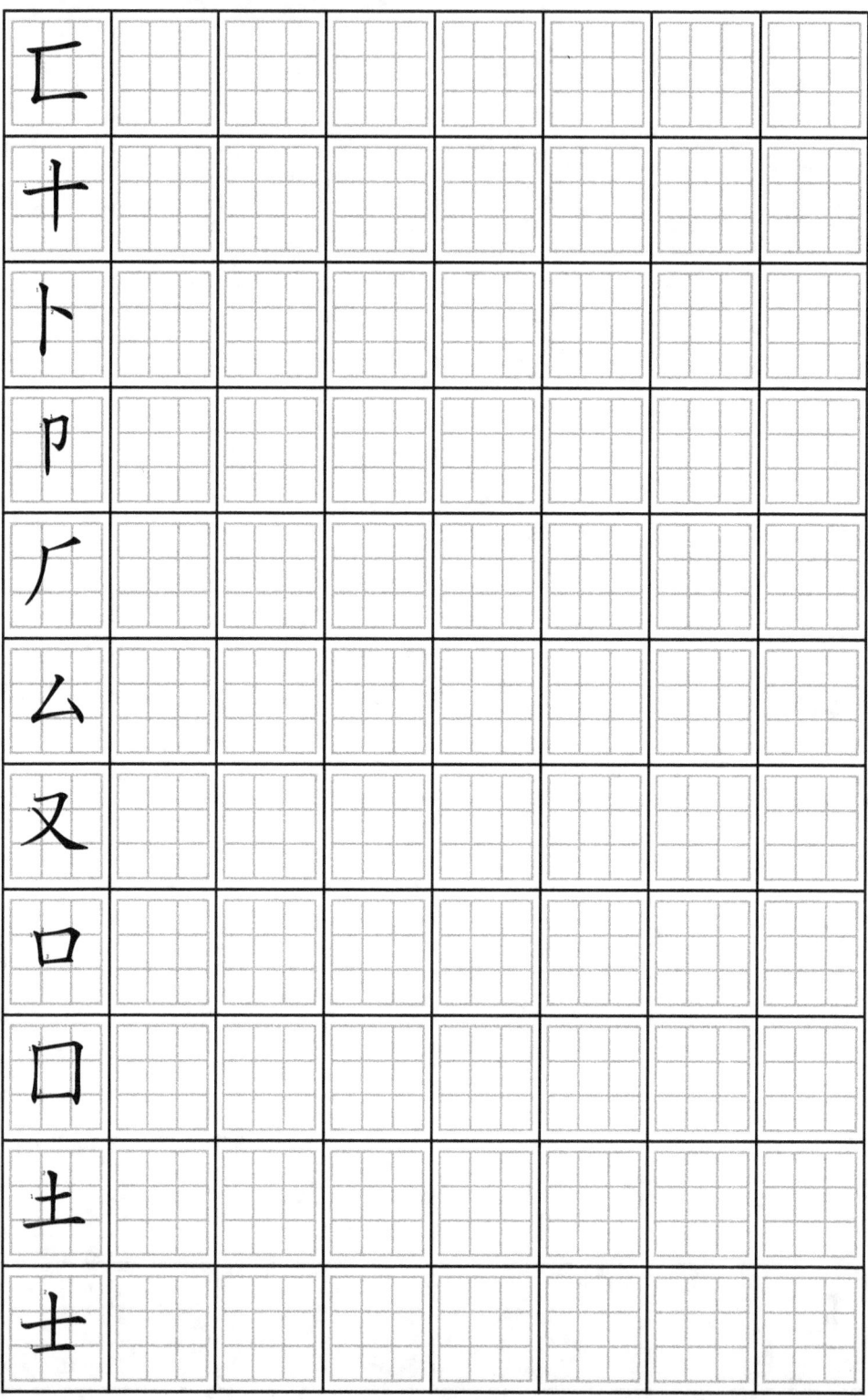

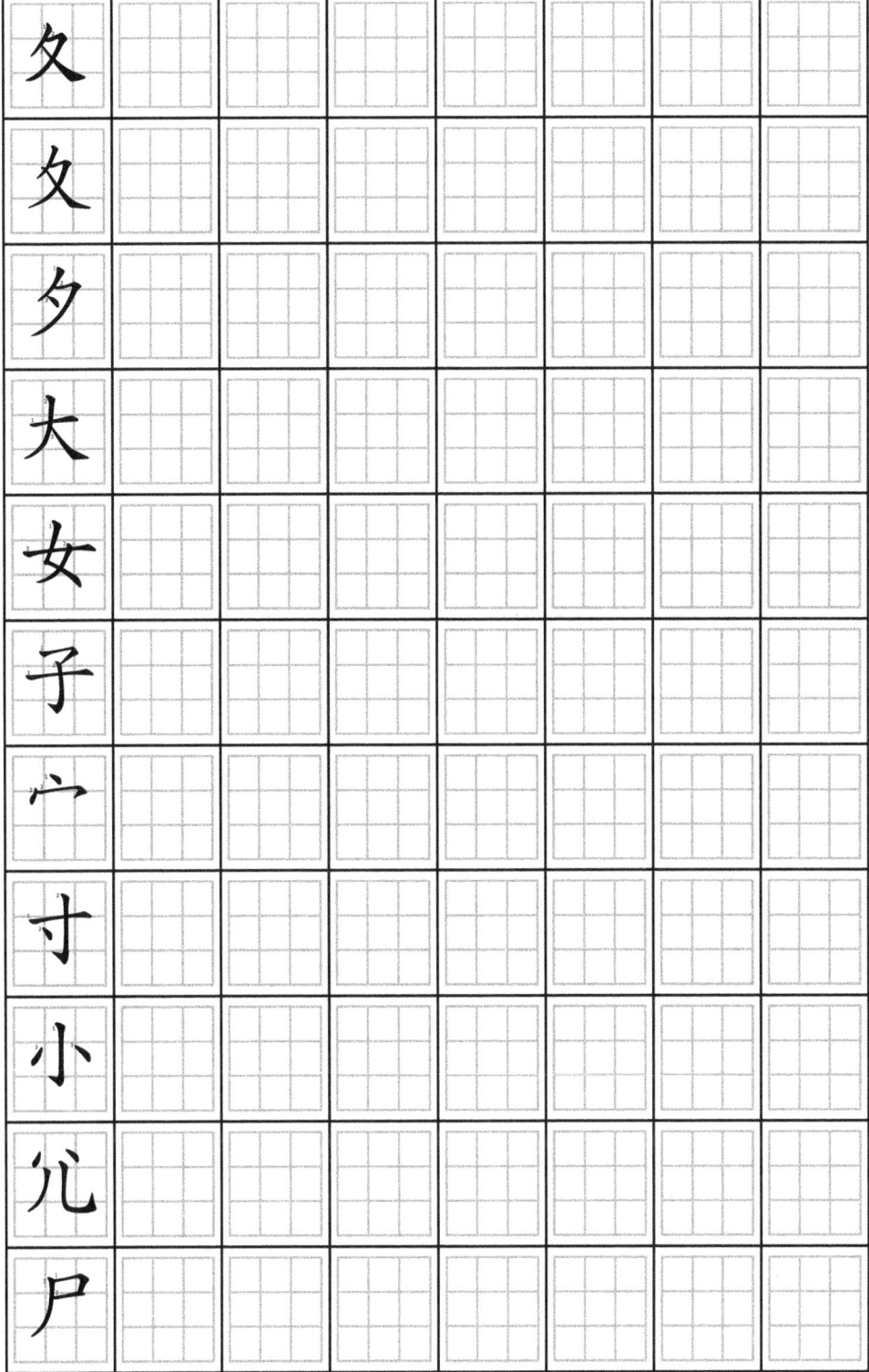

Practice Radicals

巾								
山								
巛								
工								
己								
巾								
干								
幺								
广								
廴								
廾								

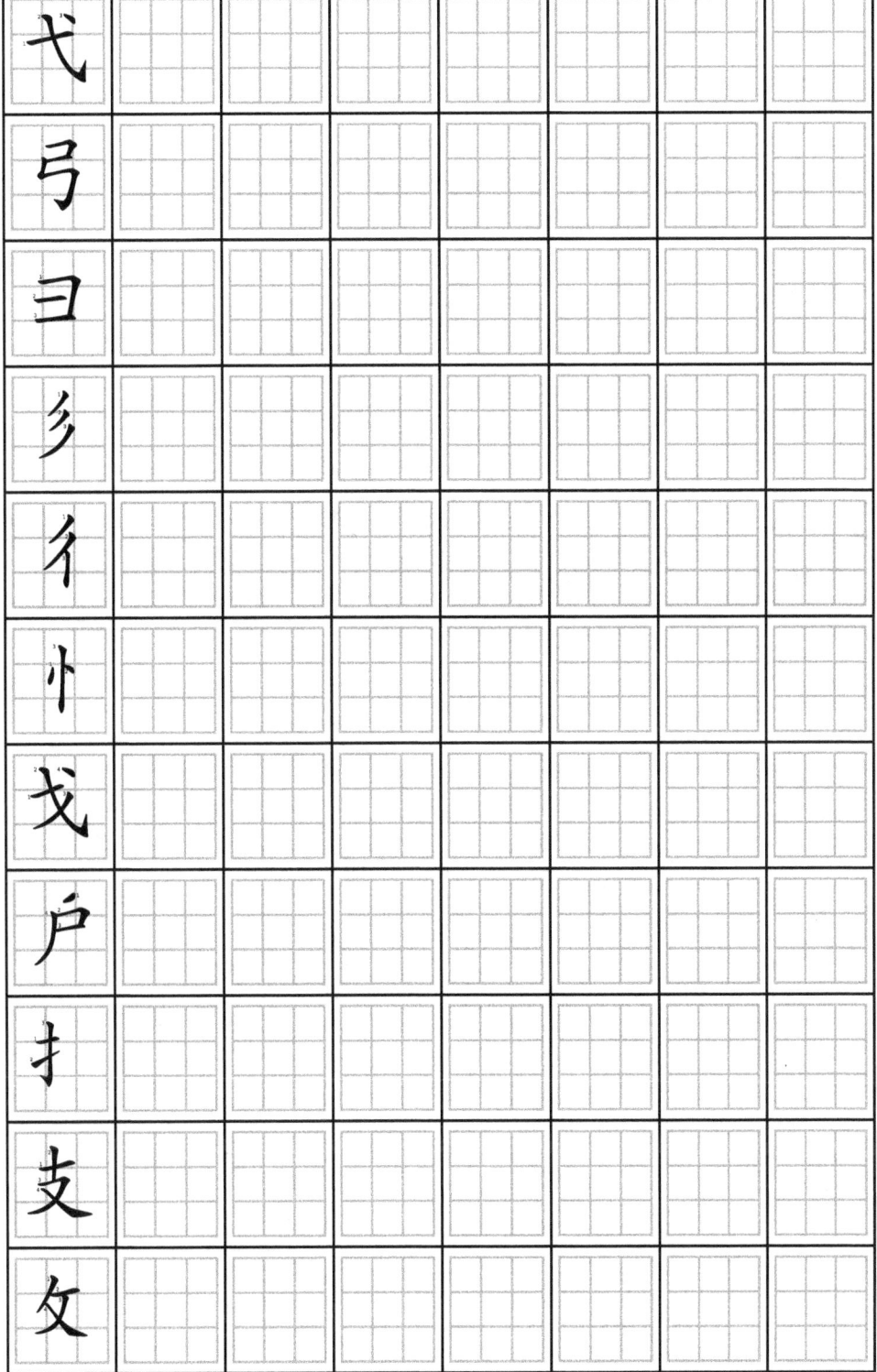

Practice Radicals

文								
斗								
斤								
方								
无								
日								
曰								
月								
木								
欠								
止								

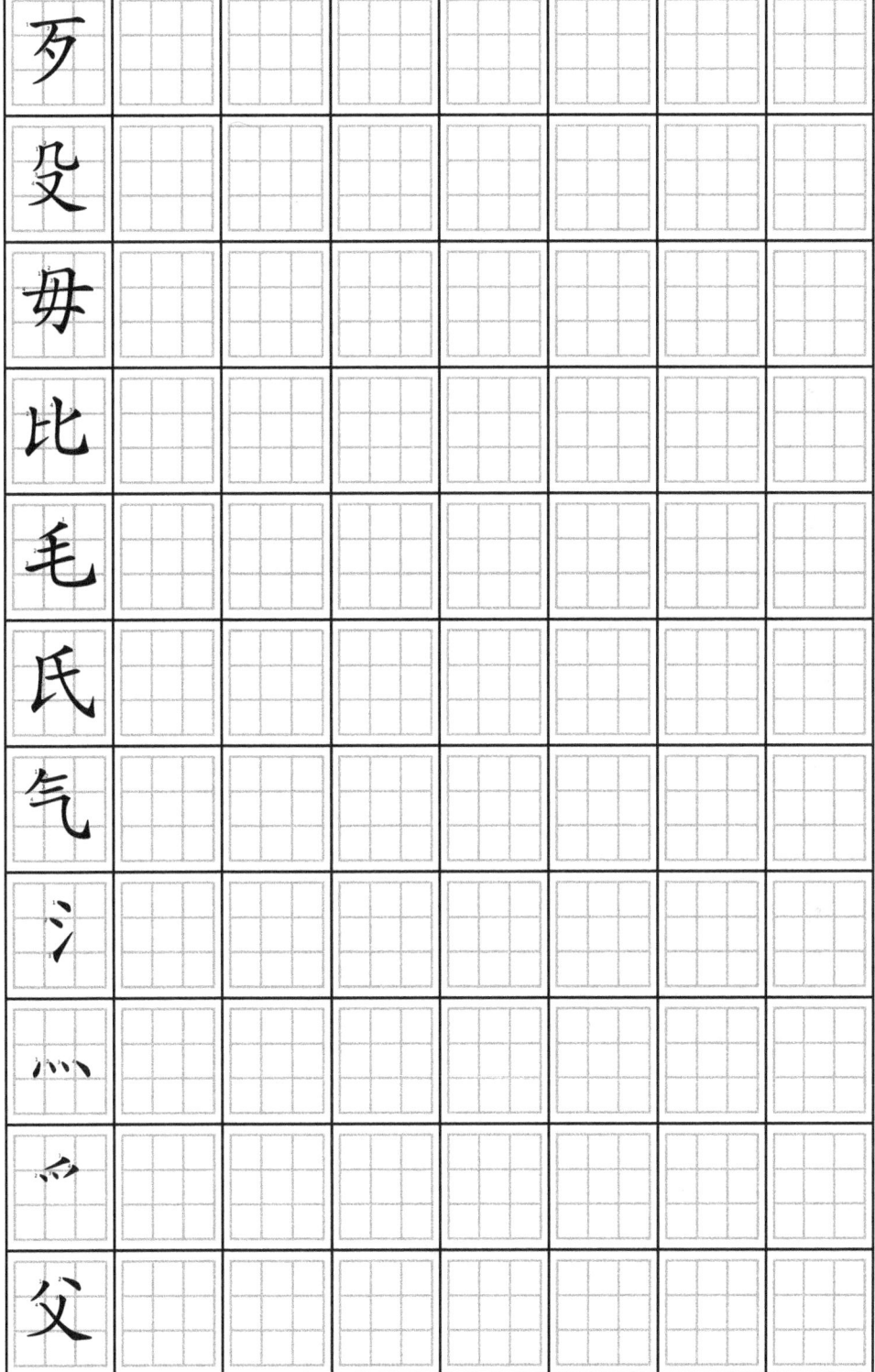

Practice Radicals

爻								
爿								
片								
牙								
牛								
犭								
玄								
玉								
瓜								
瓦								
甘								

生
用
田
疋
疒
水
白
皮
皿
目
矛

Practice Radicals

失
石
示
内
禾
穴
立
竹
米
糸
缶

网
羊
羽
老
而
未
耳
聿
肉
臣
自

Practice Radicals

| 至 |
| 白 |
| 舌 |
| 舛 |
| 舟 |
| 艮 |
| 色 |
| 艸 |
| 虍 |
| 虫 |
| 血 |

Practice Radicals

走
足
身
车
辛
辰
辶
邑
酉
采
里

金
长
门
阝
隶
佳
雨
青
非
面
革

Practice Radicals

韦								
韭								
音								
页								
风								
飞								
仒								
首								
香								
马								
骨								

高							
髟							
鬥							
鬯							
鬲							
鬼							
鱼							
鸟							
卤							
鹿							
麦							

Practice Radicals

麻
黄
黍
黑
黹
黽
鼎
鼓
鼠
鼻
齐

齿
龙
龟
龠
三
四
五
六
七
九
零

Practice Radicals

Practice the following words and utilize your knowledge of radicals.

Male and female comparisons:

男人	[nán rén]	man
男生	[nán shēng]	boy student
男孩子	[nán hái zi]	boy
儿子	[ér zi]	son
男士	[nán shì]	gentleman
男朋友	[nán péng yǒu]	boyfriend
先生	[xiān shēng]	husband
女人	[nǚ rén]	woman
女生	[nǚ shēng]	student
女孩子	[nǚ hái zi]	girl
女儿	[nǚ ér]	daughter
女士	[nǚ shì]	lady
女朋友	[nǚ péng yǒu]	girlfriend
太太	[tài tai]	wife
学生	[xué shēng]	student
孩子	[hái zi]	child
人类	[rén lèi]	mankind

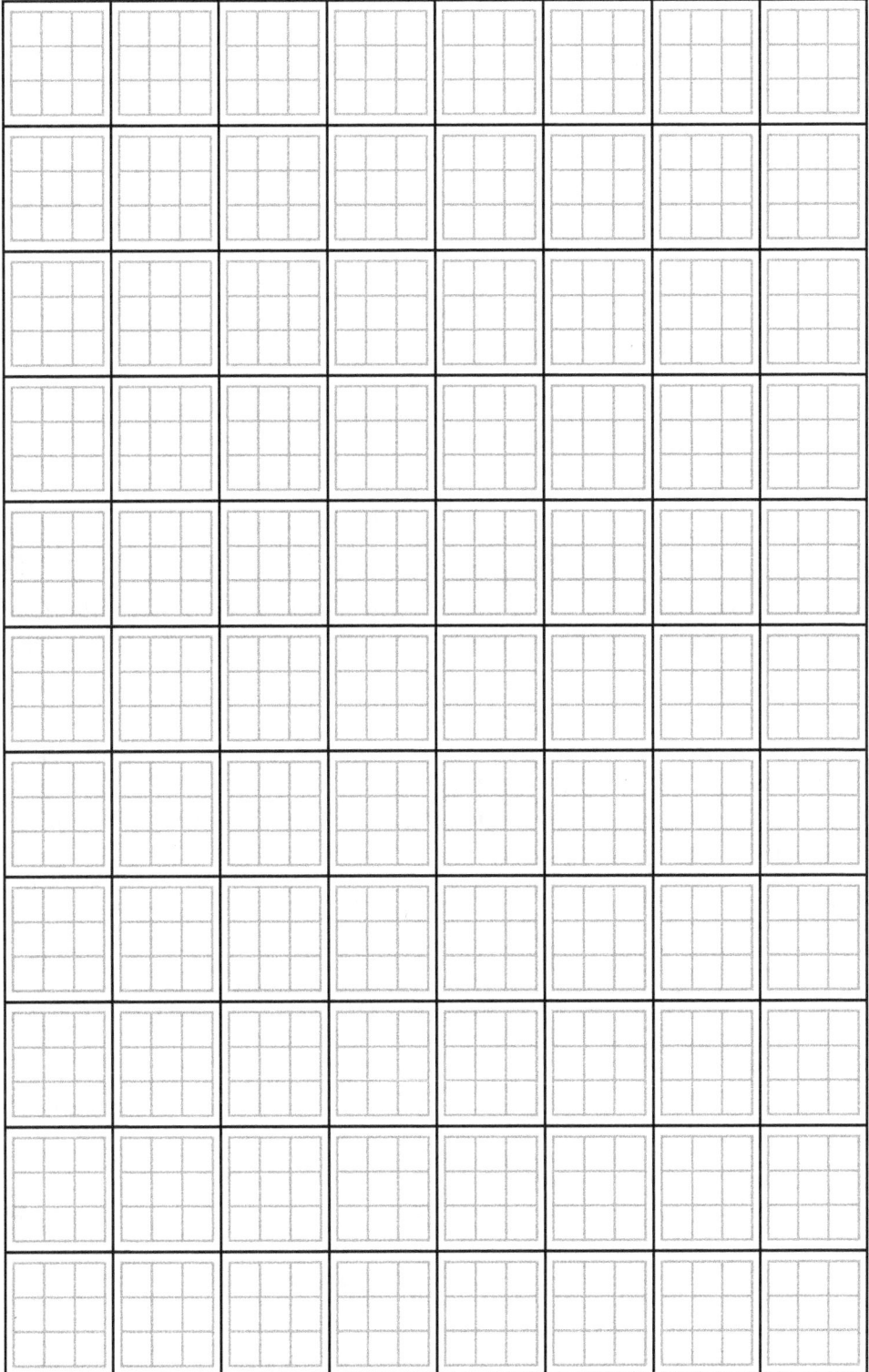

Word Index per Unit (Vocabulary used in dialog)

1. 你, 好(good), 再, 见 (p. 1)
2. 我, 叫, 什么 (名字) (p. 9)
3. 我, 叫, 什么, 名字, 是 (p. 17)
4. 您, 姓, 先生, 马, 王, 您贵姓 (p. 25)
5. 小姐, 早, 赵, 很, 吗 (p. 33)
6. 太太, 她, 陈, 早上好 (p. 41)
7. 田, 今天, 忙, 不, 太, 呢 (p. 49)
8. 人, 国, 法国人, 美国人, 我的, 的, 是的 (p. 57)
9. 谁, 他, 帅, 英国, 英国人, 先生, 你的 (p. 65)
10. 德国人, 美(pretty), 不叫, 文美, 中国, 哪, 那 (p. 73)
11. 看, 有名, 对, 意大利, 英文, 在 (p. 81)
12. 好(very), 久, 好久, 冷, 吴, 林 (p. 89)
13. 喜欢, 也, 下次, 下, 次, 那, 国家 (p. 97)
14. 去, 课, 上课, 明天, 真的, 哪里 (p. 105)
15. 他们, 多, 家人, 韩, 不是 (p. 113)
16. 累, 回家, 为什么, 要, 热 (p. 121)
17. 渴, 喝, 水, 天气, 谢谢, 不舒服 (p. 129)
18. 你们, 我们, 昨天, 早, 一样, 呢 (p. 137)
19. 高(2), 可爱, 可是, 又, 杨 (p. 145)
20. 白天, 前天, 待, 哪儿, 那儿, 外套, 当然 (p. 153)
21. 高兴, 矮, 胖, 瘦, 又, 怎么了 (p. 161)
22. 朋友, 新, 澳洲, 南非, 南 (p. 169)
23. 上班, 玩, 走路, 走, 路, 怎么, 小美 (p. 177)
24. 电影, 晚上, 看(watch), 部, 好的, 一个 (p. 185)
25. 电视, 有, 没有, 但是, 想要, 台 (p. 193)
26. 车子, 漂亮, 告诉, 这, 它 (p. 201)
27. 不好意思, 意思, 书, 贵, 本, 非常 (p. 209)
28. 都, 大, 名车, 两, 辆 (p. 217)
29. 中文, 法文, 简单, 爱, 会, 说 (p. 225)
30. 难, 进步, 学, 而且, 日文, 德文, 啊 (p. 233)
31. 玩具, 可以, 知道, 玩, 孩子, 了 (p. 241)
32. 星期三, 动物园, 想, 猫, 狗 (p. 249)
33. 多少, 种, 元, 一百, 钱, 电脑 (p. 257)
34. 笔, 几, 给, 需要, 支 (p. 265)
35. 买, 杯, 咖啡, 不错, 五, 块 (p. 273)
36. 总共, 店, 十, 冰淇淋, 糖果, 卖, 吧, 间 (p. 281)
37. 折扣, 衣服, 便宜, 一点, 件 (p. 289)
38. 红色, 黄色, 帽子, 八, 顶 (p. 297)
39. 贴纸, 跟, 应该, 分享, 蓝色, 二十, 张, 些 (p. 305)
40. 瓶, 毛, 请, 可乐, 帮 (p. 313)
41. 蛋糕, 片, 好吃, 巧克力, 有的 (p. 321)
42. 苹果, 六, 这里, 找, 绿色 (p. 329)
43. 几块, 块, 只, 现在, 那么, 多 (p. 337)
44. 妹妹, 认真, 一起, 出去, 什么时候, 时间, 问, 岁 (p. 345)
45. 弟弟, 姐姐, 照顾, 可以, 常常 (p. 353)
46. 爸爸, 妈妈, 住, 哇, 特别 (p. 361)
47. 高, 哥哥, 照片, 帅, 张 (p. 369)
48. 医生, 老师, 有钱, 做, 医院, 成功 (p. 377)
49. 大, 小孩, 十一, 家庭, 用功, 有礼貌 (p. 385)
50. **List of Radicals.** (p. 393)

Answers

Unit 1
1. 你 nǐ you
2. 再 zài again
3. 好 hǎo to be good
4. 见 jiàn to meet
5. 你好 nǐ hǎo hello
6. 再见 zài jiàn good-bye
7. 不 bù no/ not
8. 不好 bù hǎo bad
1. 再见 zài jiàn
2. 好 hǎo
3. 见 jiàn
4. 你好 nǐ hǎo
5. 再 zài
6. 你 nǐ
7. 不好 bù hǎo
8. 不 bù
1. 你
2. 好
3. 见
4. 再

Unit 2
我, wǒ, I / me
再, zài, again
叫, jiào, to be called
人, rén, people
什么, shén me, what
名字, míng zi, name
是, shì, to be
为什么, wèi shén me, why
1. 为什么 wèi shén me
2. 人 rén
3. 是 shì
4. 名字 míng zi
5. 我 wǒ
6. 叫 jiào
7. 什么 shén me
8. 再 zài
1. 我
2. 叫
3. 什
4. 么

Unit 3
1. 叫 : jiào
2. 是 : shì
3. 名字 : míng zi
4. 再见 : zài jiàn
1.Nǐ hǎo.
2.Wǒ shì Jack.
3.Nǐ jiào shén me míng zi ?
4.Zài jiàn.
5.Wǒ shì Mary.
6.Shén me?
1. Nǐ jiào shén me míng zi ?
2. Wǒ jiào Jack.
3. Wǒ shì Amy .
4. Nǐ hǎo John.

Unit 4
你, nǐ, you
您, nín, you (polite)
姓, xìng, surname
马, mǎ, horse,
先生, xiān shéng, Mr.
小姐, xiǎo jiě, Miss
王, wáng, king
贵姓, guì xìng,...your surname?
1. Nín hǎo.
2. Wǒ xìng Wáng.
3. Nín guì xìng?
4. Nín hǎo, Wáng xiān shéng.
5. Zài jiàn.
6. Wǒ shì John.
1. 马
2. 姓
3. 王
4. 先

Unit 5
马, mǎ, horse
早, zǎo, Morning!
好, hǎo, good
很, hěn, very, quite
先生, xiān shéng, Mr.
小姐, xiǎo jiě, Miss
吗, ma, question particle
早安, zǎo ān, Good morning!
1. 很 : hěn
2. 早 : zǎo
3. 吗 : ma
4. 早安 : zǎo ān
1. 我 叫 Alice。
2. 马 先生 早。
3. 我 很 好。
4. 你 好 吗?

Unit 6
太太, tài tai, wife
她, tā, she
男, nán, male
他, tā, he
好, hǎo, to be good
陈, chén, Chen
女, nǚ, female
早上, zǎo shàng, Good morning!
1. Nǐ hǎo ma ?
2. Zǎo ān!
3. Nín guì xìng?
4. Zǎo shàng hǎo, Wáng xiān shéng!
5. Tā shì wǒ tài tai.
6. Wǒ xìng Wáng.
1. 太
2. 早
3. 她
4. 是

Unit 7
忙, máng, busy
呢, ne, particle -and you?
天, tiān, day
不, bù, no/ not
今天, jīn tiān, today
明天, míng tiān, tomorrow
太, tài, too
昨天, zuó tiān, yesterday
1.Nǐ hǎo ma? 你 好 吗?
2.Nín guì xìng? 您 贵 姓?
3.Nǐ jiào shén me míng zi? 你 叫 什 么 名 字?
4.Nǐ jīn tiān máng bù máng ? 你 今天 忙 不 忙?
1. 你 今天 忙 不 忙?
2. 我 不 太 忙。
3. 我 很 忙。
4. 你 不 忙。

Unit 8
人, rén, person
国, guó, country
法国人, fǎ guó rén, Frenchman
是的, shì de, yes
法国, fǎ guó, France
美国, měi guó, America
的, de, possessive
我的, wǒ de, my/ mine
1. Nǐ shì fǎ guó rén ma ?
2. Shì de, wǒ shì fǎ guó rén.
3. Nǐ ne ?
4. Wǒ tài tai shì fǎ guó rén.
5. Wǒ de míng zi shì Dave.
6. Wáng xiān shéng shì Měi guó rén.
1. 国
2. 人
3. 的
4. 法

Unit 9
谁, shéi, who
他, tā, he/ him
的, de, possessive
帅, shuài, to be handsome
英国, yīng guó, England
你的, nǐ de, your
英国人, yīng guó rén, Englishman
先生, xiān shēng, husband
1. Yes, he is my husband.
2. Miss Lee, who is that?
3. Is that your husband?
4. He is very handsome!
1. 他 是 Terry。
2. 他 是 我 先生。
3. 他 很 帅。
4. 他 谁 是 ?

Unit 10
那, nà, that
美, měi, pretty
哪, nǎ, which
可爱, kě ài, cute
中文, Zhōng wén, Chinese
德国, dé guó, Germany
矮, ǎi, to be short
中国, zhōng guó, China
1.Tā shì Jenny.
2.Tā bú jiào Mary.
3.Tā shí něi guó rén ?
4.Tā shí Dé guó rén.
5.Nà shí May ma ?
6.Tā hěn kě ài.
1. 中
2. 那
3. 德
4. 文

Unit 11
在, zài, in, on, at
看, kàn, to look
英文, yīng wén, English
有名, yǒu míng, famous
名字, míng zi, name
日本, rì běn, Japan
对, duì, yes
法文, fǎ wén, French
1. His English name is Jimmy.
2. Which country is he from?
3. Look!
4. Yes, he is from Japan (Japanese).
1. 英国 是 他 英国 人。
2. 他 很 有名。
3. 对 他 是 中国人。
4. 你 是 哪 国 人 ?

Unit 12
天, tiān, sky
冷, lěng, cold
好, hǎo, very
天气, tiān qi, weather
吴, wú, Wu
冬天, dōng tiān, winter
久, jiǔ, long time
林, lín, Lin
1. Zǎo ān, Lín xiān sheng !
2. Dōng tiān hěn lěng !
3. Wǒ bù hǎo.
4. Jīn tiān hěn lěng !
5. Jīn tiān, nǐ hǎo mǎ ?
6. Hǎo jiǔ bù jiàn !
1. 冷
2. 久
3. 天
4. 气

Unit 13
家, jiā, home
那, nà, then
上, shàng, up
也, yě, also
国家, guó jiā, home country
次, cì, time(s)
下, xià, down
喜欢, xǐ huan, to like
1.你喜欢中国吗?
2.你好吗?
3.他是哪国人?
4.她是谁?
1.那 很 好。
2.下 次 再 见。
3.我 喜欢 你的 国家。
4.中国 很 美。

Unit 14
明天, míng tiān, tomorrow
课, kè, class
上课, shàng kè, to attend class
那里, nà lǐ, there
哪里, nǎ lǐ, where
真的, zhēn de, really
去, qù, to go
下课, xià kè, to leave class
1. Nǐ qù nǎ lǐ ?
2. Wǒ qù shàng kè.
3. Hǎo jiǔ bù jiàn.
4. Nín hǎo, Wáng xiān shéng.
5. Wǒ xǐ huan shàng kè.
6. Míng tiān jiàn.
1. 课

419

2. 真
3. 里
4. 去

Unit 15
他们, tā mén, they
韩, hán, Han
多, duō, many
你们, nǐ mén, you
韩国, hán guó, Korea
不是, bú shì, no/ not right
我们, wǒ mén, us
回家, huí jiā, return home
1. Who are they?
2. Are they going to America today?
3. No, they will go tomorrow.
4. They are Mr. Han's family.
1.他们 是 谁 ?
2.不是 他们 明天 去。
3.她 今天 我 太 美国 吗？
4.韩 先生 的 家人。

Unit 16
累, lèi, to be tired
回, huí, go back
热, rè, hot
家, jiā, home
为什么, wéi shén me, why
白天, bái tiān, daytime
要, yào, to want
走, zǒu, to walk
1. Nǐ wéi shén me hěn lèi ?
2. Nǐ wéi shén me hěn rè ?
3. Duì, wǒ tài rè !
4. Jīn tiān zhēn de tài rè !
5. Wǒ yào huí jiā.
6. Wǒ hěn lèi.
1. 家
2. 热
3. 要
4. 累

Unit 17
谢谢, xiè xiè, thank you
渴, kě, to be thirsty
喝, hē, to drink
很, hěn, very
天气, tiān qì, weather
舒服, shū fú, comfortable
水, shuǐ, water
不, bù, no/ not
1.你 不 舒服 吗？
2.你 去 哪里？
3.他们 是谁？
4.他们 今天 去 美国吗？
1. 你 不舒服 吗？
2. 今天 我 太 热。
3. 我 要 喝 水。
4. 我 好 渴。

Unit 18
你们, nǐ mén, you (plural)
今天 呢?, Jīn tiān nē ? and today?
不一样, bù yī yàng, different
晚, wǎn, to be late

我们, wǒ mén, we
昨天, zuó tiān, yesterday
早, zǎo, to be early
一样, yī yàng, same
1. Wǒ mén hěn zǎo qù shàng kè.
2. Yī yàng!
3. Jīn tiān nē?
4. Nǐ mén zuó tiān bù zài jiā mǎ?
5. Jīn tiān bù yī yàng.
6. Nǐ mén jīn tiān zǎo shàng bù zài jiā mǎ?
1. 呢
2. 样
3. 昨
4. 晚

Unit 19
高, gāo, to be tall
又..., yòu, both...and
可爱, kě ài, to be cute
胖, pàng, to be fat
可是, kě shì, but
高, Gāo, Gao
杨, Yáng, Yang
矮, ǎi, to be short
1. Yes, she is both tall and cute!
2. Yes, you are right.
3. But Miss Yang is not tall.
4. Is Miss Kao very tall?
1.她又高又可爱。
2.杨 小姐 不高。
3.好 小姐 杨 好 可爱。
4.可是 高 小姐 也 好 可爱。

Unit 20
待, dāi, to stay
外套, wài tào, overcoat
白天, bái tiān, daytime
当然, dāng rán, of course
前天, qián tiān, day before yesterday
后天, hòu tiān, day after tomorrow
那儿, nàr, there
哪儿, nǎr, where
1. Nǐ lěng bù lěng ?
2. Nǐ de wài tào zài nǎr ?
3. Dāng rán wǒ hěn lěng.
4. Wǒ dāi zài jiā.
5. Bái tiān tài lěng.
6. Jīn tiān wǒ bù lěng.
1. 待
2. 前
3. 外
4. 套

Unit 21
高兴, gāo xìng, to be happy
好看, hǎo kàn, good-looking
哭, kū, to cry
生气, shēng qì, to be angry
瘦, shòu, to be thin

怎么了, zěn me le, what's wrong?
又, yòu, furthermore·
矮, ǎi, to be short
1.你怎么了？
2.你的 外套 在 哪儿？
3.高小姐 很 高 吗？
4.你 冷不冷？
1. 你 怎么 了 ?
2.她 好 瘦。
3.我 不是 很 高兴。
4.我 太 矮 又 胖。

Unit 22
南, nán, south
新, xīn, new
朋友, péng yǒu, friend
南非, nán fēi, South Africa
澳洲, ào zhōu, Australia
男朋友, nán péng yǒu, boyfriend
女朋友, nǚ péng yǒu, girlfriend
老朋友, lǎo péng yǒu, old friend
1. Dāng rán bù shì.
2. Bù, tā shì Ào zhōu rén.
3. Tā shì fǎ guó rén ma ?
4. Tā shì wǒ tài tai.
5. Tā hěn shòu.
6. Tā shì lǎo péng yǒu.
1. 南
2. 新
3. 朋
4. 友

Unit 23
玩, wán, to enjoy
走, zǒu, to walk
路, lù, road
上班, shàng bān, go to work
怎么, zěn me, how?
走路, zǒu lù, walk (on road)
学, xué, to study
学校, xué xiào, school
1. I also like to walk.
2. How do you go to work?
3. I walk (to work); it is fun.
4. I want to go to work.
1.我 要 去 上班。
2.你 怎么 去 上班？
3.我 也 喜欢 走路。
4.你 怎么 去 学校？

Unit 24
电影, diàn yǐng, movie
看, kàn, to watch
部, bù, MW films
晚上, wǎn shàng, tonight
好的, hǎo de, good
一, yī, one
个, gè, general MW
二, èr, two
1. Jīn tiān wǎn shàng nǐ máng bù máng ?
2. Bù yào yí ge rén

qù.
3. Wéi shén me ?
4. Wǒ yào qù kàn yí bù diàn yǐng.
5. Wǒ bù máng.
6. Wǒ xǐ huān kàn diàn yǐng.
1. 看
2. 个
3. 部
4. 电

Unit 25
电视, diàn shì, television,
有, yǒu, to have
没有, méi yǒu, not to have
但是, dàn shì, but
想要, xiǎng yào, to want to
台, tái, MW machinery
电, diàn, electricity
电话, diàn huà, telephone
1.你 有 电视 吗？
2.你 要 看 电视？
3.你 朋友 有 电视 吗？
4.你 有 电视 吗？
1.你 有 电视 吗？
2.但是 我 要 看 电视。
3.我 也 想要 看 电视。
4.我 朋友 有 一台 电视。

Unit 26
这, zhè, this
它, tā, it (things)
车子, chē zǐ, car
告诉, gào sù, to tell
漂亮, piāo liàng, beautiful
开车, kāi chē, to drive
火车, huǒ chē, train
她, tā, she
1. Lín xiǎo jiě, nǐ hǎo piāo liàng!
2. Wáng xiǎo jiě, nǐ de chē zǐ hěn piāo liàng!
3. Gào sù wǒ.
4. Zhè shì xīn de ma?
5. Xiè xiè nǐ!
6. Yes, it is. Duì, tā shì.
1. 这
2. 它
3. 车
4. 开

Unit 27
便宜, pián yi, cheap
非常, fēi zháng, very
本, běn, MW books
贵, guì, expensive
书店, shū diàn, book store
意思, yì sī, meaning
书, shū, book
不好, bù hǎo, not good
1. Excuse me.
2. This is a very good book.
3. I want, but it's too expensive.
4. Do you want this book?

1.你要这本书吗？
2.不好意思。
3.我要它可是贵太。
4.我喜欢这本书。

Unit 28
都, dōu, both/all
两, liǎng, two two (MW)
大, dà, big
辆, liàng, MW (cars)
小, xiǎo, small
车, chē, car
名车, míng chē, luxury car
二, èr, two
1. Nǐ xǐ huān nǎ yí liàng chē ?
2. Wǒ xǐ huān zhè yí liàng.
3. Wǒ xǐ huān dà chē.
4. Zhè liǎng liàng ché dōu fēi cháng piāo liàng.
5. Dōu shì míng chē.
6. Zhè yí liàng chē tài xiǎo.
1. 辆
2. 小
3. 两
4. 都

Unit 29
会, huì, to be able
爱, ài, to love
说, shuō, to say/ speak
简单, jiǎn dān, easy
中文, zhōng wén, Chinese
和, hé, and
法文, fǎ wén, French
难, nán, difficult
1. 你喜欢学中文吗？
2. 你会说中文吗？
3. 法文很简单吗？
4. 中文很难学吗？
1.法文很简单。
2.都很简单。
3.我和我妈妈都会说英文。
4.两个都很简单。

Unit 30
难, nán, difficult
进步,jìn bù, to improve
学, xué, to study
而且, ér qiě, in addition
啊, a, agreement
写, xiě, to write
日文, rì wén, Japanese
德文, dé wén, German
1.Dé wén hěn nán xué.
2.Wǒ xǐ huān xué dé wén.
3.Rì wén hǎo nán xué.
4.Wǒ xǐ huān xué rì wén.
5.Wǒ méi yǒu jìn bù.
6.Yīng wén hěn jiǎn dān.
1. 且
2. 而
3. 学
4. 难

Unit 31
玩具, wán jù, toy
可以, kě yǐ, can

知道, zhī dào, to know
玩, wán, fun
孩子, hái zí, child
了, le, to urge
男孩子, nán hái zǐ ,boy
女孩子, nǚ hái zǐ, girl
1. Good boy/ girl!
2. I know, it's too expensive!
3. You cannot (have it). Do you know why?
4. This toy is fun to play with. I want it!
1.这个玩具很好玩。
2.他是好孩子。
3.你知道为什么吗？
4.太贵了。

Unit 32
想, xiǎng, would like
狗, gǒu, dog
猫, māo, cat
动物, dòng wù, animal
动物园, dòng wù yuán, zoo
星期一, xīng qī yī, Monday
星期二, xīng qī èr, Tuesday
花园, huā yuán, garden
1. Wǒ yào qù kàn diàn yǐng.
2. Wǒ xīng qī sān yào qù.
3. Nǐ xiǎng kàn nǎ yí bù diàn yǐng?
4. Wǒ yào qù dòng wù yuán.
5. Dòng wù yuán yǒu huā yuán.
6. Wǒ xǐ huān dòng wù.
1. 狗
2. 想
3. 星
4. 期

Unit 33
多少, duō shǎo, how much
种, zhǒng, kind/ type
元, yuán, dollar
钱, qián, money
一百, yì bǎi, one hundred
电脑, diàn nǎo, computer
多, duō, many/ more
少, shǎo, few/ less
1. This one is one hundred dollars.
2. OK, how much is it?
3. How much is this computer?
4. This kind of computer is very expensive.
1.这种电脑多少钱？
2.这种电视多少钱？
3.这一个一百元。
4.这种电脑很贵。

Unit 34
笔, bǐ, pen
给, gěi, to give
几, jǐ, how many
需要, xū yào, to need

支, zhī, MW thin objects
纸, zhǐ, paper
胶带, jiāo dài, tape
胶水, jiāo shuǐ, glue
1.你需要几支笔？
2.你喜欢这支笔吗。
3.这种电脑多少钱？
4.你需要胶水吗？
1. 几
2. 笔
3. 给
4. 需

Unit 35
买, mǎi, to buy
杯, bēi, cup
五, wǔ, five
块, kuài, MW dollars
咖啡, kā fēi, coffee
不错, bú cuò, pretty good
茶, chá, tea
果汁, guǒ zhī, juice
1. Good! Our coffee is excellent!
2. Morning, I want (to buy) a cup of coffee.
3. Five dollars a cup!
4. How much for a cup?
1.一杯多少钱？
2.这杯咖啡不错。
3.我要买一杯咖啡。
4.我要一杯茶。

Unit 36
总共, zǒng gòng, together
店, diàn, store
十, shí, ten
糖果, táng guǒ, candy
卖, mài, to sell
吧, ba, to suggest
间, jiān, MW (room)
冰淇淋, bīng qí lín, ice cream
1. Wǒ xǐ huan táng guǒ.
2. Wǒ xǐ huan bīng qí lín.
3. Wǒ xǐ huan zhè jiān diàn de táng guǒ.
4. Zhè jiān diàn de táng guǒ hěn bú cuò!
5. Wǒ yǒu shí kuài qián.
6. Wǒ men zǒng gòng yǒu shí kuài qián!
1. 果
2. 吧
3. 间
4. 店

Unit 37
折扣, zhé kòu, discount
衣服, yī fu, clothes
便宜, pián yi, cheap
件, jiàn, MW clothes
一点, yì diǎn, a bit
穿, chuān, to put on
帽子, mào zi, hat
袜子, wà zi, socks
1. OK, can you lower the price a bit?
2. This pice (article) of clothing is one hundred dollars.

3. Sorry, there's no discount.
4. Excuse me/ Sorry.
1.可以便宜一点吗？
2.我们没有折扣。
3.这件衣服一百元。
4.我要穿衣服。

Unit 38
八, bā, eight
红色, hóng sè, red
顶, dǐng, MW hats
黄色, huáng sè,yellow
蓝色, lán sè, blue
帽子, mào zi, hat/ cap
颜色, yán sè, color
白色, bái sè, white
1.你要这顶红色的帽子吗？
2.这顶帽子多少钱？
3.你要这顶黄色的帽子吗？
4.可以便宜一点吗？
1. 白
2. 色
3. 顶
4. 红

Unit 39
贴纸, tiē zhǐ, stickers
跟, gēn, with
应该, yīng gāi, should
分享, fēn xiǎng, to share
二十, èr shí, twenty
张, zhāng, MW paper
些, xiē, MW some/few
三十, sān shí, thirty
1. How many stickers do you have?
2. I have twenty.
3. I like these blue stickers.
4. You should share them with me.
1.你有多少张贴纸？
2.我有二十张。
3.你应该跟我分享。
4.我喜欢你的贴纸。

Unit 40
瓶, píng, bottle
可乐, kě lè, Coke
毛, máo, ten cents
帮, bāng, to help
请, qǐng, please
杯, bēi, cup
果汁, guǒ zhī, juice
啤酒, pí jiǔ, beer
1. Yì píng kě lè wǔ máo qián.
2. Xièxie!
3. Zhè zhēn de hěn pián yi.
4. Qǐng bāng wǒ mǎi yì píng?
5. Yì bēi kě lè duō shǎo qián?
6. Wǒ bù xǐ huan pí jiǔ.
1. 瓶
2. 可
3. 请
4. 帮

Unit 41
蛋糕, dàn gāo,cake
好吃, hǎo chī, delicious

421

片, piàn, slice
面包, miàn bāo, bread
蛋, dàn, egg
三明治, sān míng zhì, sandwich
草莓, cǎo méi, strawberry
1. Yes, the cake is delicious today.
2. I want two slices of cake.
3. We do have some, today we have chocolate cake.
4. Do you have chocolate cake today?
1.我要两片蛋糕。
2.今天的蛋糕很好吃。
3.今天有卖蛋糕吗?
4.今天有草莓蛋糕。

Unit 42
六, liù, six
苹果, píng guǒ, apple
这里, zhè li, here
找, zhǎo, return change
市场, shì chǎng, market
农场, nóng chǎng, farm
给, gěi, to give
绿色, lǜ sè, green
1. 你找我多少钱?
2. 今天有卖蛋糕吗?
3. 你喜欢吃苹果吗?
4. 你要喝什么?
1.　找
2.　苹
3.　市
4.　场

Unit 43
鸡块, jī kuài, chicken nugget
只, zhǐ, only/ just
多, duō, many/ much
那么, nà me, like that
现在, xiàn zài, now
块, kuài, piece
鸡, jī, chicken
鸡肉, jī ròu, chicken meat
1. At this moment I only have eight pieces.
2. Then, how many do you have (at the moment)?
3. I do not have that many at the moment.
4. I want ten chicken nuggets. Thanks!
1.现在你有几块?
2.我只有八块。
3.我要十个小鸡块。
4.我没有那么多。

Unit 44
妹妹, mèi mei, younger sister
认真, rèn zhēn, to be serious
一起, yī qǐ, together
出去, chū qù, to go out

时间, shí jiān, time
问, wèn, to ask
岁, suì, MW age
什么时候, shénme shí hòu, when
1. Nǐ mèi mei jǐ suì?
2. Nǐ jǐ suì?
3. Nǐ shì rèn zhēn de ma?
4. Bú yào wèn wǒ!
5. Wǒ xǐ huan nǐ mèi mei.
6. Nǐ xiàn zài yǒu shí jiān ma?
1.　起
2.　出
3.　岁
4.　时

Unit 45
弟弟, dì di, younger brother
姐姐, jiě jie, older sister
照顾, zhào gù, to take care of
可以, kě yǐ, can
常常, cháng cháng, often
抱, bào, to hug
兄弟, xiōng di, brothers
姐妹, jiě mèi, sisters
1. I don't have a sister or anyone who can take care of me.
2. I have two (older) sisters.
3. Yes, the two of us often play together.
4. Do you have a (younger) brother to play with?
1.我们可以一起玩吗?
2.我们常常玩。
3.我没有弟弟。
4.我有两个姐姐。

Unit 46
爸爸, bà ba, father
妈妈, mā ma, mother
住, zhù, to live
哇, wā, Wow!
特别, tè bié, special
父母, fù mǔ, parents
父, fù, father
母, mǔ, mother
1. 你妈妈是哪国人?
2. 你爸爸住在哪里?
3. 你有没有姐姐?
4. 你妹妹几岁?
1.　母
2.　住
3.　别
4.　特

Unit 47
哥哥, gē ge, older brother
照片, zhào piàn, photo
帅, shuài, to be handsome
张, zhāng, MW photo
聪明, cōng míng, to be smart
害羞, hài xiū, to be shy

像, xiàng, to resemble
强壮, qiáng zhuàng, strong
1. He is tall, skinny and handsome.
2. This is my older brother.
3. Who is this?
4. Look at this photo. It's my family.
1.你看这张照片。
2.这是谁?
3.这是我家人。
4.他是我哥哥。

Unit 48
医生, yī shēng, doctor
老师, lǎo shī, teacher
有钱, yǒu qián, to be rich
医院, yī yuàn, hospital
做, zuò, to do
成功, chéng gōng, success
护士, hù shì, nurse
工作, gōng zuò, to work
1. Tā yīng gāi hěn yǒu qián.
2. Wǒ dì di shì yī shēng.
3. Wǒ mèi mei shì hù shì.
4. Nǐ dì di shì zuò shén me de?
5. Wǒ mā ma shì lǎo shī.
6. Wǒ bú shì lǎo shī.
1.　医
2.　院
3.　老
4.　师

Unit 49
小孩, xiǎo hái, child
十一, shí yī, eleven
用功, yòng gōng, diligent
家庭, jiā tíng, household
礼貌, lǐ mào, polite
房子, fáng zi, house
十二, shí èr, twelve
十三, shí sān, thirteen
1. We have a large household.
2. How many children in your household?
3. Eleven children.
4. You are all very diligent.
1.你的家庭有几个小孩?
2.你们都很用功。
3.他很有礼貌。
4.我们家是一大家庭。

About the Author:

Daniel Schoeman is the owner of an online Mandarin language learning site and has been a student of Mandarin for the past 25 years. A graduate from the Cheng Gong University in Taiwan, he has been living in China and Taiwan continuously for the last 25 years as both scholar, researcher and educator. He compiled years of data gathered from students of Mandarin and simplified it into a comprehensible package in this book.

It is considered a collaboration between teachers and students.

Bonus Material:

We provide you free audio files for the dialogs and vocabulary. This is to assist you with the pronunciation of words (Pinyin).
You can choose any of the following options:
- You can access audio files, for all units, at the following Google drive address:
  » *https://drive.google.com/open?id=0B9YI0PJQzrWdZ1NFTmlrYy1VY1k*

or:
  » *https://drive.google.com/drive/folders/0B9YI0PJQzrWdZ1NFTmlrYy1VY1k?resourcekey=0--64aLPDK5KwNMLRRdnsVow&usp=share_link*

Simply paste the link into the URL screen of your browser and download all the audio files to your computer.
- Alternatively, you can also use a mobile device to scan either of the following QR codes:

Your mobile device must have a QR reader App installed.

Once you have scanned the code, you will be directed to the Google site where you can download the audio files as "viewer".

If you experience any difficulties, please email us at:
eyechinese@gmail.com,
and also specify book title in subject line.

www.ingramcontent.com/pod-product-compliance
Lightning Source LLC
Chambersburg PA
CBHW081146290426
44108CB00018B/2455